I0438983

REPORT OF THE RIVER MASTER OF THE DELAWARE RIVER

FOR THE PERIOD
DECEMBER 1, 2002–NOVEMBER 30, 2003

Open-File Report 2008–1372

U.S. Department of the Interior
U.S. Geological Survey

CALENDAR FOR REPORT YEAR 2003

DECEMBER 2002

S	M	T	W	T	F	S
1	2	3	4	5	6	7
8	9	10	11	12	13	14
15	16	17	18	19	20	21
22	23	24	25	26	27	28
29	30	31				

JANUARY 2003

S	M	T	W	T	F	S
			1	2	3	4
5	6	7	8	9	10	11
12	13	14	15	16	17	18
19	20	21	22	23	24	25
26	27	28	29	30	31	

FEBRUARY

S	M	T	W	T	F	S
						1
2	3	4	5	6	7	8
9	10	11	12	13	14	15
16	17	18	19	20	21	22
23	24	25	26	27	28	

MARCH

S	M	T	W	T	F	S
						1
2	3	4	5	6	7	8
9	10	11	12	13	14	15
16	17	18	19	20	21	22
23	24	25	26	27	28	29
30	31					

APRIL

S	M	T	W	T	F	S
		1	2	3	4	5
6	7	8	9	10	11	12
13	14	15	16	17	18	19
20	21	22	23	24	25	26
27	28	29	30			

MAY

S	M	T	W	T	F	S
				1	2	3
4	5	6	7	8	9	10
11	12	13	14	15	16	17
18	19	20	21	22	23	24
25	26	27	28	29	30	31

JUNE 2003

S	M	T	W	T	F	S
1	2	3	4	5	6	7
8	9	10	11	12	13	14
15	16	17	18	19	20	21
22	23	24	25	26	27	28
29	30					

JULY

S	M	T	W	T	F	S
		1	2	3	4	5
6	7	8	9	10	11	12
13	14	15	16	17	18	19
20	21	22	23	24	25	26
27	28	29	30	31		

AUGUST

S	M	T	W	T	F	S
					1	2
3	4	5	6	7	8	9
10	11	12	13	14	15	16
17	18	19	20	21	22	23
24	25	26	27	28	29	30
31						

SEPTEMBER

S	M	T	W	T	F	S
	1	2	3	4	5	6
7	8	9	10	11	12	13
14	15	16	17	18	19	20
21	22	23	24	25	26	27
28	29	30				

OCTOBER

S	M	T	W	T	F	S
			1	2	3	4
5	6	7	8	9	10	11
12	13	14	15	16	17	18
19	20	21	22	23	24	25
26	27	28	29	30	31	

NOVEMBER

S	M	T	W	T	F	S
						1
2	3	4	5	6	7	8
9	10	11	12	13	14	15
16	17	18	19	20	21	22
23	24	25	26	27	28	29
30						

Report of the River Master of the Delaware River for the period December 1, 2002–November 30, 2003

By Bruce E. Krejmas, Gary N. Paulachok, and Stephen F. Blanchard

Open-File Report 2008–1372

U.S. Department of the Interior
U.S. Geological Survey

U.S. Department of the Interior
DIRK KEMPTHORNE, Secretary

U.S. Geological Survey
Mark D. Myers, Director

U.S. Geological Survey, Reston, Virginia: 2009

For more information about the USGS and its products:
Telephone: 1-888-ASK-USGS
World Wide Web: http://www.usgs.gov/

Contents

RIVER MASTER LETTER OF TRANSMITTAL AND SPECIAL REPORT 1

DELAWARE RIVER OPERATIONS 4

    Abstract 4

    Introduction 4

    Acknowledgments 6

    Definition of Terms and Procedures 6

    Precipitation 7

    Operations 8

        December to May 8

        June to November 9

        Summary of Operations 10

    Streamflow 12

        Components of Flow, Delaware River at Montague, New Jersey 12

        Time of Travel 13

        Segregation of Flow at Montague 13

    Computation of Directed Releases 13

    Analysis of Forecasts 15

    Diversions to New York City Water Supply 15

    Storage in New York City Reservoirs 16

    Comparison of River Master Operations Data With Other Streamflow Records 16

        Releases from New York City Reservoirs.. 16

        Releases from Lake Wallenpaupack 18

        Delaware River at Montague, New Jersey 18

        Diversion Tunnels 18

    Diversions by New Jersey 19

    Conformance of Operations Under Amended Decree of the U.S. Supreme Court 19

QUALITY OF WATER IN THE DELAWARE ESTUARY 51

    Introduction 51

    Water-Quality Monitoring Program 51

    Water Quality During the 2003 Report Year 51

        Streamflow 51

        Water Temperature 53

        Specific Conductance and Chloride 54

        Dissolved Oxygen 54

        Hydrogen-Ion Activity (pH) 56

Appendix A. Docket No. D-77-20 CP (Revision 6).. 62

Appendix B. Agreement—Temporary Bottom Release Program from Cannonsville and
    Pepacton Reservoirs 66

Figures

Figure 1. Map showing Delaware River Basin above Wilmington, Delaware 5

Figure 2. Graph showing operation curves and actual combined contents for New York City reservoirs—Pepacton, Cannonsville, and Neversink—in the Delaware River Basin, December 1, 2002, to November 30, 2003 8

Figure 3. Hydrograph showing components of flow, Delaware River at Montague, New Jersey, July 1 to September 30, 2003 11

Figure 4. Boxplots showing combined storage in Pepacton, Cannonsville, and Neversink Reservoirs 12

Figure 5. Map showing location of water-quality monitoring sites on the Delaware Estuary ... 52

Graphs showing:

Figure 6. Water temperature in the Delaware Estuary at Benjamin Franklin Bridge at Philadelphia, Pennsylvania, April to November 53

Figure 7. Mean and minimum daily mean dissolved oxygen concentrations from July to September at two monitor sites on the Delaware Estuary, 1965-2003 55

Figure 8. Distribution of hourly dissolved oxygen concentrations at two monitor sites on the Delaware Estuary, July to September 2003 56

Tables

Table 1. Precipitation in the Delaware River Basin above Montague, New Jersey 20

Table 2. Conservation release rates for New York City reservoirs in the Delaware River Basin 20

Tables 3–5. Storage in:

3. Pepacton Reservoir, New York, for year ending November 30, 2003 21

4. Cannonsville Reservoir, New York, for year ending November 30, 2003 22

5. Neversink Reservoir, New York, for year ending November 30, 2003 23

Table 6. Design rates for Delaware River at Montague, New Jersey gaging station 24

Table 7. Consumption of water by New York City, 1950 to 2003 25

Table 8. New York City reservoir release design data 26

Table 9. Controlled releases from reservoirs in the upper Delaware River Basin and segregation of flow of Delaware River at Montague, New Jersey 27

Table 10. Diversions to New York City water supply 39

Tables 11–15. Daily mean discharge:

11. East Branch Delaware River at Downsville, New York 45

12. West Branch Delaware River at Stilesville, New York................................. 46

13. Neversink River at Neversink, New York... 47

14. Wallenpaupack Creek at Wilsonville, Pennsylvania 48

15. Delaware River at Montague, New Jersey 49

Table 16. Diversions by New Jersey; daily mean discharge, Delaware and Raritan Canal at Port Mercer, New Jersey.. 50

Table 17. Daily mean discharge, Delaware River at Trenton, New Jersey 57

Tables 18–19. Daily maximum and minimum chloride concentrations:
    18. Delaware River at Reedy Island Jetty, Delaware 58
    19. Delaware River at Chester, Pennsylvania... 59
Tables 20–21. Daily mean dissolved oxygen concentrations:
    20. Delaware River at Benjamin Franklin Bridge at Philadelphia, Pennsylvania 60
    21. Delaware River at Chester, Pennsylvania... 61

Conversion Factors and Vertical Datum

Multiply	By	To obtain
Length		
inch (in.)	25.4	millimeter (mm)
foot (ft)	0.3048	meter (m)
mile (mi)	1.609	kilometer (km)
Area		
square mile (mi^2)	2.590	square kilometer (km^2)
Volume		
million gallons (Mgal)	3,785	cubic meter (m^3)
million gallons (Mgal)	1.547	cubic foot per second day (ft^3/s)-d
billion gallons (Bgal)	3.785	cubic hectometer (hm^3)
cubic foot per second day (ft^3/s)-d	0.002447	cubic hectometer (hm^3)
Flow rate		
million gallons per day (Mgal/d)	1.547	cubic foot per second (ft^3/s)
million gallons per day (Mgal/d)	0.04381	cubic meter per second (m^3/s)
billion gallons per day (Bgal/d)	43.81	cubic meter per second (m^3/s)
cubic foot per second (ft^3/s)	0.02832	cubic meter per second (m^3/s)

Datum: Vertical coordinate information is referenced to the North American Vertical Datum of 1988. Horizontal coordinate information is referenced to the North American Datum of 1927.

Temperature in degrees Fahrenheit (°F) may be converted to degrees Celsius (°C) as follows: °C=(°F-32)/1.8

RIVER MASTER LETTER OF TRANSMITTAL AND SPECIAL REPORT

OFFICE OF THE DELAWARE RIVER MASTER
United States Geological Survey
415 National Center
Reston, Virginia 20192

December 12, 2008

The Honorable
John G. Roberts, Jr.
Chief Justice of the United States

The Honorable
Ruth Ann Minner
Governor of Delaware

The Honorable
Jon S. Corzine
Governor of New Jersey

The Honorable
David A. Paterson
Governor of New York

The Honorable
Edward G. Rendell
Governor of Pennsylvania

The Honorable
Michael R. Bloomberg
Mayor of the City of New York

No. 5, Original.—October Term, 1950
State of New Jersey, Complainant,
v.
State of New York and City of New York, Defendants,
Commonwealth of Pennsylvania and State of Delaware, Intervenors.

Dear Sirs and Madam:

For the record and in compliance with the provisions of the Amended Decree of the Supreme Court of the United States entered June 7, 1954, I am transmitting herewith the 50th Annual Report of the River Master of the Delaware River for the 12-month period from December 1, 2002, to November 30, 2003. In this report, this period is referred to as the River Master report year or the report year.

During the 2003 River Master report year, monthly precipitation in the upper Delaware River Basin ranged from 75 percent of the long-term average during April 2003 to 276 percent of the long-term average during September 2003. Total precipitation during the report year was 13.40 inches (131 percent) more than the long-term average. Precipitation during the December to May period, when reservoirs typically refill, was 0.47 inches less than the 62-year average. Precipitation during the report year was below normal in January, March, April, and May, and above normal in the other 8 months.

1

On December 1, 2002, when the report year began, combined storage in the New York City reservoirs in the upper Delaware River Basin was 193.745 billion gallons (Bgal) or 71.5 percent of combined storage capacity. Median combined storage on December 1, computed on the basis of 35 years of record, is 166.770 Bgal. Operations on December 1, 2002, were being conducted as stipulated by the Decree. Storage increased during December and fluctuated moderately from January to mid-March. The reservoirs were full in late March and all the reservoirs spilled. The reservoirs remained full or nearly full for the rest of the report year.

On May 28, 2003, the Delaware River Master Advisory Committee met at Hawley, Pennsylvania to discuss hydrologic conditions in the basin and operational procedures for the 2003 reservoir-release season. During the report year, the following individuals served as members of the Advisory Committee:

Delaware	John H. Talley
New Jersey	Bradley M. Campbell
New York	Erin M. Crotty
New York City	Christopher O. Ward
Pennsylvania	Cathleen Curran Myers

The River Master informed the Advisory Committee that, on the basis of information provided by New York City, the excess-release quantity beginning June 15 was 7.381 Bgal. On the basis of modifications to reservoir release programs in Delaware River Basin Commission (DRBC) Docket No. D-77-20 CP (Revision No. 6), the excess-release quantity was to be used for various purposes. On the basis of hydrologic conditions, the Parties to the Decree unanimously agreed to suspend the scheduled release of the excess-release quantity.

During the report year, the River Master and staff participated in a number of water-supply related meetings of the DRBC. The Deputy Delaware River Master met periodically with representatives of the Parties to the Decree as a non-voting member of DRBC's Flow Management Technical Advisory Committee. Issues of particular interest to the River Master involved management of reservoir releases and regulated streamflow in the upper Delaware River Basin.

The U.S. Geological Survey (USGS) continued operation of its field office of the Delaware River Master at Milford, Pennsylvania. Gary N. Paulachok, Deputy Delaware River Master, continued in charge of the office, assisted by Bruce E. Krejmas, Hydrologist.

During the year, the River Master's office at Milford continued the weekly distribution of a summary hydrologic report. These reports contain provisional data on precipitation in the upper Delaware River Basin, releases and spills from New York City reservoirs to the Delaware River, diversions to the New York City water-supply system, reservoir contents, daily segregation of flow of the Delaware River at the USGS Montague, New Jersey gaging station, and diversions by New Jersey. The reports were distributed to members of the Delaware River Master Advisory Committee and to other parties interested in Delaware River operations. A monthly summary of hydrologic conditions also was provided to Advisory Committee members.

The first section of this report documents Delaware River operations during the report year. During the year, the City of New York diverted 165.271 Bgal from the Delaware River Basin and released 55.202 Bgal from Pepacton, Cannonsville, and Neversink Reservoirs to the Delaware River. The River Master directed releases from these reservoirs to the Delaware River that totaled 3.180 Bgal.

The second section of this report describes water quality at various monitor sites on the Delaware Estuary. It includes basic data on chemical properties and physical characteristics of the water and presents summary statistics on the data.

Throughout the year, diversions to New York City's water supply, and releases designed to maintain the flow of the Delaware River at Montague, were made as directed by the River Master. Diversions by

New York City from its reservoirs in the Delaware River Basin did not exceed the limit stipulated by the Decree. Diversions by New Jersey also were within the stipulated limit.

The River Master and staff are grateful for the continued cooperation and support of the Parties to the Decree. Also, the contributions of the PPL Corporation and Mirant Corporation in informing the River Master of plans for power generation and furnishing data on reservoir releases are greatly appreciated.

Sincerely yours,

/Signed/

Stephen F. Blanchard
Delaware River Master

DELAWARE RIVER OPERATIONS

Abstract

A Decree of the Supreme Court of the United States, entered in 1954, established the position of Delaware River Master within the U.S. Geological Survey (USGS). In addition, the Decree authorizes diversions of water from the Delaware River Basin and requires compensating releases from certain reservoirs, owned by New York City, to be made under the supervision and direction of the River Master. The Decree stipulates that the River Master will furnish reports to the Court, not less frequently than annually. This report is the 50th Annual Report of the River Master of the Delaware River. It covers the 2003 River Master report year; that is, the period from December 1, 2002 to November 30, 2003.

During the report year, precipitation in the upper Delaware River Basin was 13.40 inches (131 percent) greater than the long-term average. Combined storage in Pepacton, Cannonsville, and Neversink Reservoirs was above the long-term median on December 1, 2002. Reservoir storage increased rapidly in mid-March 2003 and all the reservoirs filled and spilled. The reservoirs remained nearly full for the remainder of the report year. Delaware River operations throughout the report year were conducted as stipulated by the Decree.

Diversions from the Delaware River Basin by New York City and New Jersey were in compliance with the Decree. Reservoir releases were made as directed by the River Master at rates designed to meet the flow objective for the Delaware River at Montague, New Jersey, on 10 days during the report year. Releases were made at experimental conservation rates—or rates designed to relieve thermal stress and protect the fishery and aquatic habitat in the tailwaters of the reservoirs—on all other days.

During the report year, New York City and New Jersey complied fully with the terms of the Decree, and directives and requests of the River Master.

As part of a long-term program, the quality of water in the Delaware Estuary between Trenton, New Jersey, and Reedy Island Jetty, Delaware, was monitored at various locations. Data on water temperature, specific conductance, dissolved oxygen, and pH were collected continuously by electronic instruments at four sites. In addition, selected water-quality data were collected at 3 sites on a monthly basis and at 19 sites on a semi-monthly basis.

Introduction

An Amended Decree of the Supreme Court of the United States, entered June 7, 1954, authorized diversions of water from the Delaware River Basin and provided for releases of water from three New York City reservoirs to the upper Delaware River. The Decree stipulated that these diversions and releases were to be made under the supervision and direction of the Delaware River Master. The Decree also stipulated that reports on Delaware River operations be made to the Court not less frequently than annually. This report documents operations from December 1, 2002, to November 30, 2003, or the 2003 River Master report year. It also presents information on quality of water in the Delaware Estuary during the report year.

Some hydrologic data presented in this report are records of streamflow and water quality for USGS data-collection stations. These records were collected, computed, and furnished by the offices of the USGS at Troy, New York; Exton and New Cumberland, Pennsylvania; and West Trenton, New Jersey, in cooperation with the States of New York and New Jersey, the Commonwealth of Pennsylvania, and the City of New York. The locations of major streams and reservoirs, and selected streamflow-gaging stations in the Delaware River Basin are shown in figure 1.

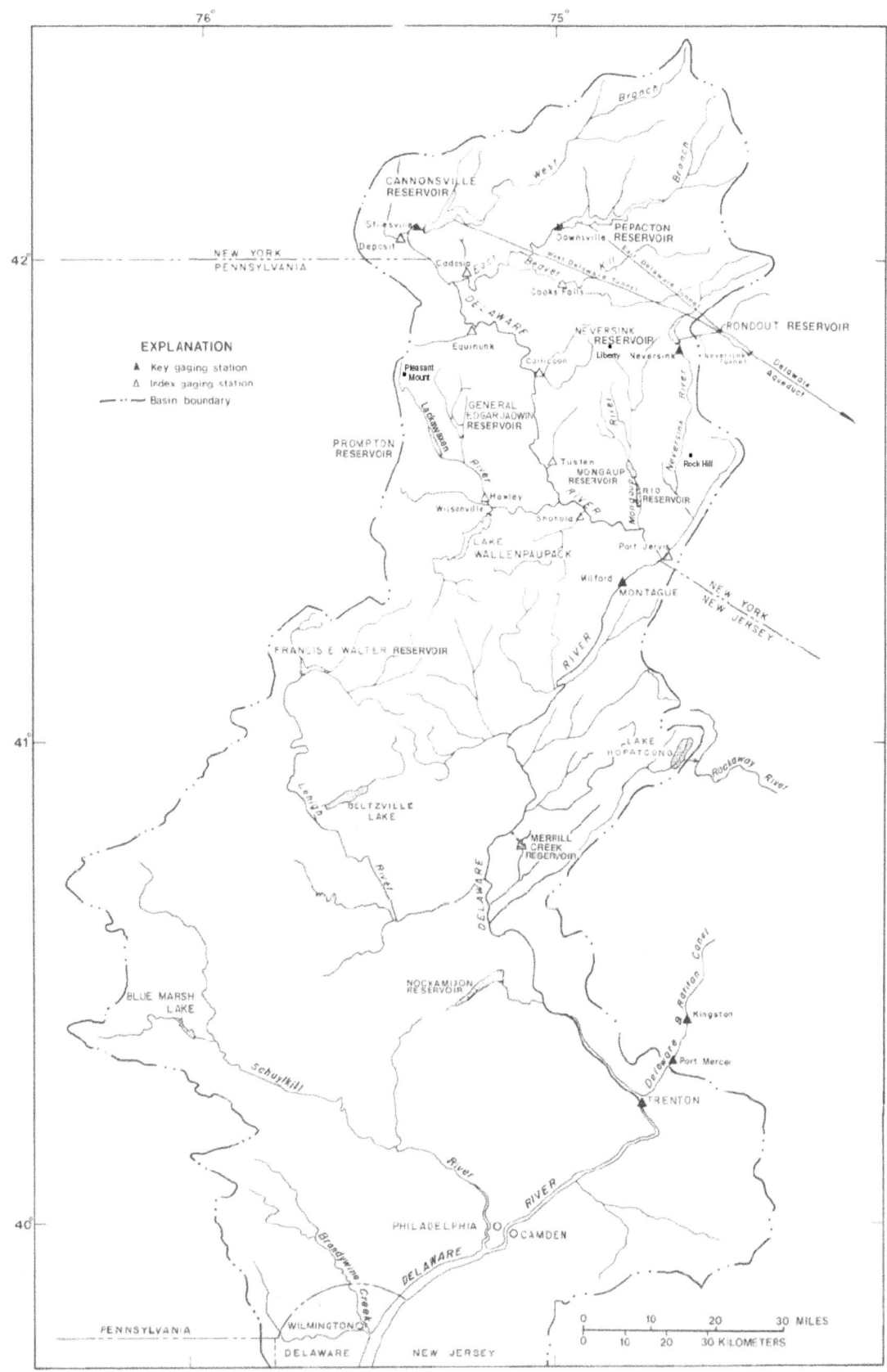

Figure 1. Delaware River Basin above Wilmington, Delaware.

Acknowledgments

The River Master's daily operation records were prepared from hydrologic data collected chiefly on a day-to-day basis. Data for these records were collected and computed by the Office of the Delaware River Master or were furnished by the following agencies and utilities: Data for Pepacton, Cannonsville, and Neversink Reservoirs by the New York City Department of Environmental Protection, Bureau of Water Supply; for Lake Wallenpaupack by PPL Corporation; and for Rio Reservoir by Mirant Corporation. Precipitation data and quantitative precipitation forecasts were provided by the National Weather Service (NWS) office in Binghamton, New York.

Definition of Terms and Procedures

The following definitions apply to various terms and procedures used in the operations documented in this report. A table for converting inch-pound units to the International System of Units (SI) is given on page vi.

- **Balancing Adjustment.**—An operating procedure to correct for inaccuracies inherent in the design of releases from New York City reservoirs to meet the Montague flow objective. The balancing adjustment is computed as 10 percent of the difference between the cumulative adjusted directed release and the cumulative directed release required for exact forecasting. The balancing adjustment is applied to the following day's release design. The maximum daily balancing adjustment is purposely limited to preclude unacceptably large variations in the adjusted flow objective.

- **Capacity.**—Total usable volume in a reservoir between the point of maximum depletion and the elevation of the lowest crest of the spillway.

- **Conservation releases.**—Controlled releases from Pepacton, Cannonsville, and Neversink Reservoirs designed to maintain specified minimum flows in stream channels below the reservoirs. The conservation rates shown in table 2 are defined as follows:

  - ◆ **Basic.**—Conservation release rates in effect prior to 1977.

  - ◆ **Augumented.**—Conservation releases at rates greater than basic, designed to protect and enhance the recreational use of waters affected by such releases. These releases initially went into effect in 1977.

  - ◆ **Experimental.**—Conservation releases that are based on the same total quantity of water as the augmented conservation releases, plus any applicable thermal stress-relief water, and designed to meet the specific needs of various experimental reservoir releases programs since 1983.

- **Daily excess-release credits.**—Daily credits and deficits during the seasonal release period (June 15 to the following March 15) are computed as the arithmetic difference between the daily mean discharge of the Delaware River at Montague, New Jersey, and 1,750 ft³/s. The daily credit cannot exceed the 24-hour period releases from Pepacton, Cannonsville, and Neversink Reservoirs routed to Montague and made in accordance with direction, except as follows: during the seasonal period, credits also are applied for part or all of other releases from these reservoirs that contribute to the daily mean discharge at Montague between 1,750 ft³/s and the applicable excess-release rate.

- **Directed releases.**—Controlled releases from New York City reservoirs in the upper Delaware River Basin, designed by the Delaware River Master to meet the Montague flow objective.

- **Diversions.**—The out-of-basin transfer of water by New York City from Pepacton, Cannonsville, and Neversink Reservoirs in the upper Delaware River Basin through the East Delaware, West Delaware, and Neversink Tunnels, respectively, to the City's water-supply system. Also, the out-of-basin transfer of water by New Jersey from the Delaware River through the Delaware and Raritan Canal.

- **Excess quantity.**—As defined by the Decree, the excess quantity of water is equal to 83 percent of the amount by which the estimated consumption in New York City during the year is less than the City's estimate of continuous safe yield (1,665 Mgal/d stipulated by the 1954 Decree) from all its sources of supply obtainable without pumping, except that the excess quantity shall not exceed 70 billion gallons. Each year, the seasonal period for release of the excess quantity begins on June 15. The flow objective for the period becomes effective at Montague on that date and remains in effect until the following March 15, or until the cumulative total of excess-release credits equals the applicable excess quantity, whichever occurs first.

- **Index gaging station.**—Particular sites on tributaries of the upper Delaware River where systematic observations of gage height and discharge are made. These stations are used mainly during the directed-release season to estimate inflows of surface water to the Delaware River.

- **Key gaging stations.**—Particular sites on the East Branch Delaware River, West Branch Delaware River, Neversink River, Delaware and Raritan Canal, and mainstem Delaware River where continuous, systematic observations of gage height and discharge are made. These stations are used on a year-round basis in River Master operations.

- **Maximum reservoir depletion.**—The minimum water surface level or elevation below which a reservoir ceases to continue to make delivery of quantities of water for all purposes for which the reservoir was designed. Sometimes this is referred to as minimum full-operating level.

- **Rate of flow.**—Mean discharge for a specified 24-hour period, in cubic feet per second or million gallons per day.

- **Rate of flow at Montague.**—Daily mean discharge of the Delaware River at Montague, New Jersey, computed on a calendar-day basis and measured at the USGS streamflow-gaging station.

- **Reservoir-controlled releases.**—Controlled releases from reservoirs passed through outlet valves in the dams or through turbines in powerplants. These releases do not include spillway overflow at the reservoirs.

- **Storage or contents.**—Usable volume of water in a reservoir. Unless otherwise indicated, volume is computed on the basis of level pool and above the point of maximum depletion.

- **Time of day.**—Time of day is expressed in 24-hour Eastern Standard Time, which during the report year included a 23-hour day on April 6 and a 25-hour day on October 26.

- **Uncontrolled runoff at Montague.**—Runoff from the 3,480 square mile drainage area above Montague, New Jersey, excluding the drainage area above Pepacton, Cannonsville, Neversink, Wallenpaupack, and Rio Dams, but including spillway overflow at these dams.

Precipitation

Precipitation in the Delaware River Basin above Montague, New Jersey, totaled 56.57 in. during the 2003 report year and was 13.40 in. greater (131 percent) than the long-term (62-year) average. Monthly precipitation ranged from 75 percent of the long-term average in April 2003 to 276 percent of average in September 2003. Data on monthly precipitation during the report year and long-term average precipitation are presented in table 1[1]. These data were computed from records collected at 10 geographically distributed stations by the NWS; the New York City Department of Environmental Protection, Bureau of Water Supply; and the River Master office.

The seasonal period from December to May typically is when surface-water and ground-water reservoirs refill. During this period in 2002–2003, average precipitation at the 10 stations was 19.81 in., which is 98 percent of the 62-year average. During June to November, average precipitation at the 10 stations was 36.76 in., which is 161 percent of the long-term average. The maximum monthly precipitation was 12.28 in. in September 2003, measured at Equinunk, Pennsylvania; the minimum monthly precipitation was 1.47 in. in January 2003, also measured at Equinunk (location shown on figure 1).

---

[1] All numbered tables in the section "Delaware River Operations" are grouped at the end of this section, beginning on page 20.

Operations

December to May

Operations on December 1, 2002, were conducted as prescribed by the Decree. The Montague flow objective was 1,750 ft³/s and the allowable diversions to New York City and New Jersey were 800 Mgal/d and 100 Mgal/d, respectively. Conservation releases from New York City reservoirs were made at the experimental release rates shown in table 2.

From December 2002 to May 2003, the first half of the report year, total precipitation was 0.47 in. below average. Monthly precipitation ranged from 75 percent of the long-term average in April 2003 to 139 percent in December 2002 (table 1). Runoff in the upper basin was above normal in March and normal during December to February, April, and May.

On December 1, 2002, when the 2003 report year began, Pepacton Reservoir contained 102.163 Bgal of water in storage above the point of maximum depletion, or 72.9 percent of the 140.190 Bgal storage capacity. Cannonsville Reservoir contained 65.510 Bgal, or 68.4 percent of the 95.706 Bgal storage capacity. Neversink Reservoir contained 26.072 Bgal, or 74.6 percent of the 34.941 Bgal storage capacity. Combined storage in these reservoirs on December 1 was 193.745 Bgal, or 71.5 percent of combined capacity. Daily storage in Pepacton, Cannonsville, and Neversink Reservoirs is shown in tables 3, 4, and 5, respectively, and combined storage during the report year is illustrated in figure 2.

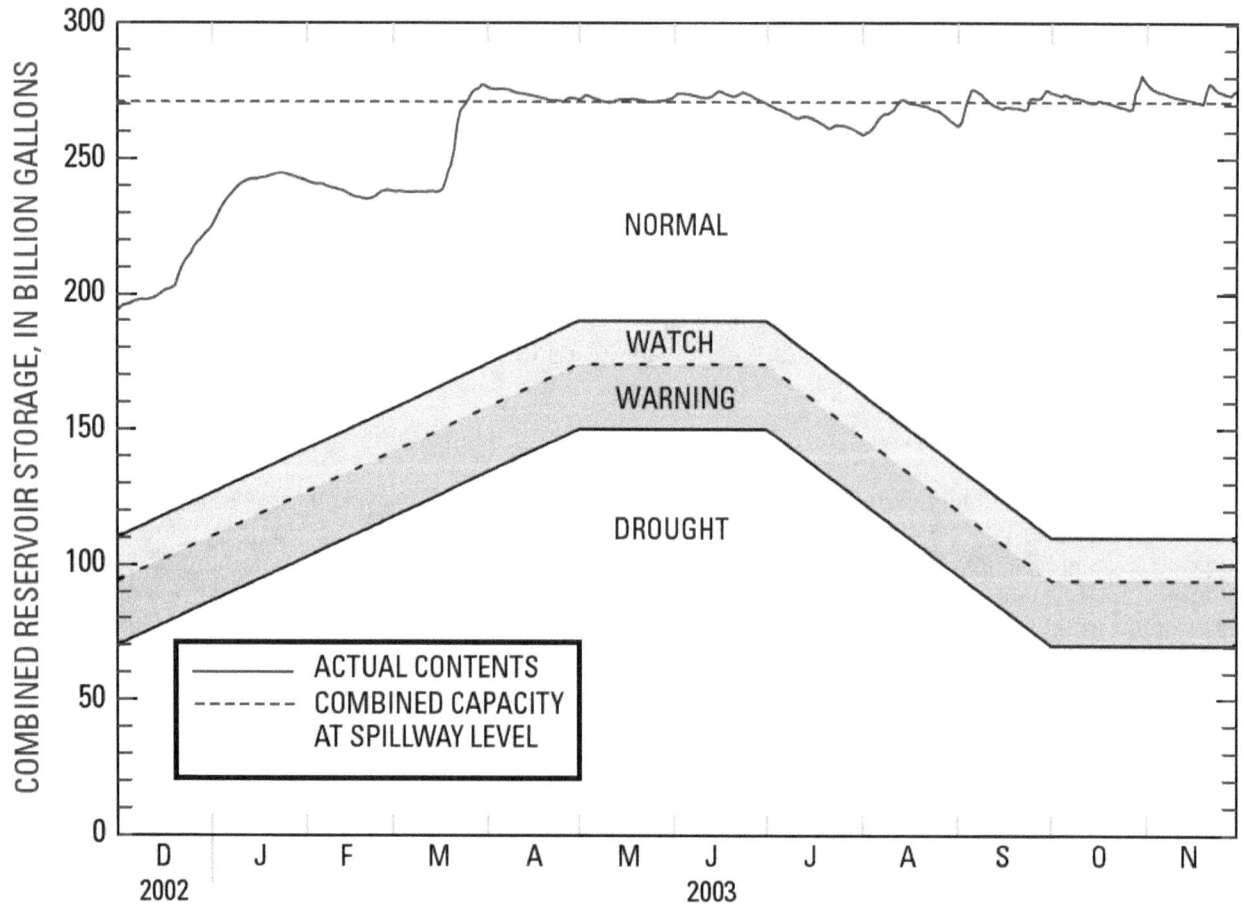

Figure 2. Operation curves and actual combined contents for New York City reservoirs—Pepacton, Cannonsville, and Neversink—in the Delaware River Basin, December 1, 2002, to November 30, 2003.

From December to May, inflow to the City's reservoirs typically exceeds outflow and, consequently, storage increases. The average inflow to Pepacton, Cannonsville, and Neversink Reservoirs for these 6 months during the 62-year period from December 1940 to May 2002 was 301.4 Bgal. During the corresponding 6 months of the report year, inflow to the three reservoirs totaled 294.6 Bgal. Evaporation loss is not included in the computations.

Combined storage increased during December and fluctuated moderately from January to mid-March. Precipitation in mid-March, in combination with snowmelt from a much above-average snowpack, resulted in a storage increase to full capacity in late March. Combined storage remained at full capacity through May.

Combined storage in the three New York City reservoirs was 192.441 Bgal on November 30, 2002 and 272.240 Bgal on May 31, 2003, a net increase of 79.799 Bgal or 29.5 percent of total capacity. The maximum combined storage from December to May was 277.282 Bgal on March 30. Typically, maximum storage in the individual reservoirs occurs on different days. Maximum storage in Pepacton Reservoir during the December to May period was 142.267 Bgal on May 3; maximum storage in Cannonsville Reservoir was 103.511 Bgal on March 23; and maximum storage in Neversink Reservoir was 35.359 Bgal on March 30, 2003. Pepacton Reservoir spilled from March 27 to May 22 and May 29–31, Cannonsville Reservoir spilled from January 16 to May 31, and Neversink Reservoir spilled from March 27 to April 15 and on May 31. A total of 123.792 Bgal of water spilled from these reservoirs during the December to May period.

During the December to May period, diversions to Rondout Reservoir by New York City totaled 71.666 Bgal (394 Mgal/d). The forecasted discharge at Montague, exclusive of water released from the City reservoirs, was greater than the flow objective on all days in the period, and no releases were directed. The observed daily mean discharge at Montague exceeded the applicable flow objective on all days. Applicable design rates for the USGS gaging station Delaware River at Montague, New Jersey, are presented in table 6.

June to November

Monthly precipitation from June to November was above average in all months. Total precipitation during the period was 36.76 in., or 13.87 in. more than the 62-year average (table 1).

Combined storage in the three New York City reservoirs was 273.084 Bgal on June 1, 2003, and 275.180 Bgal on November 30, 2003, a net increase of 2.1 Bgal or about 1 percent of total capacity. During the June to November period, maximum storage in Pepacton Reservoir was 144.211 Bgal on October 30; 101.194 Bgal in Cannonsville Reservoir on October 30; and 35.409 Bgal in Neversink Reservoir on October 30. Maximum combined storage in the three reservoirs was 280.814 Bgal on October 30. The total spill volume during this period was about 171 Bgal.

Releases were directed to meet the Montague flow objective on 10 days between June 1 and November 30, 2003, when the forecasted discharge at Montague, exclusive of water released from the New York City reservoirs, was less than the flow objective. Releases at experimental conservation rates or at rates designed to protect the fishery and aquatic habitat were made at other times during the period.

From June 1 to June 14, the Montague flow objective was 1,750 ft³/s (table 6). The forecasted flow, exclusive of releases from Pepacton, Cannonsville, and Neversink Reservoirs, did not fall below the flow objective and no releases were directed.

The New York City Department of Environmental Protection, Bureau of Water Supply, Quality, and Protection furnished the River Master with the following data for the 2003 calendar year, as stipulated by the Decree:

9

1. The estimated continuous safe yield from all the City's sources, obtainable without pumping, is 1,665 Mgal/d, or a total during calendar year 2003 of 1.665 Bgal/d x 365 days = 607.725 Bgal.

2. The estimated consumption that the City must provide for, from all its sources of supply during calendar year 2003, is 591.582 + 7.250 = 598.832 Bgal.

On the basis of the Decree and the aforementioned data, the aggregate quantity of excess-release water was 83 percent of (607.725 - 598.832), or 7.381 Bgal.

Data on water consumption by the City of New York for each calendar year since 1950, from all sources of supply, are presented in table 7.

On March 19, 2003, the reservoir releases program described in DRBC Docket No. D-77-20 CP (Revision No. 6), was revised and extended to April 30, 2004. A copy of the agreement extending the program is included in this report as Appendix A. As part of this program, 40 percent of the annual excess-release quantity was placed in a habitat protection bank. The remainder of the excess-release quantity could be used to provide an increase in the Montague flow objective or could be banked in accordance with the procedures described in the DRBC's Lower Basin Drought Management Plan.

On June 15, 2003, the beginning of the seasonal excess-release period, the Montague flow objective was increased to 1,810 ft^3/s (table 6). Storage in the New York City reservoirs remained full or nearly full throughout summer and fall as a result of above-normal precipitation and runoff, and below normal directed releases required to meet the Montague flow objective (fig. 2).

Between June 15 and November 30, 2003, the forecasted flow at Montague, exclusive of releases from the New York City reservoirs, was less than the flow objective on 10 days and releases were directed. During the June 15 to November 30 period, the observed flow was never less than the flow objective. Applicable design rates for the USGS gaging station Delaware River at Montague, New Jersey, are presented in table 6.

The total discharge measured at Montague, the portion derived from uncontrolled runoff from the drainage area below the reservoirs, the portion contributed by power reservoirs, and the portion contributed by Pepacton, Cannonsville, and Neversink Reservoirs from July to September are shown in figure 3. In developing the water budget for Montague, uncontrolled runoff was computed as the residual of observed flow minus releases and spills from all reservoirs, and, consequently, was subject to errors in observations, transit times, and routing of the various components of flow. The conservation release and spill from Rio Reservoir is included in the uncontrolled runoff component. The net effect of these uncertainties is incorporated in the computation of uncontrolled runoff. From June 1 to November 30, 2003, diversions from the three New York City Delaware Basin reservoirs to Rondout Reservoir totaled 93.605 Bgal.

Summary of Operations

From December 1, 2002, to November 30, 2003, diversions from three New York City reservoirs in the upper Delaware River Basin to Rondout Reservoir totaled 165.271 Bgal, and all releases from the three reservoirs to the Delaware River totaled 55.202 Bgal. River Master directed releases to the Delaware River from these reservoirs totaled 3.180 Bgal.

During the year, maximum storage in Pepacton Reservoir was 144.211 Bgal on October 30; 103.511 Bgal in Cannonsville Reservoir on March 23; and 35.409 Bgal in Neversink Reservoir on October 30. Maximum combined storage in the three reservoirs was 280.814 Bgal on October 30, 2003. The total combined spill for the year was 294.407 Bgal.

During the report year, minimum storage in Pepacton Reservoir was 102.163 Bgal (72.9 percent of capacity) on December 1, 2002; 65.510 Bgal (68.4 percent of capacity) in Cannonsville Reservoir on December 1, 2002; and 25.333 Bgal (72.5 percent of capacity) in Neversink Reservoir on December 20,

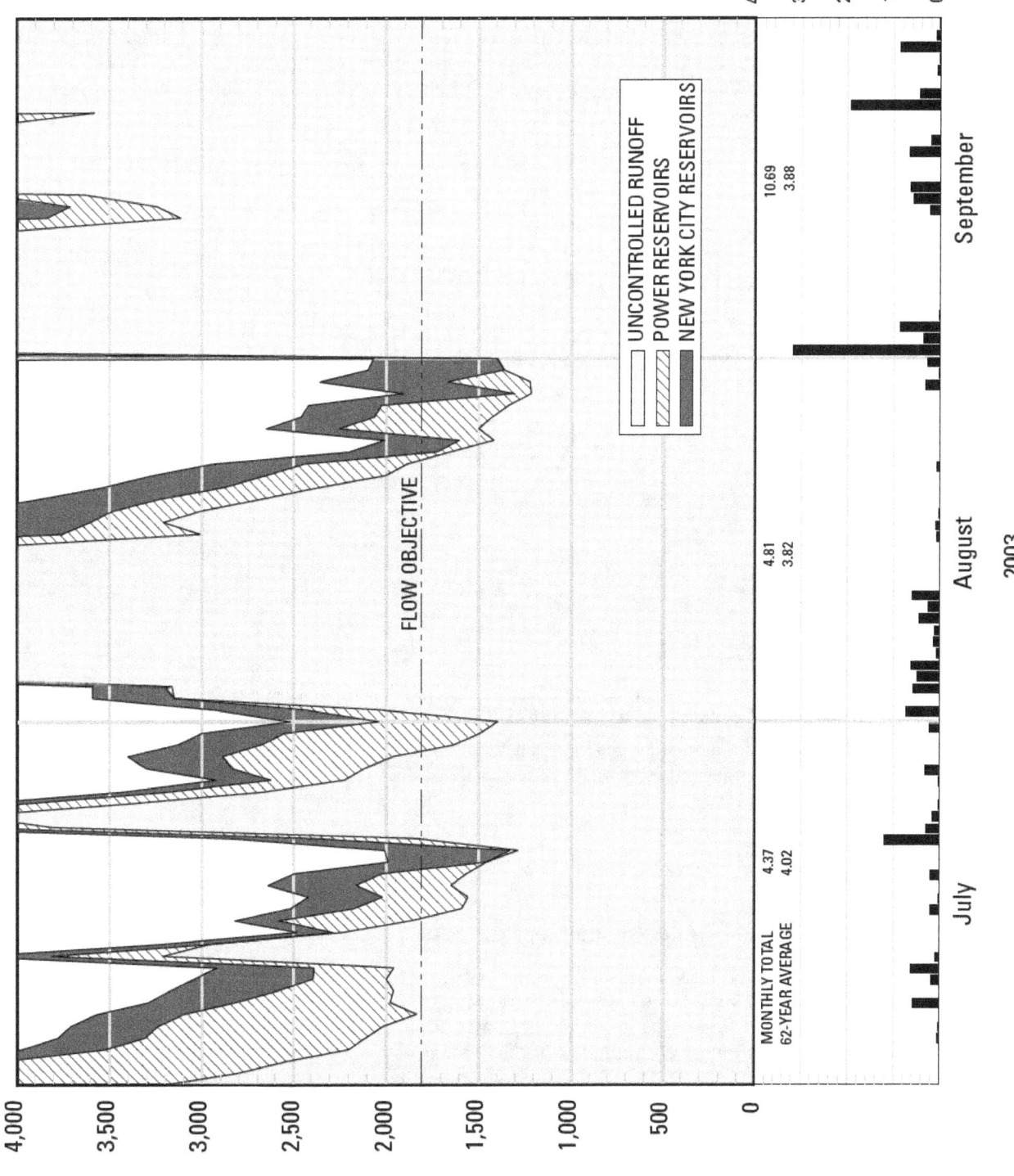

Figure 3. Components of flow, Delaware River at Montague, New Jersey, July 1 to September 30, 2003.

11

2002. Minimum combined storage in the three reservoirs was 193.745 Bgal (71.5 percent of combined capacity) on December 1, 2002.

On November 30, 2003, the end of the report year, combined storage in the three reservoirs was 275.180 Bgal or 101.6 percent of combined capacity. From December 1, 2002 to November 30, 2003, the net change in combined storage was +81.435 Bgal, or an increase equivalent to 30.1 percent of combined capacity.

The distribution of combined storage for the three reservoirs on the first day of the month, for the reference period June 1967 to November 2002, and for the report year, is shown in figure 4. Storage was above median for the report year. Storage was above the 75th percentile from April to November, 2003. New record high combined storage levels for the first day of the month were set in September, October, and November.

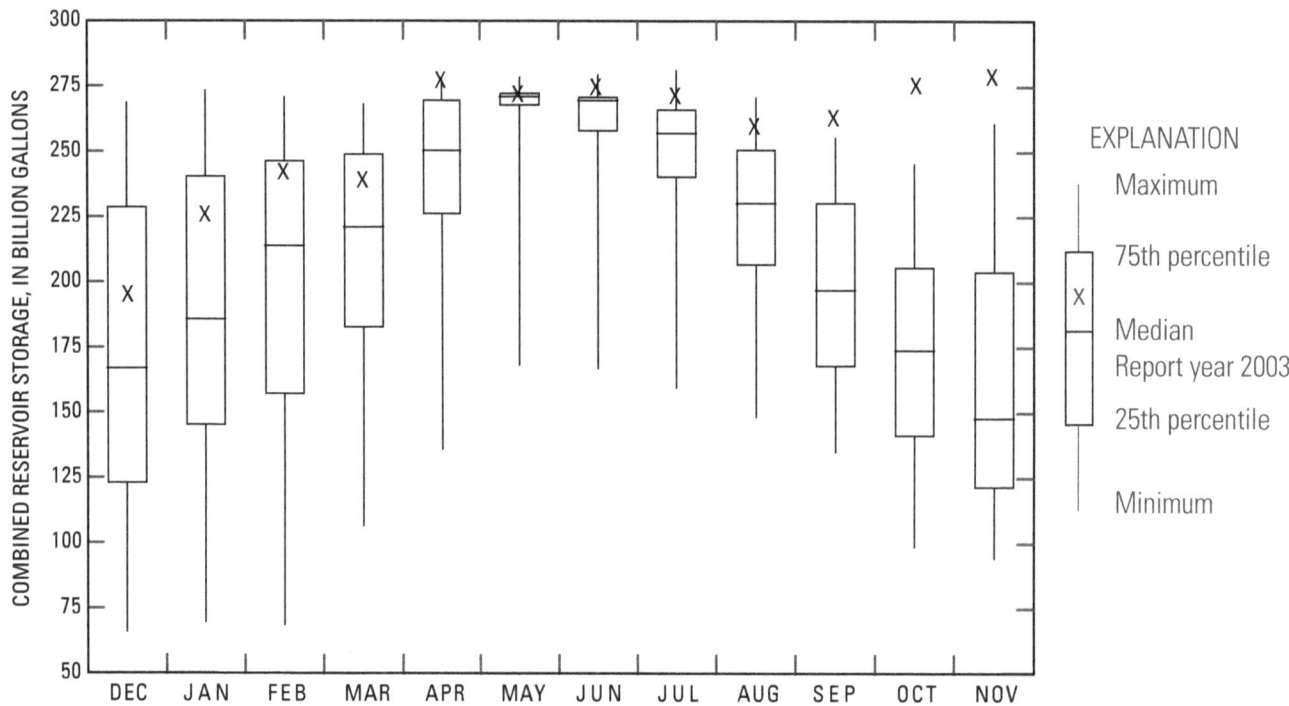

Figure 4. Combined storage in Pepacton, Cannonsville, and Neversink Reservoirs on the first day of the month, December 2002 to November 2003 (this report year), and summary statistics for the reference period, June 1967 to November 2002.

Streamflow

Components of Flow, Delaware River at Montague, New Jersey

The data and computations of the various components of flow form the basic operational records used by the River Master to carry out specific responsibilities related to the Montague formula. The operational record has two parts: forecasted flow at Montague, exclusive of controlled releases from New York City's reservoirs (table 8), and segregation of components of daily mean flow at Montague (table 9).

The following components may be present in the flow of the Delaware River at Montague:

1. Controlled releases from Lake Wallenpaupack on Wallenpaupack Creek, for the production of hydroelectric power.

2. Controlled releases from Rio Reservoir on Mongaup River, for the production of hydroelectric power.

3. Runoff from the uncontrolled area above Montague, including spills from New York City reservoirs, Lake Wallenpaupack, and Rio Reservoir.

4. Controlled releases from Pepacton, Cannonsville, and Neversink Reservoirs of New York City.

The releases from New York City's reservoirs necessary to maintain the Montague flow objective were computed on the basis of the forecasted flow at Montague, exclusive of controlled releases from the reservoirs.

Time of Travel

Following are average times for the effective travel of water from the various sources of controlled supply to Montague, New Jersey. These times were used for flow routing during the 2003 report year:

Source	Hours
Pepacton Reservoir	60
Cannonsville Reservoir	48
Neversink Reservoir	33
Lake Wallenpaupack	16
Rio Reservoir	8

The travel times were computed from reservoir and powerplant operations data and historical streamflow records. The travel times generally are suitable for use in the operations of the River Master. Occasionally, however, significant exceptions are observed. For example, when a large release from Cannonsville Reservoir follows a small release, a substantial portion of the water fills the channel en route, and the remainder may arrive at Montague as much as 66 hours after the time of release. During winter, the formation of ice cover, together with lower streamflow, gradually increases the resistance to water flow, resulting in increased travel times. Because ice-affected travel times increase gradually over several days, and releases were not directed to meet the Montague flow objective during periods of ice cover, no adjustments were made to compensate for increased travel times during these periods of the report year.

Segregation of Flow at Montague

The River Master daily operations record of reservoir releases and segregation of the various components contributing to the flow of the Delaware River at Montague, New Jersey, are presented in table 9. The data are arranged to conform to the downstream movement of water from the various sources to Montague. Summation of data along individual rows in the table is equivalent to routing the various flow contributions to Montague, using the aforementioned average travel times. Uncontrolled runoff was computed as a residual by subtracting the flow contributions of all other sources from the observed discharge at Montague.

Computation of Directed Releases

During the report year, the River Master used the following information for daily operations: (1) discharges computed from recorded or reported stream gage heights, for various 24-hour periods, absent real-time information on any changes in stage-discharge relations; (2) daily discharge from New York City's three reservoirs, measured with venturi meters; (3) precipitation reports for the previous 24 hours; (4) actual powerplant releases converted to daily discharges; (5) advance estimates of power demand converted to daily discharges; (6) advance estimates of uncontrolled runoff at Montague; and (7) average travel times for routing water from various sources. Although uncertainty is inherent in the advance estimates, this information by necessity is used in the daily design and direction of reservoir releases.

The 60-hour average travel time of water from Pepacton Reservoir to Montague is greater than the travel time of water from any other reservoir in the upper Delaware River Basin. Releases from Cannonsville and Neversink Reservoirs were timed to arrive at Montague concurrently with releases from Pepacton Reservoir. To allow for differences in travel times, daily directed releases were scheduled to begin from Pepacton Reservoir at 1200 hours, from Cannonsville Reservoir at 2400 hours, and from Neversink Reservoir at 1500 hours the following day.

Releases from the City's reservoirs required to maintain the Montague flow objective were computed from forecasts of releases from Lake Wallenpaupack and Rio Reservoir, and estimates of uncontrolled runoff at Montague. To account for the travel times from these sources to Montague, the computation requires estimates of the following components of flow two or more days in advance: (1) release of water from Lake Wallenpaupack; (2) release of water from Rio Reservoir; and (3) uncontrolled runoff at Montague. The River Master operations record for computing daily directed release requirements during periods of low flow is given in table 8.

The electric utilities furnished forecasts of power generation and releases. Because the hydroelectric plants were used chiefly for area regulation or meeting peak power demands, the forecasts were subject to various modifying factors including the vagaries of weather on electricity demand. In addition, because the power companies are members of regional power pools, demand for power outside of the local service area may unexpectedly affect generation schedules. Consequently, at times, the actual use of water for power generation differed considerably from the forecasts used in the design of reservoir releases.

For computational purposes during periods of low flow, estimates of uncontrolled runoff at Montague are treated as two components: (1) current runoff and (2) forecasted increase in runoff from precipitation. Estimates of these components are given in table 8.

During ice-free conditions, current runoff was computed using a routing and recession procedure based on discharges at 0800 hours at the following USGS gaging stations:

Station Name	Drainage Area (mi²)
Beaver Kill at Cooks Falls, New York	241
Cadosia Creek at Cadosia, New York	17.9
Oquaga Creek at Deposit, New York	67.6
Equinunk Creek at Equinunk, Pennsylvania	56.3
Callicoon Creek at Callicoon, New York	110
Tenmile River at Tusten, New York	45.6
Lackawaxen River at Hawley, Pennsylvania	290
Shohola Creek near Shohola, Pennsylvania	83.6
Neversink River at Port Jervis, New York	336

During winter, the advance estimate of uncontrolled runoff (current conditions) was made on the basis of flows at a reduced network of gaging stations and the recession curve for computed uncontrolled flow at Montague.

The forecasted runoff from precipitation is shown in table 8 under the heading "Weather Adjustment." Throughout the year, the NWS office in Binghamton, New York, furnished quantitative forecasts of average precipitation and air temperatures for the drainage basin above Montague, New Jersey. During winter, runoff was estimated on the basis of the current status of snow and ice, along with forecasted precipitation and temperature. During other periods, forecasted precipitation was used to estimate runoff.

The forecasted flow at Montague, exclusive of releases from New York City's reservoirs (table 8), is computed as the sum of forecasted releases from power reservoirs, estimated uncontrolled runoff including conservation releases from Rio Reservoir, and weather adjustments. If the computed total flow was less than the flow objective at Montague, then the deficiency was made up by River Master directed releases from the City's reservoirs.

When forecasts of precipitation or powerplant releases were revised appreciably after a release was directed, the release required from the City's reservoirs were recomputed. Commonly, this procedure resulted in a reduced release requirement for New York City reservoirs for that day. Only final figures for releases from New York City reservoirs are given in table 8.

Analysis of Forecasts

Forecasts of streamflow at Montague, developed on the basis of anticipated contributions from the components described previously (excluding releases from New York City's reservoirs), differed on most days from observed flow. Occasionally, variations in the components were partially compensating and observed flows were in excellent agreement with forecasted flows.

The forecasted flow of the Delaware River at Montague, exclusive of releases from New York City reservoirs, was less than the flow objective on 10 days from July 20 to September 3, 2003.

On any given day, the forecasted releases and actual releases can differ considerably. The ranges of actual daily releases for these 10 days are as follows: daily releases at Lake Wallenpaupack differed by 72 ft³/s less to 394 ft³/s more than forecasted releases, and daily releases at Rio Reservoir differed by 0 ft³/s less to 301 ft³/s more than forecasted releases. On the basis of observed flows at Montague, total directed releases from New York City's reservoirs during the report year were 2,302 (ft³/s-d) more than that required for exact forecasting.

Analysis of the precipitation forecasts shows that the total precipitation amount forecasted for the 3-day design periods is reasonably accurate, but often the actual timing of precipitation events may be earlier or later than forecasted. The accuracy of the runoff forecasts is affected greatly by the timing of precipitation events. In addition, if the actual storm track differs from the forecasted track, then the amount and timing of runoff can be substantially different than predicted.

Diversions to New York City Water Supply

The 1954 Amended Decree authorizes New York City to divert water from the Delaware River Basin at a rate not to exceed the equivalent of 800 Mgal/d. The Decree specifies that the diversion rate shall be computed as the aggregate total diversion beginning June 1 of each year divided by the number of days elapsed since the preceding May 31.

Daily diversions during the report year from Pepacton, Cannonsville, and Neversink Reservoirs to the New York City water-supply system (Rondout Reservoir) are given in table 10. A running account of the average rates of combined diversions from the three reservoirs, computed as prescribed by the Decree, also is shown. The following tabulation shows allowable maximum diversion rates and average actual diversions for various periods during the report year.

Effective dates	Allowable diversion (Mgal/d)	Average actual diversion (Mgal/d)
June 1, 2002, to May 31, 2003	800	492
June 1, 2003, to November 30, 2003	800	512

During the report year, a total of 165.271 Bgal of water was diverted to the New York City water-supply system. The allowable diversion was 330.560 Bgal.

Storage in New York City Reservoirs

The following tabulation summarizes the "point of maximum depletion" and other pertinent levels and contents of Pepacton, Cannonsville, and Neversink Reservoirs. This information was provided by the New York City Board of Water Supply.

Level	Pepacton Reservoir		Cannonsville Reservoir		Neversink Reservoir	
	Elevation (ft)	Contents (Bgal)	Elevation (ft)	Contents (Bgal)	Elevation (ft)	Contents (Bgal)
Full pool or spillway crest	1,280.00	*140.190	1,150.00	*95.706	1,440.00	*34.941
Point of maximum depletion	1,152.00	*3.511	1,040.00	*1.020	1,319.00	*0.525
Sill of diversion tunnel	1,143.00	*4.200	+1,035.00	*1.564	1,314.00	
Sill of river outlet tunnel	1,126.50		1,020.50		1,314.00	
Dead storage		1.800		0.328		1.680

*Contents shown are quantities stored between listed elevations.

+Elevation of mouth of inlet channel of diversion works.

Daily storage in Pepacton, Cannonsville, and Neversink Reservoirs, above the "point of maximum depletion" or minimum full-operating level, is given in tables 3, 4, and 5.

On December 1, 2002, combined storage in the three reservoirs was 193.745 Bgal, or 71.5 percent of combined capacity. As noted previously, storage fluctuated moderately during winter and then increased to full capacity in late March. In 2003, Pepacton Reservoir spilled a total of 109.370 Bgal from March 27 to May 22; May 29 to June 28; August 12–19; September 2–12; and September 23 to November 30. Cannonsville Reservoir spilled a total of 170.052 Bgal from January 16 to July 1; August 12–20; and September 4 to November 30, 2003. Neversink Reservoir spilled a total of 14.985 Bgal from March 27 to April 15; May 31 to June 7; June 13–17; June 22–23; August 12–13; September 28 to October 5; and October 29 to November 8, 2003. Combined storage reached a maximum for the year on October 30, 2003, when all three reservoirs were spilling. Storage did not decline seasonally during the report year. Combined storage was 275.180 Bgal, or 101.6 percent of combined capacity, on November 30, 2003.

Comparison of River Master Operations Data With Other Streamflow Records

River Master operations are conducted on a day-to-day basis, and, by necessity, use preliminary data on streamflow. In this section, records used in River Master operations are compared to final data published for USGS gaging stations. Data on releases were reported in million gallons per day and converted to cubic feet per second for use in the comparisons.

Releases from New York City Reservoirs

River Master operations data on controlled releases from Pepacton, Cannonsville, and Neversink Reservoirs to the Delaware River were furnished by the New York City Department of Environmental Protection. These data were obtained from calibrated instruments connected to venturi meters installed in the outlet conduits of the reservoirs.

The USGS gaging station on East Branch Delaware River at Downsville, New York, is 0.5 mile downstream from Downsville Dam (fig. 1). Discharge measured at this station includes releases from Pepacton Reservoir and a small amount of seepage and any runoff that enters the stream channel between the dam and the gaging station. The drainage area is 371 mi^2 at the dam and 372 mi^2 at the gaging station.

The following tabulation compares releases from Pepacton Reservoir (table 9), reported by New York City, to the final records for the USGS gaging station on East Branch Delaware River at Downsville, New York (table 11), for the flow objectives shown.

Flow objective (ft^3/s)	45	70	95
Number of USGS daily mean discharge values used in comparison	110	15	50
New York City-measured mean flow (ft^3/s)	45.4	69.8	94.3
USGS-computed mean flow (ft^3/s)	45.0	67.2	88.2
Percent difference	+0.9	+3.9	+6.9

The differences at the flow rates shown are less than 7 percent. The instruments connected to the venturi meters were recalibrated periodically by New York City to improve the accuracy of the recorded flow data.

The USGS gaging station on West Branch Delaware River at Stilesville, New York, is 1.4 miles downstream from Cannonsville Dam (fig. 1). Discharge measured at this station includes releases from Cannonsville Reservoir and runoff from 2 mi^2 of drainage area between the dam and the gaging station. The drainage area is 454 mi^2 at the dam and 456 mi^2 at the gaging station.

The following tabulation compares releases from Cannonsville Reservoir (table 9), reported by New York City, to the final records for the USGS gaging station on West Branch Delaware River at Stilesville, New York (table 12), for the flow objectives shown.

Flow objective (ft^3/s)	45	200–400
Number of USGS daily mean discharge values used in comparison	40	30
New York City-measured mean flow (ft^3/s)	45.1	280
USGS-computed mean flow (ft^3/s)	59.5	274
Percent difference	-24.2	+2.2

The gaging-station records are rated fair at flows greater than 100 ft^3/s and poor at flows less than 100 ft^3/s. A rating of "fair" means that about 95 percent of the daily discharges are within 15 percent of the true discharge, whereas "poor" means that daily discharges have less than "fair" accuracy. The records include runoff from the area between the dam and the gaging station, and seepage near the base of the dam. On January 21, 1998, the seepage was measured at 3.9 ft^3/s.

The USGS gaging station on Neversink River at Neversink, New York, is 1,650 feet downstream from Neversink Dam (fig. 1). Discharge measured at this station includes releases from Neversink Reservoir and, during storms, a small amount of runoff that originates between the dam and the gaging station. The drainage area is 92.5 mi^2 at the dam and 92.6 mi^2 at the gaging station.

The following tabulation compares releases from Neversink Reservoir (table 9), reported by New York City, to the final records for the USGS gaging station on Neversink River at Neversink, New York (table 13), for the flow objectives shown.

Flow objective (ft³/s)	25	53
Number of USGS daily mean discharge values used in comparison	174	85
New York City-measured mean flow (ft³/s)	24.8	52.6
USGS-computed mean flow (ft³/s)	26.1	55.4
Percent difference	-5.0	-5.1

Releases from Lake Wallenpaupack

Records of daily discharge through the Wallenpaupack powerplant were furnished by PPL Corporation and published by USGS as Wallenpaupack Creek at Wilsonville, Pennsylvania (table 14). These discharges represent the flow through the turbines of the powerplant and were computed on a midnight-to-midnight basis. For River Master operations, flows were computed on a 24-hour basis beginning at 0800 hours to compensate for the 16-hour travel time to Montague, New Jersey (table 9).

From December 2002 to November 2003, the River Master's record agrees with the published USGS record except for some very small differences that result mainly from differences in timeframe and rounding of computations. Overall, the records agree to within 0.2 percent for the year.

Delaware River at Montague, New Jersey

The River Master's operations record for the Delaware River at Montague, New Jersey (table 9), showed 1.5 percent more discharge for the report year than the published USGS record for the gaging station (table 15). Daily values for the two records were in good agreement, except during ice-affected periods.

Diversion Tunnels

Records of diversions through the East Delaware, West Delaware, and Neversink Tunnels (fig. 1) were furnished by the New York City Department of Environmental Protection. These records were obtained from the City's calibrated instruments connected to venturi meters installed in the tunnel conduits. The measured flows were transmitted electronically, on a 15-second interval, to the Department's computer at the West of Hudson Control Center. On 5-minute intervals, release and diversion quantities for the preceding 5-minute period were computed using the instantaneous rate-of-flow data from each instrument. These 5-minute quantities were then summed to compute daily total flows, which were reported to the River Master's office on a daily basis. On a weekly basis, the diversion figures were checked against the flow meter totalizer readings and were corrected when necessary.

The East Delaware Tunnel is used to divert water from Pepacton Reservoir to Rondout Reservoir. Conditions in the outlet channel of the East Delaware Tunnel were unfavorable for flow measurements during the report year because of high water levels in Rondout Reservoir.

The generating plant at the downstream end of the East Delaware Tunnel operated most days of the report year. When the powerplant was not in operation, some water leaked through the wicket gates and was not recorded on the totalizer. A current-meter measurement made in 1989 shows that the (assumed constant) rate of leakage is about 8.0 Mgal/d. Because the powerplant was not in operation for the equivalent of 152 days during the 2003 report year, the unmeasured leakage was estimated to be about 1.2 Bgal.

The West Delaware Tunnel is used to divert water from Cannonsville Reservoir to Rondout Reservoir. Inspections of the channel below the outlet, when valves were closed, revealed only negligible leakage. A hydroelectric powerplant uses water diverted through the West Delaware Tunnel, but the plant operates only when diversions are less than 300 Mgal/d. When the powerplant is not operating, the valves on the pipelines to the plant are closed, and there is no leakage through the system.

The Neversink Tunnel is used to divert water from Neversink Reservoir to Rondout Reservoir. A hydroelectric plant uses water diverted through the Neversink Tunnel. When the powerplant is not operating and the main valve on the diversion tunnel is open, leakage develops that is not recorded on the venturi instruments. One current-meter measurement made in 1999 showed a leakage rate of 16.2 ft^3/s (10.5 Mgal/d). When the powerplant is operating, the leakage is included in the recorded flow. No leakage occurs when the main valve on the tunnel is closed. During the 2003 report year, the powerplant operated part of the day on most days and was not operated the equivalent of 216 days. Using the leakage rate noted above and records of power-plant operation, nearly 2.3 Bgal of water was diverted but not recorded.

Diversions by New Jersey

The Amended Decree authorizes New Jersey to divert water from the Delaware River and its tributaries in New Jersey, to areas outside the Delaware River Basin, without compensating releases. These diversions may not exceed 100 Mgal/d as a monthly average, and the daily mean diversion may not exceed 120 Mgal/d. The USGS gaging station on Delaware and Raritan Canal at Port Mercer, New Jersey (fig. 1), is used as the official control point for measuring diversions by New Jersey (table 16).

The following tabulation gives the allowable diversion by New Jersey, the period it was in effect, and the maximum monthly diversion during the report year.

Effective dates	Allowable monthly average diversion (Mgal/d)	Maximum monthly average diversion (Mgal/d)	Month of maximum average diversion
Dec. 1, 2002, to Nov. 30, 2003	100	99.3	April 2003

The maximum daily mean diversion was 106 Mgal on May 11, 2003. Diversions by New Jersey did not exceed the limits prescribed by the Decree.

Conformance of Operations as Provided Under The Amended Decree of The U.S. Supreme Court Entered June 7, 1954

From December 1, 2002, to November 30, 2003, operations of the Delaware River Master were conducted as stipulated by the Decree.

Diversions from the Delaware River Basin to the New York City water-supply system did not exceed those authorized by the Decree. Under compensating releases of the Montague Formula, New York City released water from its reservoirs at rates designed by the River Master to maintain the applicable flow objectives at Montague, New Jersey. During the report year, New York City complied fully with all directives and requests of the River Master.

Diversions from the Delaware River Basin by New Jersey were within limits stipulated by the Decree. New Jersey complied fully with all directives and requests of the River Master.

Table 1. Precipitation in the Delaware River Basin above Montague, New Jersey

[All values, except percentages, in inches]

| Month | December 1940 to November 2002 Monthly Average | December 2002 to November 2003 | | | |
| | | Amount | Percent of average | Excess (+) or deficit (-) | |
				Month	Cumulative
December	3.35	4.66	139	+1.31	+1.31
January	2.98	2.64	89	-.34	+.97
February	2.63	2.97	113	+.34	+1.31
March	3.36	3.03	90	-.33	+.98
April	3.74	2.80	75	-.94	+.04
May	4.22	3.71	88	-.51	-.47
June	3.99	6.57	165	+2.58	+2.11
July	4.02	4.37	109	+.35	+2.46
August	3.82	4.81	126	+.99	+3.45
September	3.88	10.69	276	+6.81	+10.26
October	3.39	5.94	175	+2.55	+12.81
November	3.79	4.38	116	+.59	+13.40
12 months	43.17	56.57	131	+13.40	

Table 2. Conservation release rates for New York City reservoirs in the Delaware River Basin

[All values in cubic feet per second]

| Reservoir | Effective dates | Conservation release rates | | |
		Basic	Augmented	Experimental
Pepacton	December 1 to March 31	6	50	45
	April 1–7	6	70	45
	April 8–30	19	70	45
	May 1–31	19	70	70
	June 1 to August 31	19	70	95
	September 1–30	19	70	70
	October 1–31	19	70	45
	November 1–30	6	50	45
Cannonsville	December 1 to March 31	8	33	45
	April 1–15	8	45	45
	April 16 to May 31	23	45	45
	June 1–14	23	45	160
	June 15 to August 15	23	325	160
	August 16 to September 15	23	45	160
	September 16 to October 31	23	45	45
	November 1–30	23	33	45
Neversink	December 1 to March 31	5	25	25
	April 1–7	5	45	25
	April 8–30	15	45	25
	May 1 to September 30	15	45	53
	October 1–31	15	45	25
	November 1–30	5	25	25

Table 3. Storage in Pepacton Reservoir, New York, for year ending November 30, 2003

[Storage in millions of gallons above elevation 1,152.00 ft. Add 7,711 million gallons for total contents above sill of outlet tunnel, elevation 1,126.50 ft. Storage at spillway level is 140,190 million gallons]

(River Master daily operations record; gage reading at 0800 hours;

DAY	DEC	JAN	FEB	MAR	APR	MAY	JUN	JUL	AUG	SEP	OCT	NOV
1	102,163	112,283	116,144	114,030	141,839	140,709	140,950	139,822	134,588	137,729	141,727	142,286
2	102,601	113,453	115,892	114,047	141,672	141,431	141,431	139,565	134,967	138,664	141,431	141,876
3	103,011	114,363	115,625	114,163	141,672	142,267	141,505	139,271	135,167	140,449	141,338	141,653
4	103,042	115,210	115,459	114,030	141,616	142,136	141,468	139,032	135,511	142,323	141,246	141,486
5	103,074	115,959	115,442	114,080	141,635	141,894	141,412	138,866	136,345	142,845	141,449	141,319
6	103,105	116,578	115,310	114,147	141,616	141,764	141,319	138,793	137,127	142,267	141,338	141,227
7	103,090	117,048	115,160	114,213	141,579	141,431	141,005	138,480	137,674	141,783	141,190	140,931
8	103,058	117,467	115,061	114,246	141,560	140,950	140,913	138,406	138,186	141,486	140,894	140,746
9	103,011	117,905	114,745	114,296	141,245	140,820	140,727	138,150	138,076	140,987	140,764	140,913
10	102,869	118,377	114,562	114,279	140,950	140,672	140,653	137,894	138,498	140,597	140,634	140,950
11	102,759	118,344	114,329	114,153	140,820	140,523	140,783	137,637	138,866	140,319	140,542	140,838
12	102,853	118,276	114,097	114,130	140,838	140,783	140,894	137,802	139,969	140,061	140,431	140,820
13	102,822	118,124	113,915	114,113	140,820	140,913	141,098	137,930	140,987	139,951	140,375	140,672
14	102,869	117,989	113,650	114,097	140,783	140,913	141,245	138,003	141,042	139,767	140,301	140,672
15	103,105	117,669	113,470	113,865	140,764	140,875	141,412	137,820	140,727	139,601	140,468	140,579
16	103,294	117,417	113,091	113,849	140,727	140,764	141,375	137,656	140,301	139,712	140,690	140,560
17	103,404	117,199	112,794	114,195	140,727	140,727	141,079	137,510	140,282	139,785	140,672	140,505
18	103,420	116,947	112,580	115,293	140,653	140,672	140,838	137,182	140,282	139,712	140,616	140,449
19	103,484	117,098	112,267	117,249	140,560	140,560	140,709	136,926	140,227	139,658	140,560	140,505
20	103,594	117,316	111,972	119,053	140,542	140,486	140,560	136,526	140,061	139,804	140,597	142,733
21	105,209	117,467	112,086	122,378	140,449	140,375	140,783	136,145	139,969	139,712	140,560	142,939
22	106,292	117,702	112,267	127,233	140,449	140,319	141,079	136,417	139,822	139,601	140,523	142,435
23	107,108	117,854	112,564	130,865	140,579	140,172	141,319	136,526	139,656	139,804	140,505	142,043
24	107,734	117,972	113,091	133,527	140,597	140,024	141,098	136,435	139,473	141,079	140,468	141,764
25	108,217	117,854	113,486	135,602	140,375	139,896	140,950	136,454	139,418	141,061	140,449	141,727
26	109,137	117,619	113,816	137,528	140,356	139,748	140,838	136,290	139,179	140,950	140,412	141,598
27	109,770	117,383	113,865	139,271	140,690	139,748	140,616	136,054	138,848	140,987	140,764	141,486
28	110,338	117,132	113,997	140,449	140,764	139,859	140,468	135,873	138,627	141,635	143,013	141,375
29	110,827	116,914		141,227	140,746	140,024	140,227	135,584	138,333	142,249	143,313	142,062
30	111,317	116,695		142,193	140,764	140,338	140,024	135,185	138,186	141,969	144,211	142,062
31	111,726	116,394		142,174		140,523		134,877	137,985		142,864	
Change	+10,062	+4,668	-2,397	+28,177	-1,410	-241	-499	-5,147	+3,108	+3,984	+895	-802
Equiv. Mgal/d	+324.6	+150.6	-85.6	+908.9	-47.0	-7.8	-16.6	-166.0	+100.3	+132.8	+28.9	-26.7
Equiv. ft³/s	+502	+233	-132	+1,406	-72.7	-12.0	-25.7	-257	+155	+205	+44.7	-41.4

Change for year +40,398 Mgal   Equivalent for year +110.7 Mgal/d   Equivalent for year +171 ft³/s

Table 4. Storage in Cannonsville Reservoir, New York, for year ending November 30, 2003

[Storage in millions of gallons above elevation 1,040.00 ft. Add 2,584 million gallons for total contents above sill outlet tunnel, elevation 1,020.50 ft. Storage at spillway level is 95,706 million gallons]
(River Master daily operations record; gage reading at 0800 hours)

DAY	DEC	JAN	FEB	MAR	APR	MAY	JUN	JUL	AUG	SEP	OCT	NOV
1	65,510	85,571	96,543	96,671	99,472	97,814	96,945	96,109	90,929	92,131	97,637	100,115
2	66,057	86,655	96,527	96,527	99,167	97,701	97,347	95,722	91,036	92,664	97,718	99,424
3	66,554	87,739	96,494	96,478	99,054	98,023	97,460	95,387	91,400	94,885	97,395	98,941
4	66,923	88,663	96,559	96,414	98,893	97,959	97,492	95,113	91,477	95,835	97,090	98,539
5	67,292	89,545	96,704	96,382	98,989	97,798	97,460	94,992	92,116	98,056	97,251	98,249
6	67,649	90,382	96,816	96,317	99,102	97,621	97,428	94,778	92,786	98,571	97,251	98,168
7	68,351	91,112	96,655	96,317	99,070	97,492	97,363	94,489	93,394	98,523	96,784	97,991
8	68,682	91,797	96,430	96,301	98,845	97,347	97,363	94,200	93,699	98,249	96,880	97,750
9	69,040	92,420	96,511	96,237	98,667	97,154	97,331	93,653	94,170	97,846	97,186	97,492
10	69,225	93,014	96,623	96,189	98,539	97,025	97,251	93,349	94,428	97,315	97,186	97,235
11	69,384	93,668	96,671	96,221	98,249	96,864	97,025	93,272	94,656	96,896	97,106	97,315
12	69,742	94,276	96,687	96,221	98,088	96,880	97,057	93,759	95,220	96,671	97,009	97,251
13	70,152	94,763	96,655	96,269	97,959	96,977	97,170	93,820	95,786	96,543	96,945	97,315
14	70,642	95,067	96,366	96,237	97,846	97,186	97,669	93,683	95,996	96,495	96,864	97,412
15	71,278	95,326	96,173	96,173	97,653	97,347	98,426	93,471	95,851	96,447	97,009	97,347
16	72,033	95,539	95,996	96,350	97,637	97,379	98,426	93,181	95,754	96,768	97,540	97,347
17	72,576	95,996	96,157	96,559	97,589	97,363	98,249	92,862	95,738	96,623	97,557	97,299
18	73,013	96,286	96,302	97,830	97,412	97,331	98,040	92,512	95,851	96,382	97,476	97,267
19	73,450	96,382	96,398	99,070	97,267	97,218	97,862	92,284	95,883	96,124	97,412	97,138
20	74,022	96,575	96,463	99,730	97,202	97,122	97,685	91,994	95,803	96,028	97,444	98,748
21	75,804	96,639	96,495	101,178	97,090	97,073	97,846	91,629	95,722	96,028	97,122	100,614
22	77,421	96,671	96,511	103,447	97,041	96,977	98,136	91,888	95,584	96,044	97,057	100,132
23	78,664	96,687	96,703	103,511	97,025	96,671	98,345	92,390	95,387	96,366	97,009	99,376
24	79,686	96,623	96,977	102,208	96,993	96,623	98,265	92,482	95,204	97,782	97,122	98,716
25	80,557	96,559	97,267	101,210	97,057	96,735	98,072	92,573	94,992	97,862	96,913	98,571
26	81,770	96,575	97,283	100,663	96,993	96,784	97,701	92,512	94,763	97,798	96,784	98,217
27	82,579	96,639	97,267	100,389	97,653	96,848	97,186	92,360	94,367	97,637	96,864	98,104
28	83,056	96,623	96,977	99,955	97,943	96,880	96,864	92,131	93,911	97,605	98,313	98,072
29	83,735	96,575		99,521	98,007	96,864	96,623	91,888	93,272	98,088	99,086	98,265
30	84,400	96,511		99,730	97,927	96,832	96,350	91,584	92,846	98,104	101,194	98,394
31	84,921	96,559		99,762		96,800		91,264	92,436		100,888	
Change	+20,086	+11,638	+418	+2,785	-1,835	-1,127	-450	-5,086	+1,172	+5,668	+2,784	-2,494
Equiv. Mgal/d	+647.9	+375.4	+14.9	+89.8	-61.2	-36.4	-15.0	-164.1	+37.8	+188.9	+89.8	-83.1
Equiv. ft³/s	+1,002	+581	+23.1	+139	-94.6	-56.2	-23.2	-254	+58.5	+292	+139	-128.6

Change for year +33,559 Mgal   Equivalent for year +91.9 Mgal/d   Equivalent for year +142 ft³/s

22

Table 5. Storage in Neversink Reservoir, New York, for year ending November 30, 2003

[Storage in millions of gallons above elevation 1,319.00 ft. Add 525 million gallons for total contents above sill of outlet tunnel, elevation 1,314.00 ft. Storage at spillway level is 34,941 million gallons]
(River Master daily operations record; gage reading at 0800 hours)

DAY	DEC	JAN	FEB	MAR	APR	MAY	JUN	JUL	AUG	SEP	OCT	NOV
1	26,072	27,124	28,870	27,128	35,179	33,393	35,189	34,552	33,360	32,311	35,041	35,229
2	26,165	27,503	28,795	27,206	35,189	33,211	35,299	34,492	33,504	32,514	35,001	35,194
3	26,261	27,849	28,716	27,356	35,174	33,158	35,189	34,448	33,548	33,499	34,936	35,174
4	26,190	28,084	28,588	27,202	35,174	33,129	35,155	34,355	34,086	34,184	34,936	35,140
5	26,123	28,263	28,557	27,172	35,165	33,081	35,140	34,306	34,433	34,675	35,115	35,125
6	26,093	28,434	28,398	27,107	35,145	32,972	35,120	34,282	34,739	34,700	34,931	35,174
7	26,018	28,579	28,207	27,026	35,135	33,048	35,085	34,155	34,798	34,552	34,798	35,150
8	25,963	28,716	28,084	27,116	35,125	33,115	34,956	34,106	34,645	34,350	34,739	35,130
9	25,913	28,852	27,931	27,206	35,120	33,168	34,843	34,033	34,443	34,116	34,680	34,917
10	25,821	28,972	27,774	27,275	35,120	33,235	34,863	34,130	34,527	33,886	34,472	34,724
11	25,733	29,110	27,606	27,326	35,115	33,317	34,793	34,037	34,818	33,630	34,243	34,532
12	25,703	29,226	27,498	27,412	35,155	33,485	34,759	33,920	34,956	33,336	33,993	34,360
13	25,633	29,325	27,292	27,485	35,160	33,635	34,936	33,969	34,966	33,038	33,746	34,155
14	25,587	29,424	27,077	27,503	35,150	33,765	35,120	33,993	34,858	32,752	33,485	33,944
15	25,620	29,491	26,949	27,563	34,971	33,803	35,110	33,925	34,818	32,514	33,341	33,717
16	25,587	29,572	26,842	27,653	34,877	33,896	35,080	33,833	34,586	32,643	33,331	33,485
17	25,574	29,643	26,770	27,792	34,715	33,979	34,986	33,741	34,404	32,800	33,173	33,249
18	25,483	29,720	26,676	28,114	34,630	34,072	34,931	33,688	34,219	32,886	32,957	33,005
19	25,379	29,769	26,557	28,650	34,492	34,160	34,877	33,586	34,023	33,022	32,723	32,805
20	25,333	29,850	26,566	29,052	34,340	34,228	34,803	33,523	33,920	32,991	32,529	33,857
21	25,733	29,914	26,604	30,027	34,194	34,311	34,788	33,446	33,823	32,805	32,306	34,448
22	25,900	29,986	26,638	31,860	34,013	34,301	34,833	33,408	33,688	32,552	32,075	34,562
23	26,030	29,964	26,762	32,995	33,979	34,370	34,981	33,630	33,543	32,420	31,832	34,572
24	26,118	29,910	26,923	33,374	33,983	34,399	34,936	33,504	33,432	33,620	31,592	34,517
25	26,236	29,810	27,035	33,828	33,886	34,517	34,892	33,369	33,461	33,669	31,331	34,453
26	26,409	29,692	27,098	34,350	33,784	34,635	34,818	33,427	33,365	33,606	31,058	34,389
27	26,536	29,563	27,163	34,926	33,760	34,788	34,700	33,432	33,201	33,760	30,923	34,238
28	26,651	29,450	27,133	35,165	33,760	34,808	34,675	33,437	33,009	34,340	33,538	34,096
29	26,769	29,293		35,184	33,615	34,724	34,630	33,446	32,815	35,229	34,448	34,586
30	26,868	29,164		35,359	33,528	34,798	34,596	33,446	32,634	35,080	35,409	34,724
31	26,988	29,012		35,234		34,917		33,456	32,477		35,289	
Change	+1,046	+2,024	-1,879	-8,101	-1,706	+1,389	-321	-1,140	-979	+2,603	+209	-565
Equiv. Mgal/d	+33.7	+65.3	-67.1	+261.3	-56.9	+44.8	-10.7	-36.8	-31.6	+86.8	+6.7	-18.8
Equiv. ft³/s	+52.2	+101	-104	+404	-88.0	+69.3	-16.6	-56.9	-48.9	+134	+10.4	-29.1

Change for year +8,782 Mgal   Equivalent for year +24.1 Mgal/d   Equivalent for year +37.2 ft³/s

Table 6. Design rates for Delaware River at Montague, New Jersey, gaging station, December 1, 2002, to November 30, 2003

[Rates in cubic feet per second]

Effective dates	Montague Design Rate
December 1, 2002, to June 14, 2003	1,750
June 15 to November 30, 2003	1,810

Table 7. Consumption of water by New York City, 1950 to 2003
Data furnished by New York City, Department of Environmental Protection, Bureau of Water Supply

[Mgal/d, million gallons per day; Bgal, billion gallons]

Year	Average daily consumption			Annual Consumption (Bgal)
	City Proper (Mgal/d)	Outside Communities (Mgal/d)	Total (Mgal/d)	
1950	953.3	29.1	982.4	358.576
51	1,041.9	28.1	1,070.0	390.550
52	1,087.0	32.7	1,119.7	409.810
53	1,093.9	44.6	1,138.5	415.552
54	1,063.4	46.3	1,109.7	405.040
1955	1,109.9	45.3	1,155.2	421.648
56	1,111.3	48.9	1,160.2	424.633
57	1,169.0	57.2	1,226.2	447.563
58	1,152.9	49.6	1,202.5	438.912
59	1,204.3	60.3	1,264.6	461.579
1960	1,199.4	58.9	1,258.3	460.529
61	1,221.0	64.0	1,285.0	469.022
62	1,207.6	68.8	1,276.4	465.896
63	1,218.0	76.7	1,294.7	472.582
64	1,189.2	79.4	1,268.6	464.295
1965	1,052.1	71.2	1,123.3	409.995
66	1,044.9	73.2	1,118.1	408.128
67	1,135.3	71.0	1,206.3	440.302
68	1,242.0	78.2	1,320.2	483.175
69	1,328.7	80.1	1,408.8	514.229
1970	1,400.3	90.4	1,490.7	544.116
71	1,423.6	87.9	1,511.5	551.695
72	1,412.4	83.0	1,495.4	547.340
73	1,448.9	95.4	1,544.3	563.681
74	1,441.8	96.3	1,538.1	561.409
1975	1,415.0	92.1	1,507.1	550.093
76	1,435.0	95.8	1,530.8	560.264
77	1,483.0	104.7	1,587.7	579.510
78	1,479.4	103.0	1,582.4	577.566
79	1,513.0	104.6	1,617.6	590.426
1980	1,506.3	110.1	1,616.3	591.582
81	1,309.5	100.0	1,409.5	514.475
82	1,383.0	104.8	1,487.8	543.060
83	1,424.2	112.6	1,536.8	561.010
84	1,465.2	113.9	1,579.1	577.963
1985	1,325.4	106.5	1,431.9	522.656
86	1,351.1	115.2	1,466.3	535.200
87	1,447.1	119.8	1,566.9	571.885
88	1,484.3	125.6	1,609.9	589.090
89	1,402.0	113.4	1,515.4	553.158
1990	1,424.4	122.4	1,546.8	564.577
91	1,469.9	123.6	1,593.5	581.628
92	1,368.7	113.9	1,482.6	542.632
93	1,368.9	118.8	1,487.7	543.011
94	1,357.8	119.2	1,477.0	539.105
1995	1,326.1	123.1	1,449.2	528.958
96	1,283.5	120.2	1,403.7	512.351
97	1,201.3	123.5	1,324.8	483.552
98	1,220.0	124.7	1,344.7	490.816
99	1,237.2	128.6	1,365.8	498.517
2000	1,240.4	124.9	1,365.3	499.700
01	1,184.0	128.4	1,312.4	479.026
02	1,135.6	121.1	1,256.7	458.696
03	1,093.7	115.9	1,209.6	441.516

Table 8. New York City reservoir release design data (River Master daily operation record)

[ft³/s, cubic feet per second; (ft³/s)-d, cubic feet per second days; Col., Column]

Advance estimate of discharge of Delaware River at Montague, New Jersey, exclusive of New York City reservoir releases

Date of advance estimate	Powerplant release forecasts		Uncontrolled runoff		Montague date	Discharge (ft³/s)	Indicated deficiency (ft³/s)	Balancing adjustment (ft³/s)	Directed release (ft³/s)	Computation of balancing adjustment						
	Lake Wallenpaupack (ft³/s)	Rio Reservoir (ft³/s)	Current condition (ft³/s)	Weather adjustment (ft³/s)						Adjusted directed release		Actual deficiency		Cumulative difference (ft³/s)-d	Balancing adjustment (ft³/s)
										Daily (ft³/s)	Cumulative (ft³/s)-d	Daily (ft³/s)	Cumulative (ft³/s)-d		
2003	Col. 1	Col. 2	Col. 3	Col. 4	2003	Col. 5	Col. 6	Col. 7	Col. 8	Col. 9	Col. 10	Col. 11	Col. 12	Col. 13	Col. 14

MONTAGUE DESIGN RATE = 1,750 (ft³/s) DECEMBER 1, 2002, to JUNE 14, 2003

The estimate discharge at Montague was greater than the Montague design rate from December 1, 2002, to June 14, 2003.

MONTAGUE DESIGN RATE = 1,810 (ft³/s) JUNE 15, 2003, to NOVEMBER 30, 2003

The estimate discharge at Montague was greater than the Montague design rate from June 15, 2003, to July 19, 2003.

	Col. 1	Col. 2	Col. 3	Col. 4		Col. 5	Col. 6	Col. 7	Col. 8	Col. 9	Col. 10	Col. 11	Col. 12	Col. 13	Col. 14
July 17	0	0	1,215	65	July 20	1,280	530	0	530	531	531	351	351	+180	-18
18	0	0	1,081	51	21	1,132	678	0	678	678	1,209	478	829	+380	-38

The estimated discharge at Montague was greater than the Montague design rate from July 22, 2003, to August 2, 2003.

| July 31 | 0 | | 1,090 | 323 | Aug. 3 | 1,413 | 397 | -38 | 359 | 359 | 1,568 | 0 | 829 | 739 | -60 |

The estimated discharge at Montague was greater than the Montague design rate from August 4, 2003, to August 23, 2003.

| Aug. 21 | 0 | 64 | 1,715 | 31 | Aug. 24 | 1,810 | 0 | -60 | 0 | 0 | 1,568 | 83 | 912 | 656 | -60 |
| 22 | 96 | 0 | 1,572 | 5 | 25 | 1,673 | 137 | -60 | 77 | 77 | 1,645 | 206 | 1,118 | 527 | -53 |

The estimated discharge at Montague was greater than the Montague design rate from August 26, 2003, to August 28, 2003.

Aug. 26	64	0	1,058	32	Aug. 29	1,154	656	-53	603	603	2,248	503	1,621	627	-60
27	0	0	1,042	23	30	1,065	745	-53	692	690	2,938	140	1,761	1,177	-60
28	0	0	968	51	31	1,019	791	-53	738	738	3,676	448	2,209	1,467	-60
29	0	0	919	168	Sept. 1	1,087	723	-53	670	670	4,346	410	2,619	1,727	-60
30	0	0	1,074	200	2	1,274	536	-60	476	478	4,824	0	2,619	2,205	-60
31	559	0	1,075	19	3	1,653	157	-60	97	97	4,921	0	2,619	2,302	-60

The estimated discharge at Montague was greater than the Montague design rate from September 4, 2003, to November 30, 2003.

Col. 1 - Furnished by power company.
Col. 2 - Furnished by power company.
Col. 3 - Computed from index stations.
Col. 4 - Computed increase in runoff based on quantitative precipitation forecasts.
Col. 5 = Col. 1 + Col. 2 + Col. 3 + Col. 4.

Col. 6 = Design rate - Col. 5, when positive; otherwise Col. 6 = 0.
Col. 7 = Col. 14 (4 days earlier).
Col. 8 = Design rate - Col. 5 + Col. 7, when positive; otherwise Col. 8 = 0.
Col. 9 = Col. 7 from Table 9.
Col. 10 = Summation of Col. 9.

Col. 11 = Design rate - (Col. 9 + Col. 10 from Table 9), when positive; otherwise Col. 11 = 0.
Col. 12 = Summation of Col. 11.
Col. 13 = Col. 10 - Col. 12.
Col. 14 = Col. 13 divided by -10, limited to ±60.

Table 9. Controlled releases from reservoirs in the upper Delaware River Basin and segregation of flow of Delaware River at Montague, New Jersey (River Master daily operation record)

[Mean discharge in cubic feet per second for 24 hours; Col., Column]

	Controlled Releases from New York City Reservoirs					Controlled Releases from Power Reservoirs			Segregation of Flow, Delaware River at Montague, New Jersey					
	Directed	Pepacton	Cannonsville	Neversink		Lake Wallenpaupack	Rio Reservoir		Controlled Releases			Computed uncontrolled	Total
	Amount								New York City Reservoirs		Power-plants		
									Directed	Other			
Date 2002	Col. 1	Col. 2	Col. 3	Col. 4	Date 2002	Col. 5	Col. 6	Date 2002	Col. 7	Col. 8	Col. 9	Col. 10	Col. 11
Nov. 28	0	46	46	25	Nov. 30	236	124	Dec. 1	0	117	360	4,463	4,940
29	0	46	46	25	Dec. 1	340	415	2	0	117	755	4,218	5,090
30	0	46	46	25	2	633	383	3	0	117	1,016	3,647	4,780
Dec. 1	0	46	46	25	3	834	372	4	0	117	1,206	2,917	4,240
2	0	46	46	25	4	625	319	5	0	117	944	2,919	3,980
3	0	46	46	25	5	633	213	6	0	117	846	2,887	3,850
4	0	46	46	25	6	553	220	7	0	117	773	2,850	3,740
5	0	45	45	25	7	283	124	8	0	116	407	2,727	3,250
6	0	46	45	25	8	336	0	9	0	116	336	2,758	3,210
7	0	46	45	25	9	656	78	10	0	116	734	2,910	3,760
8	0	46	45	25	10	645	53	11	0	116	698	2,696	3,510
9	0	46	79	25	11	681	89	12	0	150	770	3,320	4,240
10	0	46	145	25	12	679	71	13	0	216	750	3,794	4,760
11	0	46	145	25	13	1,005	142	14	0	216	1,147	5,137	6,500
12	0	46	121	25	14	711	170	15	0	192	881	7,697	8,770
13	0	46	70	25	15	478	199	16	0	141	677	7,872	8,690
14	0	46	45	25	16	839	394	17	0	116	1,233	6,221	7,570
15	0	46	45	25	17	774	411	18	0	116	1,185	5,279	6,580
16	0	46	45	25	18	760	415	19	0	116	1,175	4,429	5,720
17	0	46	45	25	19	730	426	20	0	116	1,156	5,018	6,290
18	0	45	45	25	20	587	426	21	0	115	1,013	9,372	10,500
19	0	45	45	25	21	270	418	22	0	115	688	10,197	11,000
20	0	45	45	25	22	348	546	23	0	115	894	8,331	9,340
21	0	45	45	25	23	767	472	24	0	115	1,239	6,986	8,340
22	0	45	45	25	24	811	415	25	0	115	1,226	6,339	7,680
23	0	45	45	25	25	1,009	422	26	0	115	1,431	5,564	7,110
24	0	45	45	25	26	1,266	426	27	0	115	1,692	5,513	7,320
25	0	63	45	25	27	1,196	426	28	0	133	1,622	5,285	7,040
26	0	71	45	25	28	1,373	408	29	0	141	1,781	4,878	6,800
27	0	71	45	25	29	963	397	30	0	141	1,360	4,409	5,910
28	0	71	45	25	30	918	408	31	0	141	1,326	4,463	5,930
Total	0	1,511	1,737	775		21,939	9,382		0	4,023	31,321	155,096	190,440

Col. 2 - 24 hours beginning 1200 of date shown.
Col. 3 - 24 hours ending 2400 one day later.
Col. 4 - 24 hours beginning 1500 one day later.
Col. 5 - 24 hours beginning 0800 of date shown.
Col. 6 - 24 hours beginning 1600 of date shown.

Col. 7 = Col. 2 + Col. 3 + Col. 4 in response to direction (Col. 1).
Col. 8 = Col. 2 + Col. 3 + Col. 4 - Col. 7.
Col. 9 = Col. 5 + Col. 6.
Col. 10 = Col. 11 - Col. 7 - Col. 8 - Col. 9.
Col. 11 = 24 hours of calendar day shown.

Table 9. Controlled releases from reservoirs in the upper Delaware River Basin and segregation of flow of Delaware River at Montague, New Jersey—continued (River Master daily operation record)

[Mean discharge in cubic feet per second for 24 hours; Col., Column]

Controlled Releases from New York City Reservoirs					Controlled Releases from Power Reservoirs			Segregation of Flow, Delaware River at Montague, New Jersey					
Directed		Pepacton	Cannonsville	Neversink		Lake Wallenpaupack	Rio Reservoir		Controlled Releases			Computed uncontrolled	Total
Date	Amount				Date			Date	New York City Reservoirs Directed	Other	Power-plants		
2002/2003	Col. 1	Col. 2	Col. 3	Col. 4	2002/2003	Col. 5	Col. 6	2003	Col. 7	Col. 8	Col. 9	Col. 10	Col. 11
Dec. 29	0	68	45	25	Dec. 31	1,017	426	Jan. 1	0	138	1,443	5,169	6,750
30	0	45	45	25	Jan. 1	1,631	521	2	0	115	2,152	12,233	14,500
31	0	45	43	25	2	1,615	883	3	0	113	2,498	14,989	17,600
Jan. 1	0	45	45	25	3	1,000	890	4	0	115	1,890	11,595	13,600
2	0	45	45	25	4	1,049	507	5	0	115	1,556	9,629	11,300
3	0	45	45	25	5	1,040	461	6	0	115	1,501	8,244	9,860
4	0	46	45	25	6	956	770	7	0	116	1,726	7,038	8,880
5	0	46	45	25	7	771	879	8	0	116	1,650	6,454	8,220
6	0	46	45	25	8	830	812	9	0	116	1,642	6,172	7,930
7	0	46	45	25	9	877	528	10	0	116	1,405	5,979	7,500
8	0	46	45	25	10	674	415	11	0	116	1,089	5,645	6,850
9	0	46	45	25	11	839	408	12	0	116	1,247	5,077	6,440
10	0	48	45	25	12	796	387	13	0	118	1,183	4,949	6,250
11	0	48	45	25	13	788	387	14	0	118	1,175	4,417	5,710
12	0	48	45	25	14	873	418	15	0	118	1,291	4,091	5,500
13	0	48	45	25	15	790	248	16	0	118	1,038	3,844	5,000
14	0	48	45	25	16	680	248	17	0	118	928	3,554	4,600
15	0	45	45	25	17	658	248	18	0	115	906	3,679	4,700
16	0	45	45	25	18	585	248	19	0	115	833	3,652	4,600
17	0	45	45	25	19	599	241	20	0	115	840	3,645	4,600
18	0	45	45	25	20	659	230	21	0	115	889	3,696	4,700
19	0	45	45	25	21	873	177	22	0	115	1,050	3,735	4,900
20	0	45	45	25	22	951	170	23	0	115	1,121	3,764	5,000
21	0	45	45	25	23	1,010	174	24	0	115	1,184	3,601	4,900
22	0	45	45	25	24	958	121	25	0	115	1,079	3,606	4,800
23	0	45	45	25	25	972	128	26	0	115	1,100	3,585	4,800
24	0	45	45	25	26	923	121	27	0	115	1,044	3,541	4,700
25	0	45	45	25	27	836	124	28	0	115	960	3,425	4,500
26	0	45	45	25	28	914	160	29	0	115	1,074	3,511	4,700
27	0	46	45	25	29	958	121	30	0	116	1,079	3,305	4,500
28	0	46	45	25	30	867	138	31	0	116	1,005	3,179	4,300
Total	0	1,441	1,393	775	Total	27,989	11,589		0	3,609	39,578	169,003	212,190

Col. 2 - 24 hours beginning 1200 of date shown.
Col. 3 - 24 hours ending 2400 one day later.
Col. 4 - 24 hours beginning 1500 one day later.
Col. 5 - 24 hours beginning 0800 of date shown.
Col. 6 - 24 hours beginning 1600 of date shown.

Col. 7 = Col. 2 + Col. 3 + Col. 4 in response to direction (Col. 1).
Col. 8 = Col. 2 + Col. 3 + Col. 4 - Col. 7.
Col. 9 = Col. 5 + Col. 6.
Col. 10 = Col. 11 - Col. 7 - Col. 8 - Col. 9.
Col. 11 = 24 hours of calendar day shown.

Table 9. Controlled releases from reservoirs in the upper Delaware River Basin and segregation of flow of Delaware River at Montague, New Jersey—continued (River Master daily operation record)

[Mean discharge in cubic feet per second for 24 hours; Col., Column]

Controlled Releases from New York City Reservoirs					Controlled Releases from Power Reservoirs			Segregation of Flow, Delaware River at Montague, New Jersey					
Directed		Pepacton	Cannonsville	Neversink	Date	Lake Wallenpaupack	Rio Reservoir	Date	Controlled Releases			Computed uncontrolled	Total
Date	Amount								New York City Reservoirs		Power-plants		
									Directed	Other			
2003	Col. 1	Col. 2	Col. 3	Col. 4	2003	Col. 5	Col. 6	2003	Col. 7	Col. 8	Col. 9	Col. 10	Col. 11
Jan. 29	0	46	45	25	Jan. 31	614	53	Feb. 1	0	116	667	2,917	3,700
30	0	46	45	25	Feb. 1	599	106	2	0	116	705	2,779	3,600
31	0	45	45	25	2	682	96	3	0	115	778	2,707	3,600
Feb. 1	0	45	45	25	3	620	106	4	0	115	726	2,859	3,700
2	0	45	45	25	4	495	106	5	0	115	601	3,684	4,400
3	0	45	45	25	5	737	103	6	0	115	840	4,545	5,500
4	0	45	45	25	6	702	103	7	0	115	805	4,080	5,000
5	0	45	45	25	7	646	106	8	0	115	752	3,833	4,700
6	0	45	45	25	8	532	106	9	0	115	638	3,547	4,300
7	0	45	45	25	9	581	163	10	0	115	744	3,241	4,100
8	0	45	45	25	10	612	106	11	0	115	718	3,267	4,100
9	0	45	45	25	11	569	106	12	0	115	675	3,210	4,000
10	0	45	45	25	12	562	106	13	0	115	668	3,317	4,100
11	0	45	45	25	13	667	103	14	0	115	770	3,115	4,000
12	0	45	45	25	14	503	89	15	0	115	592	3,093	3,800
13	0	45	45	25	15	615	110	16	0	115	725	3,060	3,900
14	0	45	45	25	16	860	117	17	0	115	977	3,008	4,100
15	0	45	45	25	17	772	103	18	0	115	875	3,010	4,000
16	0	45	45	25	18	487	103	19	0	115	590	2,995	3,700
17	0	45	45	25	19	556	138	20	0	115	694	2,991	3,800
18	0	45	45	25	20	536	138	21	0	115	674	3,011	3,800
19	0	45	45	25	21	855	426	22	0	115	1,281	2,804	4,200
20	0	45	45	25	22	700	422	23	0	115	1,122	3,863	5,100
21	0	45	45	25	23	779	53	24	0	115	832	5,753	6,700
22	0	45	45	25	24	630	53	25	0	115	683	6,202	7,000
23	0	45	45	25	25	435	426	26	0	115	861	6,024	7,000
24	0	45	45	25	26	490	174	27	0	115	664	5,521	6,300
25	0	46	51	25	27	552	457	28	0	122	1,009	4,869	6,000
Total	0	1,263	1,266	700		17,388	4,278		0	3,229	21,666	103,305	128,200

Col. 2 - 24 hours beginning 1200 of date shown.
Col. 3 - 24 hours ending 2400 one day later.
Col. 4 - 24 hours beginning 1500 one day later.
Col. 5 - 24 hours beginning 0800 of date shown.
Col. 6 - 24 hours beginning 1600 of date shown.

Col. 7 = Col. 2 + Col. 3 + Col. 4 in response to direction (Col. 1).
Col. 8 = Col. 2 + Col. 3 + Col. 4 - Col. 7.
Col. 9 = Col. 5 + Col. 6.
Col. 10 = Col. 11 - Col. 7 - Col. 8 - Col. 9.
Col. 11 = 24 hours of calendar day shown.

Table 9. Controlled releases from reservoirs in the upper Delaware River Basin and segregation of flow of Delaware River at Montague, New Jersey—continued (River Master daily operation record)

[Mean discharge in cubic feet per second for 24 hours; Col., Column]

Controlled Releases from New York City Reservoirs					Controlled Releases from Power Reservoirs				Segregation of Flow, Delaware River at Montague, New Jersey					
Directed		Pepacton	Cannonsville	Neversink	Date	Lake Wallenpaupack	Rio Reservoir	Date	Controlled Releases			Computed uncontrolled	Total	
Date	Amount								New York City Reservoirs		Power-plants			
									Directed	Other				
2003	Col. 1	Col. 2	Col. 3	Col. 4	2003	Col. 5	Col. 6	2003	Col. 7	Col. 8	Col. 9	Col. 10	Col. 11
Feb. 26	0	46	45	25	Feb. 28	470	142	Mar. 1	0	116	612	4,672	5,400
27	0	46	45	25	Mar. 1	189	89	2	0	116	278	4,406	4,800
28	0	45	45	25	2	156	89	3	0	115	245	5,040	5,400
Mar. 1	0	45	45	25	3	475	89	4	0	115	564	4,921	5,600
2	0	45	45	25	4	619	89	5	0	115	708	4,577	5,400
3	0	45	45	25	5	403	82	6	0	115	485	4,600	5,200
4	0	45	45	25	6	499	170	7	0	115	669	4,516	5,300
5	0	45	45	25	7	561	74	8	0	115	635	3,950	4,700
6	0	45	45	25	8	168	89	9	0	115	257	4,028	4,400
7	0	45	45	25	9	222	96	10	0	115	318	3,957	4,390
8	0	45	45	25	10	566	78	11	0	115	644	3,661	4,420
9	0	45	45	25	11	408	82	12	0	115	490	3,355	3,960
10	0	45	45	25	12	362	78	13	0	115	440	3,505	4,060
11	0	45	45	25	13	450	121	14	0	115	571	3,334	4,020
12	0	45	45	25	14	443	138	15	0	115	581	3,214	3,910
13	0	45	45	25	15	0	99	16	0	115	99	3,796	4,010
14	0	45	45	25	16	12	461	17	0	115	473	6,612	7,200
15	0	45	45	25	17	12	514	18	0	115	526	13,159	13,800
16	0	45	45	25	18	0	518	19	0	115	518	24,167	24,800
17	0	45	45	25	19	0	652	20	0	115	652	22,433	23,200
18	0	45	45	25	20	651	727	21	0	115	1,378	36,507	38,000
19	0	45	45	25	21	465	1,599	22	0	115	2,064	47,721	49,900
20	0	45	45	25	22	436	1,702	23	0	115	2,138	44,147	46,400
21	0	45	45	25	23	463	1,426	24	0	115	1,889	32,396	34,400
22	0	45	45	25	24	394	1,238	25	0	115	1,632	24,953	26,700
23	0	45	45	25	25	677	979	26	0	115	1,656	21,929	23,700
24	0	45	45	25	26	828	840	27	0	115	1,668	19,917	21,700
25	0	45	45	25	27	601	840	28	0	115	1,441	16,844	18,400
26	0	45	45	25	28	768	826	29	0	115	1,594	14,891	16,600
27	0	45	45	25	29	963	859	30	0	115	1,822	20,363	22,300
28	0	45	45	25	30	1,014	1,064	31	0	115	2,078	20,007	22,200
Total	0	1,397	1,395	775		13,275	15,850		0	3,567	29,125	431,578	464,270

Col. 2 - 24 hours beginning 1200 of date shown.
Col. 3 - 24 hours ending 2400 one day later.
Col. 4 - 24 hours beginning 1500 one day later.
Col. 5 - 24 hours beginning 0800 of date shown.
Col. 6 - 24 hours beginning 1600 of date shown.

Col. 7 = Col. 2 + Col. 3 + Col. 4 in response to direction (Col. 1).
Col. 8 = Col. 2 + Col. 3 + Col. 4 - Col. 7.
Col. 9 = Col. 5 + Col. 6.
Col. 10 = Col. 11 - Col. 7 - Col. 8 - Col. 9.
Col. 11 = 24 hours of calendar day shown.

Table 9. Controlled releases from reservoirs in the upper Delaware River Basin and segregation of flow of Delaware River at Montague, New Jersey—continued (River Master daily operation record)

[Mean discharge in cubic feet per second for 24 hours; Col., Column]

Controlled Releases from New York City Reservoirs					Controlled Releases from Power Reservoirs			Segregation of Flow, Delaware River at Montague, New Jersey					
Directed		Pepacton	Cannonsville	Neversink		Lake Wallenpaupack	Rio Reservoir		Controlled Releases			Computed uncontrolled	Total
Date	Amount				Date			Date	New York City Reservoirs		Power-plants		
									Directed	Other			
2003	Col. 1	Col. 2	Col. 3	Col. 4	2003	Col. 5	Col. 6	2003	Col. 7	Col. 8	Col. 9	Col. 10	Col. 11
Mar. 29	0	45	45	25	Mar. 31	1,087	755	Apr. 1	0	115	1,842	16,743	18,700
30	0	45	45	25	Apr. 1	922	933	2	0	115	1,855	14,330	16,300
31	0	45	45	25	2	1,070	833	3	0	115	1,903	13,482	15,500
Apr. 1	0	45	45	25	3	1,080	557	4	0	115	1,637	12,648	14,400
2	0	45	45	25	4	1,038	734	5	0	115	1,772	12,113	14,000
3	0	45	45	25	5	911	699	6	0	115	1,610	12,275	14,000
4	0	45	45	23	6	1,571	752	7	0	113	2,323	10,964	13,400
5	0	43	43	25	7	1,270	667	8	0	111	1,937	10,852	12,900
6	0	45	45	25	8	1,295	553	9	0	115	1,848	10,037	12,000
7	0	45	45	25	9	1,348	564	10	0	115	1,912	9,273	11,300
8	0	45	45	25	10	1,304	553	11	0	115	1,857	9,228	11,200
9	0	45	45	25	11	872	652	12	0	115	1,524	10,461	12,100
10	0	45	45	25	12	0	326	13	0	115	326	11,159	11,600
11	0	45	45	25	13	101	511	14	0	115	612	9,773	10,500
12	0	45	45	25	14	624	376	15	0	115	1,000	8,485	9,600
13	0	45	45	25	15	724	238	16	0	115	962	7,613	8,690
14	0	45	45	25	16	757	270	17	0	115	1,027	6,828	7,970
15	0	45	45	25	17	719	277	18	0	115	996	6,159	7,270
16	0	45	45	25	18	412	379	19	0	115	791	5,664	6,570
17	0	45	45	25	19	0	379	20	0	115	379	5,266	5,760
18	0	45	45	25	20	0	390	21	0	115	390	4,935	5,440
19	0	45	45	25	21	534	546	22	0	115	1,080	4,545	5,740
20	0	45	45	25	22	516	550	23	0	115	1,066	4,559	5,740
21	0	45	45	25	23	520	454	24	0	115	974	4,431	5,520
22	0	45	45	25	24	539	216	25	0	115	755	4,110	4,980
23	0	45	45	25	25	595	177	26	0	115	772	3,873	4,760
24	0	45	45	25	26	0	184	27	0	115	184	5,711	6,010
25	0	45	45	25	27	2	145	28	0	115	147	7,618	7,880
26	0	45	45	25	28	0	0	29	0	115	0	6,795	6,910
27	0	45	45	25	29	0	0	30	0	115	0	6,095	6,210
Total	0	1,348	1,348	748		19,811	13,670		0	3,444	33,481	256,025	292,950

Col. 2 - 24 hours beginning 1200 of date shown.
Col. 3 - 24 hours ending 2400 one day later.
Col. 4 - 24 hours beginning 1500 one day later.
Col. 5 - 24 hours beginning 0800 of date shown.
Col. 6 - 24 hours beginning 1600 of date shown.

Col. 7 = Col. 2 + Col. 3 + Col. 4 in response to direction (Col. 1).
Col. 8 = Col. 2 + Col. 3 + Col. 4 - Col. 7.
Col. 9 = Col. 5 + Col. 6.
Col. 10 = Col. 11 - Col. 7 - Col. 8 - Col. 9.
Col. 11 = 24 hours of calendar day shown.

Table 9. Controlled releases from reservoirs in the upper Delaware River Basin and segregation of flow of Delaware River at Montague, New Jersey—continued (River Master daily operation record)

[Mean discharge in cubic feet per second for 24 hours; Col., Column]

Controlled Releases from New York City Reservoirs					Controlled Releases from Power Reservoirs			Segregation of Flow, Delaware River at Montague, New Jersey					
Directed		Pepacton	Cannonsville	Neversink		Lake Wallenpaupack	Rio Reservoir		Controlled Releases			Computed uncontrolled	Total
Date	Amount				Date			Date	New York City Reservoirs		Power-plants		
2003	Col. 1	Col. 2	Col. 3	Col. 4	2003	Col. 5	Col. 6	2003	Directed Col. 7	Other Col. 8	Col. 9	Col. 10	Col. 11
Apr. 28	0	45	45	25	Apr. 30	28	0	May 1	0	115	28	5,587	5,730
29	0	45	45	32	May 1	130	0	2	0	122	130	5,178	5,430
30	0	50	45	53	2	0	0	3	0	148	0	8,322	8,470
May 1	0	70	45	53	3	0	71	4	0	168	71	9,611	9,850
2	0	70	45	53	4	0	0	5	0	168	0	8,422	8,590
3	0	70	45	53	5	0	0	6	0	168	0	7,382	7,550
4	0	70	45	53	6	0	0	7	0	168	0	6,622	6,790
5	0	70	45	53	7	0	0	8	0	168	0	5,882	6,050
6	0	70	45	53	8	0	0	9	0	168	0	5,562	5,730
7	0	70	45	53	9	69	0	10	0	168	69	4,763	5,000
8	0	70	45	53	10	0	0	11	0	168	0	4,282	4,450
9	0	70	45	53	11	0	0	12	0	168	0	4,382	4,550
10	0	70	45	53	12	0	0	13	0	168	0	5,802	5,970
11	0	70	45	53	13	1	0	14	0	168	1	5,471	5,640
12	0	70	45	53	14	1	0	15	0	168	1	5,231	5,400
13	0	70	45	53	15	0	0	16	0	168	0	4,872	5,040
14	0	70	45	53	16	1	85	17	0	168	86	4,496	4,750
15	0	70	45	53	17	0	0	18	0	168	0	4,122	4,290
16	0	70	45	53	18	0	14	19	0	168	14	3,758	3,940
17	0	70	45	53	19	126	18	20	0	168	144	3,468	3,780
18	0	70	45	53	20	353	0	21	0	168	353	3,199	3,720
19	0	70	45	53	21	174	0	22	0	168	174	3,198	3,540
20	0	70	45	53	22	146	0	23	0	168	146	3,116	3,430
21	0	70	45	53	23	204	0	24	0	168	204	2,898	3,270
22	0	70	45	53	24	0	0	25	0	168	0	3,032	3,200
23	0	70	45	53	25	0	0	26	0	168	0	4,142	4,310
24	0	70	45	53	26	0	0	27	0	168	0	5,942	6,110
25	0	70	45	53	27	138	0	28	0	168	138	5,314	5,620
26	0	70	45	53	28	197	28	29	0	168	225	4,867	5,260
27	0	70	45	53	29	269	0	30	0	168	269	4,413	4,850
28	0	70	45	53	30	260	0	31	0	168	260	3,972	4,400
Total	0	2,100	1,395	1,594		2,097	216		0	5,089	2,313	157,308	164,710

Col. 2 - 24 hours beginning 1200 of date shown.
Col. 3 - 24 hours ending 2400 one day later.
Col. 4 - 24 hours beginning 1500 one day later.
Col. 5 - 24 hours beginning 0800 of date shown.
Col. 6 - 24 hours beginning 1600 of date shown.

Col. 7 = Col. 2 + Col. 3 + Col. 4 in response to direction (Col. 1).
Col. 8 = Col. 2 + Col. 3 + Col. 4 - Col. 7.
Col. 9 = Col. 5 + Col. 6.
Col. 10 = Col. 11 - Col. 7 - Col. 8 - Col. 9.
Col. 11 = 24 hours of calendar day shown.

Table 9. Controlled releases from reservoirs in the upper Delaware River Basin and segregation of flow of Delaware River at Montague, New Jersey—continued (River Master daily operation record)

[Mean discharge in cubic feet per second for 24 hours; Col., Column; Cumul., Cumulative]

Controlled Releases from New York City Reservoirs					Controlled Releases from Power Reservoirs			Segregation of Flow, Delaware River at Montague, New Jersey							
Directed		Pepacton	Cannonsville	Neversink		Lake Wallenpaupack	Rio Reservoir		Controlled Releases			Computed uncontrolled	Total	Excess Release Credits	
Date	Amount				Date			Date	New York City Reservoirs		Power-plants			Daily	Cumul.
2003					2003			2003	Directed	Other					
	Col. 1	Col. 2	Col. 3	Col. 4		Col. 5	Col. 6		Col. 7	Col. 8	Col. 9	Col. 10	Col. 11	Col. 12	Col. 13
May 29	0	70	45	53	May 31	48	71	June 1	0	168	119	9,353	9,640	0	0
30	0	70	45	53	June 1	1,685	0	2	0	168	1,685	17,747	19,600	0	0
31	0	74	45	53	2	1,621	14	3	0	172	1,635	13,193	15,000	0	0
June 1	0	94	45	53	3	1,714	142	4	0	192	1,856	10,752	12,800	0	0
2	0	94	45	53	4	1,678	113	5	0	192	1,791	9,917	11,900	0	0
3	0	94	45	53	5	1,676	142	6	0	192	1,818	8,690	10,700	0	0
4	0	94	45	53	6	1,230	71	7	0	192	1,301	8,097	9,590	0	0
5	0	94	45	53	7	1,068	174	8	0	192	1,242	9,666	11,100	0	0
6	0	94	45	53	8	1,037	418	9	0	192	1,455	8,213	9,860	0	0
7	0	94	45	53	9	682	372	10	0	192	1,054	7,164	8,410	0	0
8	0	94	45	53	10	707	312	11	0	192	1,019	6,129	7,340	0	0
9	0	94	45	53	11	1,026	213	12	0	192	1,239	6,009	7,440	0	0
10	0	94	45	53	12	1,317	248	13	0	192	1,565	7,683	9,440	0	0
11	0	94	45	53	13	861	248	14	0	192	1,109	9,999	11,300	0	0
12	0	94	45	53	14	808	248	15	0	192	1,056	14,052	15,300	0	0
13	0	94	45	53	15	710	124	16	0	192	834	11,074	12,100	0	0
14	0	94	45	53	16	456	195	17	0	192	651	8,947	9,790	0	0
15	0	94	45	53	17	442	138	18	0	192	580	7,758	8,530	0	0
16	0	94	45	53	18	595	344	19	0	192	939	6,839	7,970	0	0
17	0	94	45	53	19	573	170	20	0	192	743	6,085	7,020	0	0
18	0	94	45	53	20	486	89	21	0	192	575	10,433	11,200	0	0
19	0	94	45	53	21	1,176	675	22	0	192	1,851	18,457	20,500	0	0
20	0	94	45	53	22	1,703	550	23	0	192	2,253	19,155	21,600	0	0
21	0	94	45	53	23	1,721	787	24	0	192	2,508	13,900	16,600	0	0
22	0	94	45	53	24	1,680	238	25	0	192	1,918	10,290	12,400	0	0
23	0	94	45	53	25	1,721	121	26	0	192	1,842	8,366	10,400	0	0
24	0	94	45	53	26	1,719	199	27	0	192	1,918	6,790	8,900	0	0
25	0	94	45	54	27	1,719	149	28	0	193	1,868	5,909	7,970	0	0
26	0	212	492	84	28	1,692	113	29	0	788	1,805	4,157	6,750	0	0
27	0	158	308	84	29	1,688	128	30	0	550	1,816	3,734	6,100	0	0
Total	0	2,934	2,060	1,653		35,239	6,806		0	6,647	42,045	288,558	337,250	0	

Col. 2 - 24 hours beginning 1200 of date shown.
Col. 3 - 24 hours ending 2400 one day later.
Col. 4 - 24 hours beginning 1500 one day later.
Col. 5 - 24 hours beginning 0800 of date shown.
Col. 6 - 24 hours beginning 1600 of date shown.

Col. 7 = Col. 2 + Col. 3 + Col. 4 in response to direction (Col. 1).
Col. 8 = Col. 2 + Col. 3 + Col. 4 - Col. 7.
Col. 9 = Col. 5 + Col. 6.
Col. 10 = Co . 11 - Col. 7 - Col. 8 - Col. 9.
Col. 11 = 24 hours of calendar day shown.

Col. 12 = Col. 11 - Col. 8 - 1,750 ft³/s computed arithmetically, but not greater than Col. 7; except that part of Col. 8 contributing to the excess-release increment of Col. 11.

Col. 13 = Season limit of cumulative credit beginning June 15, 2003 = 11,418 (ft³/s)·d A total of 6,851 (ft³/s)-d is available for release.

Table 9. Controlled releases from reservoirs in the upper Delaware River Basin and segregation of flow of Delaware River at Montague, New Jersey—continued (River Master daily operation record)

[Mean discharge in cubic feet per second for 24 hours; Col., Column; Cumul., Cumulative]

Controlled Releases from New York City Reservoirs

Directed Date 2003	Directed Amount Col. 1	Pepac-ton Col. 2	Cannons-ville Col. 3	Never-sink Col. 4
June 28	0	153	308	82
29	0	153	308	53
30	0	99	306	53
July 1	0	94	306	53
2	0	94	306	74
3	0	94	306	74
4	0	94	306	74
5	0	94	306	74
6	0	94	399	90
7	0	94	466	85
8	0	94	384	53
9	0	94	280	53
10	0	94	118	53
11	0	94	45	53
12	0	94	91	53
13	0	94	196	53
14	0	94	226	79
15	0	94	311	70
16	0	94	328	53
17	530	94	384	53
18	678	94	531	53
19	0	94	300	68
20	0	94	299	53
21	0	94	176	53
22	0	94	128	53
23	0	94	101	54
24	0	94	125	77
25	0	94	283	88
26	0	94	333	87
27	0	94	302	53
28	0	94	302	53
Total	**1,208**	**3,037**	**8,560**	**1,977**

Controlled Releases from Power Reservoirs

Date 2003	Lake Wallenpau-pack Col. 5	Rio Reservoir Col. 6
June 30	1,676	184
July 1	1,697	145
2	1,445	113
3	1,139	184
4	1,193	0
5	1,220	0
6	1,132	128
7	723	113
8	515	110
9	315	78
10	428	0
11	561	43
12	0	0
13	0	53
14	629	89
15	525	60
16	463	0
17	515	0
18	459	0
19	0	0
20	0	43
21	529	0
22	431	21
23	689	0
24	579	0
25	518	0
26	348	50
27	718	0
28	923	0
29	1,043	0
30	1,060	0
Total	**21,473**	**1,414**

Segregation of Flow, Delaware River at Montague, New Jersey

Date 2003	Controlled Releases NYC Reservoirs Directed Col. 7	Controlled Releases NYC Reservoirs Other Col. 8	Controlled Releases Power-plants Col. 9	Computed uncontrolled Col. 10	Total Col. 11	Excess Release Credits Daily Col. 12	Excess Release Credits Cumul. Col. 13
July 1	0	543	1,860	3,207	5,610	0	0
2	0	514	1,842	2,804	5,160	0	0
3	0	458	1,558	2,534	4,550	0	0
4	0	453	1,323	2,204	3,980	0	0
5	0	474	1,193	2,113	3,780	0	0
6	0	474	1,220	2,016	3,710	0	0
7	0	474	1,260	1,836	3,570	0	0
8	0	474	836	1,980	3,290	0	0
9	0	583	625	1,962	3,170	0	0
10	0	645	393	2,002	3,040	0	0
11	0	531	428	1,961	2,920	0	0
12	0	427	604	3,209	4,240	0	0
13	0	265	0	2,965	3,230	0	0
14	0	192	53	2,235	2,480	0	0
15	0	238	718	1,864	2,820	0	0
16	0	343	585	1,592	2,520	0	0
17	0	399	463	1,558	2,420	0	0
18	0	475	515	1,650	2,640	0	0
19	0	475	459	1,566	2,500	0	0
20	531	0	0	1,459	1,990	240	240
21	678	0	43	1,289	2,010	260	500
22	0	462	529	1,829	2,820	0	500
23	0	446	452	3,812	4,710	0	500
24	0	323	689	4,258	5,270	0	500
25	0	275	579	3,396	4,250	0	500
26	0	249	518	2,663	3,430	0	500
27	0	296	398	2,226	2,920	0	500
28	0	465	718	2,117	3,300	0	500
29	0	514	923	1,963	3,400	0	500
30	0	449	1,043	1,638	3,130	0	500
31	0	449	1,060	1,491	3,000	0	500
Total	**1,209**	**12,365**	**22,887**	**69,399**	**105,860**		

Col. 2 - 24 hours beginning 1200 of date shown.
Col. 3 - 24 hours ending 2400 one day later.
Col. 4 - 24 hours beginning 1500 one day later.
Col. 5 - 24 hours beginning 0800 of date shown.
Col. 6 - 24 hours beginning 1600 of date shown.

Col. 7 = Col. 2 + Col. 3 + Col. 4 in response to direction (Col. 1).
Col. 8 = Col. 2 + Col. 3 + Col. 4 - Col. 7.
Col. 9 = Col. 5 + Col. 6.
Col. 10 = Col. 11 - Col. 7 - Col. 8 - Col. 9.
Col. 11 = 24 hours of calendar day shown.

Col. 12 = Col. 11 - Col. 8 - 1,750 ft^3/s computed arithmetically, but not greater than Col. 7; except that part of Col. 8 contributing to the excess-release increment of Col. 11.

Col. 13 = Season limit of cumulative credit beginning June 15, 2003 = 11,418 $(ft^3/s) \cdot d$. A total of 6,851 $(ft^3/s) \cdot d$ is available for release.

Table 9. Controlled releases from reservoirs in the upper Delaware River Basin and segregation of flow of Delaware River at Montague, New Jersey—continued (River Master daily operation record)

[Mean discharge in cubic feet per second for 24 hours; Col., Column; Cumul., Cumulative]

Controlled Releases from New York City Reservoirs					Controlled Releases from Power Reservoirs			Segregation of Flow, Delaware River at Montague, New Jersey							
Directed		Pepacton	Cannonsville	Neversink		Lake Wallenpaupack	Rio Reservoir		Controlled Releases			Computed uncontrolled	Total	Excess Release Credits	
Date	Amount				Date			Date	New York City Reservoirs		Power-plants			Daily	Cumul.
									Directed	Other					
2003	Col. 1	Col. 2	Col. 3	Col. 4	2003	Col. 5	Col. 6	2003	Col. 7	Col. 8	Col. 9	Col. 10	Col. 11	Col. 12	Col. 13
July 29	0	94	328	57	July 31	544	0	Aug. 1	0	479	644	1,397	2,520	0	500
30	0	94	333	71	Aug. 1	394	0	2	0	498	394	2,038	2,930	0	500
31	359	94	297	53	2	0	0	3	359	85	43	3,146	3,590	359	859
Aug. 1	0	94	240	53	3	0	43	4	0	387	43	3,160	3,590	0	859
2	0	94	198	53	4	250	0	5	0	345	250	4,975	5,570	0	859
3	0	94	198	70	5	185	0	6	0	362	185	6,493	7,040	0	859
4	0	94	175	53	6	245	0	7	0	322	245	6,653	7,220	0	859
5	0	94	159	53	7	290	11	8	0	306	301	5,023	5,630	0	859
6	0	94	122	53	8	434	124	9	0	269	558	4,663	5,490	0	859
7	0	94	105	53	9	232	18	10	0	252	250	5,518	6,020	0	859
8	0	94	243	53	10	367	89	11	0	390	456	5,384	6,230	0	859
9	0	94	299	53	11	0	330	12	0	446	330	11,424	12,200	0	859
10	0	94	320	53	12	0	816	13	0	467	816	9,717	11,000	0	859
11	0	387	520	57	13	422	730	14	0	964	1,152	7,374	9,490	0	859
12	0	727	741	84	14	773	624	15	0	1,552	1,397	5,511	8,460	0	859
13	0	710	784	53	15	392	929	16	0	1,547	1,321	4,112	6,980	0	859
14	0	713	709	68	16	382	369	17	0	1,490	751	3,009	5,250	0	859
15	0	461	495	68	17	329	71	18	0	1,024	400	3,206	4,630	0	859
16	0	330	387	70	18	386	89	19	0	787	475	3,008	4,270	0	859
17	0	246	343	70	19	482	71	20	0	659	553	2,678	3,890	0	859
18	0	246	342	70	20	415	103	21	0	658	518	2,364	3,540	0	859
19	0	244	306	68	21	455	191	22	0	618	646	2,006	3,270	0	859
20	0	173	258	68	22	501	53	23	0	499	554	1,887	2,940	0	859
21	0	169	251	53	23	0	71	24	0	473	71	1,656	2,200	60	919
22	77	105	248	53	24	96	89	25	0	329	185	1,419	2,010	60	979
23	0	94	248	53	25	684	71	26	77	395	755	1,500	2,650	0	979
24	0	94	248	53	26	545	92	27	0	395	637	1,428	2,460	0	979
25	0	94	246	53	27	576	113	28	0	393	689	1,338	2,420	0	979
26	603	94	456	53	28	0	89	29	603	0	89	1,218	1,910	160	1,139
27	692	94	543	53	29	394	53	30	690	0	447	1,223	2,360	610	1,749
28	738	94	591	53	30	0	0	31	738	0	0	1,362	2,100	350	2,099
Total	2,469	6,297	10,733	1,828		9,873	5,239		2,467	16,391	15,112	115,890	149,860		

Col. 2 - 24 hours beginning 1200 of date shown.
Col. 3 - 24 hours ending 2400 one day later.
Col. 4 - 24 hours beginning 1500 one day later.
Col. 5 - 24 hours beginning 0800 of date shown.
Col. 6 - 24 hours beginning 1600 of date shown.

Col. 7 = Col. 2 + Col. 3 + Col. 4 in response to direction (Col. 1).
Col. 8 = Col. 2 + Col. 3 + Col. 4 - Col. 7.
Col. 9 = Col. 5 + Col. 6.
Col. 10 = Col. 11 - Col. 7 - Col. 8 - Col. 9.
Col. 11 = 24 hours of calendar day shown.

Col. 12 = Col. 11 - Col. 8 - 1,750 ft³/s computed arithmetically, but not greater than Col. 7; except that part of Col. 8 contributing to the excess-release increment of Col. 11.

Col. 13 = Season limit of cumulative credit beginning June 15, 2003 = 11,418 (ft³/s)·d² A total of 6,851 (ft³/s)·d is available for release.

35

Table 9. Controlled releases from reservoirs in the upper Delaware River Basin and segregation of flow of Delaware River at Montague, New Jersey—continued (River Master daily operation record)

[Mean discharge in cubic feet per second for 24 hours; Col., Column; Cumul, Cumulative]

Controlled Releases from New York City Reservoirs					Controlled Releases from Power Reservoirs			Segregation of Flow, Delaware River at Montague, New Jersey							
Directed		Pepac-ton	Cannons-ville	Never-sink		Lake Wallenpau-pack	Rio Reservoir		Controlled Releases			Computed uncon-trolled	Total	Excess Release Credits	
Date 2003	Amount Col. 1	Col. 2	Col. 3	Col. 4	Date 2003	Col. 5	Col. 6	Date 2003	NYC Reservoirs Directed Col. 7	Other Col. 8	Power-plants Col. 9	Col. 10	Col. 11	Daily Col. 12	Cumul. Col. 13
Aug. 29	670	94	523	53	Aug. 31	0	0	Sep. 1	670	0	0	1,400	2,070	320	2,419
30	476	94	331	53	Sept. 1	87	74	2	478	0	161	10,061	10,700	478	2,897
31	97	90	244	53	2	487	301	3	97	290	788	25,125	26,300	97	2,994
Sept. 1	0	88	243	53	3	596	518	4	0	384	1,114	27,002	28,500	0	2,994
2	0	684	617	53	4	478	833	5	0	1,354	1,311	31,335	34,000	0	2,994
3	0	569	945	53	5	485	660	6	0	1,567	1,145	18,588	21,300	0	2,994
4	0	70	45	53	6	436	578	7	0	168	1,014	13,918	15,100	0	2,994
5	0	70	45	53	7	399	514	8	0	168	913	10,719	11,800	0	2,994
6	0	70	45	53	8	597	284	9	0	168	881	8,451	9,500	0	2,994
7	0	70	45	53	9	535	142	10	0	168	677	6,965	7,810	0	2,994
8	0	93	342	53	10	637	152	11	0	488	789	5,673	6,950	0	2,994
9	0	374	630	53	11	639	213	12	0	1,057	852	3,971	5,880	0	2,994
10	0	351	484	53	12	614	117	13	0	888	731	3,111	4,730	0	2,994
11	0	70	333	53	13	350	124	14	0	456	474	3,240	4,170	0	2,994
12	0	70	232	53	14	435	195	15	0	355	630	3,635	4,620	0	2,994
13	0	70	232	53	15	831	266	16	0	355	1,097	11,048	12,500	0	2,994
14	0	70	275	53	16	1,543	628	17	0	398	2,171	8,831	11,400	0	2,994
15	0	175	472	53	17	1,576	603	18	0	700	2,179	6,081	8,960	0	2,994
16	0	453	684	53	18	1,556	603	19	0	1,190	2,159	5,081	8,430	0	2,994
17	0	495	688	53	19	1,567	138	20	0	1,236	1,705	5,229	8,170	0	2,994
18	0	493	521	53	20	1,595	71	21	0	1,067	1,666	4,107	6,840	0	2,994
19	0	90	289	53	21	1,567	209	22	0	432	1,776	3,582	5,790	0	2,994
20	0	70	217	53	22	1,201	85	23	0	340	1,286	10,074	11,700	0	2,994
21	0	70	217	53	23	1,436	170	24	0	340	1,606	24,254	26,200	0	2,994
22	0	70	217	53	24	1,432	401	25	0	340	1,833	15,227	17,400	0	2,994
23	0	70	217	53	25	1,434	468	26	0	340	1,902	11,358	13,600	0	2,994
24	0	70	136	53	26	1,432	362	27	0	259	1,794	9,147	11,200	0	2,994
25	0	70	48	53	27	85	333	28	0	171	418	11,511	12,100	0	2,994
26	0	70	48	53	28	0	816	29	0	171	816	17,613	18,600	0	2,994
27	0	70	48	53	29	0	723	30	0	171	723	14,406	15,300	0	2,994
Total	1,243	5,263	9,413	1,590		24,030	10,581		1,245	15,021	34,611	330,743	381,620		

Col. 2 - 24 hours beginning 1200 of date shown.
Col. 3 - 24 hours ending 2400 one day later.
Col. 4 - 24 hours beginning 1500 one day later.
Col. 5 - 24 hours beginning 0800 of date shown.
Col. 6 - 24 hours beginning 1600 of date shown.

Col. 7 = Col. 2 + Col. 3 + Col. 4 in response to direction (Col. 1).
Col. 8 = Col. 2 + Col. 3 + Col. 4 - Col. 7.
Col. 9 = Col. 5 + Col. 6.
Col. 10 = Col. 11 - Col. 7 - Col. 8 - Col. 9.
Col. 11 = 24 hours of calendar day shown.

Col. 12 = Col. 11 - Col. 8 - 1,750 ft³/s computed arithmetically, but not greater than Col. 7; except that part of Col. 8 contributing to the excess-release increment of Col. 11.

Col. 13 = Season limit of cumulative credit beginning June 15, 2003 = 11,418 (ft³/s)·d. A total of 6,851 (ft³/s)·d is available for release.

Table 9. Controlled releases from reservoirs in the upper Delaware River Basin and segregation of flow of Delaware River at Montague, New Jersey—continued (River Master daily operation record)

[Mean discharge in cubic feet per second for 24 hours; Col., Column; Cumul, Cumulative]

Controlled Releases from New York City Reservoirs					Controlled Releases from Power Reservoirs			Segregation of Flow, Delaware River at Montague, New Jersey							
Directed		Pepacton	Cannonsville	Neversink		Lake Wallenpaupack	Rio Reservoir		Controlled Releases			Computed uncontrolled	Total	Excess Release Credits	
Date	Amount				Date			Date	New York City Reservoirs		Power-plants			Daily	Cumul.
									Directed	Other					
2003	Col. 1	Col. 2	Col. 3	Col. 4	2003	Col. 5	Col. 6	2003	Col. 7	Col. 8	Col. 9	Col. 10	Col. 11	Col. 12	Col. 13
Sept. 28	0	70	48	53	Sept. 30	0	915	Oct. 1	0	171	915	11,314	12,400	0	2,994
29	0	70	46	43	Oct. 1	0	922	2	0	159	922	9,519	10,600	0	2,994
30	0	65	43	25	2	0	826	3	0	133	826	8,281	9,240	0	2,994
Oct. 1	0	45	45	25	3	0	418	4	0	115	418	7,187	7,720	0	2,994
2	0	45	45	25	4	0	202	5	0	115	202	7,813	8,130	0	2,994
3	0	45	45	25	5	0	238	6	0	115	238	8,347	8,700	0	2,994
4	0	45	45	25	6	0	209	7	0	115	209	7,026	7,350	0	2,994
5	0	45	45	25	7	0	482	8	0	115	482	6,213	6,810	0	2,994
6	0	45	45	25	8	0	426	9	0	115	426	5,549	6,090	0	2,994
7	0	45	45	25	9	0	500	10	0	115	500	4,995	5,610	0	2,994
8	0	45	45	25	10	0	454	11	0	115	454	4,631	5,200	0	2,994
9	0	45	45	25	11	12	426	12	0	115	438	4,207	4,760	0	2,994
10	0	45	45	25	12	125	355	13	0	115	480	3,855	4,450	0	2,994
11	0	45	45	25	13	659	135	14	0	115	794	3,541	4,450	0	2,994
12	0	45	45	25	14	597	213	15	0	115	810	6,475	7,400	0	2,994
13	0	45	45	25	15	525	468	16	0	115	993	10,392	11,500	0	2,994
14	0	45	45	25	16	506	379	17	0	115	885	8,300	9,300	0	2,994
15	0	45	45	25	17	421	284	18	0	115	705	6,950	7,770	0	2,994
16	0	45	45	25	18	0	287	19	0	115	287	6,288	6,690	0	2,994
17	0	45	45	25	19	69	284	20	0	115	353	6,372	6,840	0	2,994
18	0	45	45	25	20	487	280	21	0	115	767	6,028	6,910	0	2,994
19	0	45	45	25	21	512	411	22	0	115	923	5,472	6,510	0	2,994
20	0	45	45	25	22	506	408	23	0	115	914	5,151	6,180	0	2,994
21	0	45	45	25	23	468	440	24	0	115	908	4,767	5,790	0	2,994
22	0	45	45	25	24	488	323	25	0	115	811	4,324	5,250	0	2,994
23	0	45	45	25	25	0	230	26	0	115	230	4,155	4,500	0	2,994
24	0	45	45	25	26	79	309	27	0	115	388	6,437	6,940	0	2,994
25	0	45	45	25	27	712	848	28	0	115	1,560	26,825	28,500	0	2,994
26	0	45	45	25	28	803	1,511	29	0	115	2,314	33,571	36,000	0	2,994
27	0	45	45	25	29	768	2,138	30	0	115	2,906	46,879	49,900	0	2,994
28	0	45	45	25	30	656	1,461	31	0	115	2,117	32,068	34,300	0	2,994
Total	0	1,465	1,397	821		8,393	16,782		0	3,683	25,175	312,932	341,790	0	

Col. 2 - 24 hours beginning 1200 of date shown.
Col. 3 - 24 hours ending 2400 one day later.
Col. 4 - 24 hours beginning 1500 one day later.
Col. 5 - 24 hours beginning 0800 of date shown.
Col. 6 - 24 hours beginning 1600 of date shown.

Col. 7 = Col. 2 + Col. 3 + Col. 4 in response to direction (Col. 1).
Col. 8 = Col. 2 + Col. 3 + Col. 4 - Col. 7.
Col. 9 = Col. 5 + Col. 6.
Col. 10 = Col. 11 - Col. 7 - Col. 8 - Col. 9.
Col. 11 = 24 hours of calendar day shown.

Col. 12 = Col. 11 - Col. 8 - 1,750 ft³/s computed arithmetically, but not greater than Col. 7; except that part of Col. 8 contributing to the excess-release increment of Col. 11.

Col. 13 = Season limit of cumulative credit beginning June 15, 2003 = 11,418 (ft³/s)-d. A total of 6,851 (ft³/s)-d is available for release.

Table 9. Controlled releases from reservoirs in the upper Delaware River Basin and segregation of flow of Delaware River at Montague, New Jersey—continued (River Master daily operation record)

[Mean discharge in cubic feet per second for 24 hours; Col., Column; Cumul, Cumulative]

| Controlled Releases from New York City Reservoirs | | | | | Controlled Releases from Power Reservoirs | | | Segregation of Flow, Delaware River at Montague, New Jersey | | | | | | | |
Directed Date 2003	Directed Amount Col. 1	Pepacton Col. 2	Cannonsville Col. 3	Neversink Col. 4	Date 2003	Lake Wallenpaupack Col. 5	Rio Reservoir Col. 6	Date 2003	Controlled Releases NYC Reservoirs Directed Col. 7	Controlled Releases NYC Reservoirs Other Col. 8	Controlled Releases Power-plants Col. 9	Computed uncontrolled Col. 10	Total Col. 11	Excess Release Credits Daily Col. 12	Excess Release Credits Cumul. Col. 13
Oct. 29	0	45	45	25	Oct. 31	584	1,117	Nov. 1	0	115	1,701	22,384	24,200	0	2,994
30	0	45	45	25	Nov. 1	0	809	2	0	115	809	17,476	18,400	0	2,994
31	0	45	45	25	2	136	855	3	0	115	991	14,494	15,600	0	2,994
Nov. 1	0	45	45	25	3	658	844	4	0	115	1,502	11,883	13,500	0	2,994
2	0	45	43	25	4	826	865	5	0	113	1,691	10,396	12,200	0	2,994
3	0	45	43	25	5	1,055	833	6	0	113	1,888	10,899	12,900	0	2,994
4	0	45	43	25	6	1,036	447	7	0	113	1,483	10,404	12,000	0	2,994
5	0	45	43	25	7	1,054	454	8	0	113	1,508	8,479	10,100	0	2,994
6	0	45	43	25	8	1,055	351	9	0	113	1,406	7,281	8,800	0	2,994
7	0	45	43	25	9	1,051	362	10	0	113	1,413	6,584	8,110	0	2,994
8	0	45	43	25	10	1,086	259	11	0	113	1,345	6,312	7,770	0	2,994
9	0	45	43	25	11	1,045	252	12	0	113	1,297	6,270	7,680	0	2,994
10	0	45	43	25	12	1,066	645	13	0	113	1,711	6,356	8,180	0	2,994
11	0	45	43	25	13	1,093	486	14	0	113	1,579	5,748	7,440	0	2,994
12	0	45	43	25	14	1,096	152	15	0	113	1,248	5,459	6,820	0	2,994
13	0	45	43	25	15	1,025	294	16	0	113	1,319	5,078	6,510	0	2,994
14	0	45	43	25	16	986	199	17	0	113	1,185	4,712	6,010	0	2,994
15	0	45	43	25	17	623	234	18	0	113	857	4,730	5,700	0	2,994
16	0	45	43	25	18	642	326	19	0	113	968	4,849	5,930	0	2,994
17	0	45	43	25	19	760	362	20	0	113	1,122	20,665	21,900	0	2,994
18	0	45	43	25	20	754	663	21	0	113	1,417	29,170	30,700	0	2,994
19	0	45	43	25	21	587	156	22	0	113	743	22,044	22,900	0	2,994
20	0	45	43	25	22	568	355	23	0	113	923	17,064	18,100	0	2,994
21	0	45	43	25	23	414	479	24	0	113	893	13,894	14,900	0	2,994
22	0	45	43	25	24	506	681	25	0	113	1,187	12,200	13,500	0	2,994
23	0	45	43	25	25	439	688	26	0	113	1,127	11,260	12,500	0	2,994
24	0	45	45	25	26	410	553	27	0	115	963	9,622	10,700	0	2,994
25	0	45	46	25	27	66	550	28	0	116	616	9,268	10,000	0	2,994
26	0	45	46	25	28	758	631	29	0	116	1,389	16,095	17,600	0	2,994
27	0	45	46	25	29	764	681	30	0	116	1,445	17,739	19,300	0	2,994
Total	0	1,350	1,309	750		22,143	15,583		0	3,409	37,726	348,815	389,950		

Col. 2 - 24 hours beginning 1200 of date shown.
Col. 3 - 24 hours ending 2400 one day later.
Col. 4 - 24 hours beginning 1500 one day later.
Col. 5 - 24 hours beginning 0800 of date shown.
Col. 6 - 24 hours beginning 1600 of date shown.

Col. 7 = Col. 2 + Col. 3 + Col. 4 in response to direction (Col. 1).
Col. 8 = Col. 2 + Col. 3 + Col. 4 - Col. 7.
Col. 9 = Col. 5 + Col. 6.
Col. 10 = Col. 11 - Col. 7 - Col. 8 - Col. 9.
Col. 11 = 24 hours of calendar day shown.

Col. 12 = Col. 11 - Col. 8 - 1,750 ft³/s computed arithmetically, but not greater than Col. 7; except that part of Col. 8 contributing to the excess-release increment of Col. 11.

Col. 13 = Season limit of cumulative credit beginning June 15, 2003 = 11,418 (ft³/s)·d. A total of 6,851 (ft³/s)·d is available for release.

38

Table 10. Diversions to New York City water supply
Million gallons per day for 24 hour period beginning 0800 local time
(River Master daily operation record)

Date 2002	East Delaware Tunnel	West Delaware Tunnel	Neversink Tunnel	Average June 1, 2002, to date	Date 2003	East Delaware Tunnel	West Delaware Tunnel	Neversink Tunnel	Average June 1, 2002, to date
Dec. 1	0	0	0	586	Jan. 1	0	0	0	546
2	19	0	0	583	2	0	0	0	544
3	300	0	121	582	3	0	0	0	541
4	302	0	161	582	4	0	0	0	539
5	300	0	135	581	5	0	0	0	536
6	301	0	160	580	6	0	0	0	534
7	300	0	150	579	7	0	0	0	531
8	301	0	122	579	8	0	0	0	529
9	305	0	150	578	9	0	0	0	527
10	321	0	150	577	10	450	0	0	526
11	296	0	156	577	11	449	0	0	526
12	298	0	181	576	12	449	0	0	526
13	305	0	164	576	13	450	0	0	525
14	305	0	154	575	14	451	0	0	525
15	143	0	149	574	15	450	0	0	525
16	308	0	142	573	16	450	0	0	524
17	319	0	175	573	17	450	0	0	524
18	326	0	182	572	18	0	0	0	522
19	324	0	154	572	19	0	0	0	520
20	299	0	120	571	20	0	0	0	517
21	299	0	89	570	21	0	0	0	515
22	299	0	70	569	22	0	0	0	513
23	301	0	103	568	23	0	0	0	511
24	283	0	76	567	24	298	48	122	511
25	0	0	0	565	25	400	0	137	511
26	0	0	0	562	26	400	0	133	511
27	0	0	0	559	27	400	0	152	511
28	0	0	0	557	28	400	0	221	511
29	0	0	0	554	29	400	0	191	512
30	0	0	0	551	30	400	0	199	512
31	0	0	0	549	31	400	0	176	512
Total	6,554	0	3,064			6,697	48	1,331	

39

Table 10. Diversions to New York City water supply—continued
Million gallons per day for 24 hour period beginning 0800 local time
(River Master daily operation record)

Date 2003	East Delaware Tunnel	West Delaware Tunnel	Neversink Tunnel	Average June 1, 2002, to date
Feb. 1	400	0	136	512
2	400	0	138	513
3	401	0	166	513
4	399	0	191	513
5	400	0	245	514
6	400	249	260	515
7	400	295	170	517
8	400	1	211	517
9	400	0	216	517
10	400	0	200	518
11	400	0	163	518
12	400	0	246	518
13	399	250	265	520
14	450	295	170	521
15	450	295	146	523
16	450	1	121	523
17	450	0	160	523
18	450	0	163	524
19	450	0	27	524
20	0	0	0	522
21	0	0	0	520
22	0	0	0	518
23	0	0	0	516
24	0	0	0	514
25	0	0	0	512
26	0	0	0	510
27	228	263	112	510
28	300	296	88	511
Total	8,427	1,945	3,594	

Date 2003	East Delaware Tunnel	West Delaware Tunnel	Neversink Tunnel	Average June 1, 2002, to date
Mar. 1	298	296	0	511
2	300	296	23	512
3	300	296	255	513
4	300	296	34	513
5	300	296	164	514
6	298	296	157	515
7	299	196	0	515
8	272	196	0	515
9	285	196	0	515
10	301	196	0	515
11	295	196	0	515
12	295	196	0	514
13	300	196	0	514
14	299	196	0	514
15	296	196	0	514
16	296	196	0	514
17	284	221	0	514
18	247	149	0	514
19	290	260	0	514
20	150	99	0	513
21	0	0	0	511
22	0	0	0	510
23	0	0	0	508
24	0	0	0	506
25	0	0	0	504
26	0	0	0	503
27	0	0	0	501
28	0	0	0	499
29	0	0	0	498
30	0	0	0	496
31	0	0	0	494
	5,705	4,465	633	

40

Table 10. Diversions to New York City water supply—continued

Million gallons per day for 24 hour period beginning 0800 local time
(River Master daily operation record)

Date 2003	East Delaware Tunnel	West Delaware Tunnel	Neversink Tunnel	Average June 1, 2002, to date	Date 2003	East Delaware Tunnel	West Delaware Tunnel	Neversink Tunnel	Average June 1, 2002, to date
Apr. 1	0	0	0	493	May 1	35	246	188	492
2	0	0	0	491	2	0	293	221	492
3	0	0	0	490	3	0	296	127	492
4	0	0	0	488	4	0	296	166	492
5	0	0	0	486	5	13	296	191	492
6	0	0	0	485	6	344	296	5	492
7	0	0	0	483	7	438	296	0	493
8	390	0	0	483	8	501	295	0	494
9	500	0	0	483	9	501	295	0	495
10	500	176	0	484	10	501	295	0	495
11	500	195	0	484	11	501	295	0	496
12	500	195	0	485	12	501	295	0	497
13	500	195	0	486	13	501	0	0	497
14	459	37	264	487	14	502	0	0	497
15	450	0	286	487	15	501	0	0	497
16	450	0	385	488	16	448	0	0	497
17	450	0	270	489	17	448	0	0	497
18	450	0	281	490	18	448	0	0	497
19	451	0	280	491	19	448	0	0	497
20	451	0	281	491	20	449	0	0	496
21	452	0	298	492	21	448	0	0	496
22	318	0	178	492	22	448	295	0	497
23	300	0	201	492	23	448	73	0	497
24	299	0	197	492	24	448	0	0	497
25	299	0	229	492	25	448	0	0	497
26	300	0	252	492	26	448	0	79	497
27	297	0	109	492	27	218	0	145	497
28	297	0	225	492	28	0	0	199	496
29	188	0	167	492	29	0	0	58	495
30	283	0	191	492	30	0	0	0	493
					31	0	0	0	492
Total	9,084	798	4,094			9,986	3,862	1,379	

41

Table 10. Diversions to New York City water supply—continued
Million gallons per day for 24 hour period beginning 0800 local time
(River Master daily operation record)

Date 2003	East Delaware Tunnel	West Delaware Tunnel	Neversink Tunnel	Average June 1, 2003, to date	Date 2003	East Delaware Tunnel	West Delaware Tunnel	Neversink Tunnel	Average June 1, 2003, to date
June 1	0	0	0	0	July 1	398	425	109	377
2	0	0	0	0	2	398	331	118	391
3	0	0	0	0	3	398	296	110	404
4	0	0	0	0	4	255	189	94	408
5	0	0	0	0	5	210	157	60	408
6	344	0	0	57	6	388	296	143	420
7	431	0	316	156	7	388	296	102	430
8	435	0	283	226	8	388	295	103	439
9	197	0	125	237	9	397	295	6	446
10	0	0	216	235	10	397	295	141	456
11	0	0	193	231	11	258	181	157	459
12	0	0	24	214	12	0	281	0	455
13	0	0	0	197	13	21	296	0	452
14	0	0	0	183	14	280	296	96	457
15	0	0	0	171	15	275	296	100	461
16	200	0	200	185	16	272	296	111	466
17	378	0	200	208	17	450	296	61	473
18	401	0	198	230	18	452	296	129	482
19	401	0	205	250	19	452	296	68	489
20	199	0	200	257	20	452	296	69	495
21	0	0	204	255	21	250	141	131	496
22	0	0	204	252	22	462	114	0	497
23	248	0	196	261	23	460	296	226	506
24	291	0	196	270	24	450	296	65	512
25	259	196	196	285	25	450	296	0	516
26	350	194	222	304	26	450	296	0	520
27	398	194	100	318	27	450	296	0	524
28	398	194	103	332	28	450	296	0	528
29	398	194	103	344	29	450	296	0	532
30	398	269	93	358	30	450	296	0	535
					31	450	296	107	541
Total	5,726	1,241	3,777			11,301	8,624	2,306	

Table 10. Diversions to New York City water supply—continued
Million gallons per day for 24 hour period beginning 0800 local time
(River Master daily operation record)

Date 2003	East Delaware Tunnel	West Delaware Tunnel	Neversink Tunnel	Average June 1, 2003, to date
Aug. 1	400	296	109	545
2	400	296	104	549
3	400	296	109	553
4	45	17	259	549
5	0	0	154	543
6	0	0	334	540
7	0	0	379	538
8	25	0	382	536
9	100	98	220	534
10	100	99	177	532
11	100	100	335	532
12	0	9	382	530
13	179	0	382	531
14	320	0	240	531
15	300	102	387	534
16	300	121	372	538
17	300	0	342	539
18	300	0	337	540
19	300	100	193	541
20	300	100	194	542
21	300	197	206	544
22	299	198	203	545
23	308	198	174	547
24	308	199	0	547
25	309	199	141	548
26	310	295	217	551
27	310	295	226	554
28	304	292	226	557
29	306	292	235	560
30	307	294	207	563
31	303	291	211	566
Total	7,233	4,384	7,437	

Date 2003	East Delaware Tunnel	West Delaware Tunnel	Neversink Tunnel	Average June 1, 2003, to date
Sept. 1	307	294	205	568
2	38	20	9	563
3	0	0	0	557
4	0	0	250	554
5	0	0	367	552
6	0	0	383	550
7	0	0	383	548
8	376	0	384	550
9	390	0	358	552
10	437	0	374	555
11	443	0	383	558
12	448	0	386	560
13	448	0	386	563
14	444	0	387	565
15	205	0	128	563
16	0	0	0	558
17	0	0	0	553
18	0	0	0	548
19	20	0	285	546
20	295	0	383	547
21	291	0	384	548
22	297	0	385	549
23	295	0	386	550
24	298	0	384	551
25	278	0	385	552
26	0	0	64	548
27	0	0	0	544
28	0	0	0	539
29	0	0	252	537
30	0	0	287	535
Total	5,310	314	7,578	

Table 10. Diversions to New York City water supply—continued
Million gallons per day for 24 hour period beginning 0800 local time
(River Master daily operation record)

Date 2003	East Delaware Tunnel	West Delaware Tunnel	Neversink Tunnel	Average June 1, 2003, to date
Oct. 1	3	0	284	533
2	0	261	253	533
3	0	296	195	532
4	0	296	158	532
5	0	296	379	533
6	0	296	382	534
7	293	1	253	534
8	286	0	235	534
9	317	0	383	535
10	311	0	383	536
11	294	0	384	537
12	299	0	385	538
13	297	0	385	540
14	302	0	386	541
15	301	0	385	542
16	300	0	385	543
17	293	0	386	544
18	297	0	386	545
19	296	0	387	546
20	297	0	387	547
21	303	0	387	548
22	303	0	387	549
23	301	0	387	550
24	292	0	388	550
25	291	0	389	551
26	296	0	390	552
27	62	0	116	550
28	0	0	0	546
29	0	0	0	542
30	0	0	0	539
31	0	0	0	535
Total	6,034	1,446	9,205	

Date 2003	East Delaware Tunnel	West Delaware Tunnel	Neversink Tunnel	Average June 1, 2003, to date
Nov. 1	0	0	0	532
2	0	0	0	528
3	0	0	0	525
4	0	0	0	522
5	338	0	0	521
6	449	0	0	520
7	449	0	0	520
8	0	0	352	519
9	0	0	360	518
10	189	0	360	518
11	287	0	381	519
12	292	0	382	520
13	301	0	385	521
14	301	0	385	522
15	296	0	386	523
16	292	0	381	524
17	293	0	393	525
18	232	0	312	525
19	0	0	129	522
20	0	0	353	521
21	0	0	344	520
22	0	0	341	519
23	0	0	338	518
24	0	0	338	517
25	0	0	342	516
26	0	0	343	515
27	0	0	341	514
28	0	0	341	513
29	0	0	342	512
30	0	0	341	512
Total	3,719	0	7,970	

Table 11. Daily mean discharge, East Branch Delaware River at Downsville, New York (station number 01417000), for year ending November 30, 2003 (U.S. Geological Survey published record)

[All values except total in cubic feet per second, ft³/s; total in cubic feet per second days, (ft³/s)-d; e, estimated]

DAY	DEC	JAN	FEB	MAR	APR	MAY	JUN	JUL	AUG	SEP	OCT	NOV
1	40	47	45	44	2,110	333	863	87	88	76	1,750	2,900
2	38	47	45	44	1,790	1,600	1,310	87	87	424	1,430	2,270
3	39	47	45	44	1,640	2,620	1,330	87	87	1,120	1,230	1,800
4	39	47	45	44	1,540	2,260	1,270	87	87	e4,600	1,230	1,490
5	40	47	45	44	1,560	1,800	1,140	87	88	4,550	1,390	1,280
6	41	47	45	44	1,550	1,390	959	87	89	2,910	1,220	988
7	41	47	45	44	1,460	910	586	88	90	2,000	915	614
8	41	47	45	45	1,290	566	440	87	90	1,410	606	474
9	41	47	45	45	801	429	286	87	90	930	451	637
10	42	47	45	45	538	279	367	87	90	587	348	670
11	42	47	45	45	452	208	507	88	222	211	254	507
12	43	47	45	44	441	462	635	87	600	71	172	458
13	43	47	45	45	399	525	855	87	1,310	69	116	349
14	43	49	45	44	366	511	1,260	87	1,260	68	115	306
15	44	48	45	47	351	450	1,380	87	801	114	261	268
16	44	45	45	48	345	368	1,200	88	454	301	399	222
17	44	45	45	46	339	279	848	87	356	484	351	196
18	45	45	44	46	256	205	538	87	300	497	288	179
19	45	45	44	46	190	141	370	87	257	308	303	428
20	46	46	43	47	128	87	293	87	198	68	315	4,370
21	46	46	43	48	78	69	594	94	156	67	268	4,390
22	46	45	44	49	69	73	1,010	84	131	67	229	3,070
23	46	46	44	49	89	64	1,070	85	89	312	185	2,360
24	46	46	44	49	86	65	748	89	89	1,030	150	1,860
25	51	46	44	48	77	64	549	88	90	922	122	1,750
26	72	46	44	47	128	64	547	90	90	862	99	1,480
27	71	46	47	47	314	63	352	90	90	905	1,150	1,280
28	71	46	44	335	324	64	171	90	90	2,340	4,220	1,280
29	71	45		1,370	288	65	146	90	90	2,810	7,090	2,430
30	56	45		2,630	288	128	119	87	90	2,270	7,330	2,380
31	46	45		2,520		318		87	90		4,330	
Total	1,463	1,436	1,250	8,093	19,287	16,460	21,743	2,717	7,739	32,383	38,317	42,686
Mean	47.2	46.3	44.6	261	643	531	725	87.6	250	1,079	1,236	1,423

Year total 193,574 (ft³/s)-d

Mean 530 ft³/s

Table 12. Daily mean discharge, West Branch Delaware River at Stilesville, New York (station number 01425000), for year ending November 30, 2003 (U.S. Geological Survey published record)

[All values except total in cubic feet per second, ft³/s; total in cubic feet per second days, (ft³/s)-d]

DAY	DEC	JAN	FEB	MAR	APR	MAY	JUN	JUL	AUG	SEP	OCT	NOV
1	56	58	356	551	2,860	1,250	682	368	291	253	1,490	3,620
2	56	67	361	471	2,510	1,280	935	299	243	272	1,320	2,900
3	56	63	354	417	2,330	1,480	1,010	296	200	602	962	2,400
4	56	61	400	338	2,230	1,380	1,010	296	204	1,360	885	2,030
5	56	59	508	309	2,300	1,230	974	296	179	1,760	949	1,770
6	56	59	544	307	2,450	1,100	933	296	159	2,180	910	1,660
7	56	58	440	286	2,340	968	904	374	138	2,040	843	1,470
8	56	58	366	292	2,160	842	897	434	106	1,900	888	1,280
9	56	59	401	308	1,970	730	845	374	228	1,690	895	1,140
10	63	58	446	297	1,800	615	769	278	289	1,530	862	1,020
11	133	58	471	266	1,540	522	725	148	306	1,060	809	947
12	143	58	467	265	1,420	556	766	69	538	790	743	960
13	129	57	428	270	1,300	645	773	67	848	609	673	966
14	98	58	300	263	1,190	808	1,410	190	910	567	615	1,000
15	65	57	216	248	1,200	877	1,920	217	781	700	852	969
16	57	63	168	264	1,190	882	1,820	299	532	989	1,120	921
17	56	143	228	470	1,130	847	1,600	314	423	1,100	1,100	897
18	55	246	280	1,380	1,050	810	1,420	370	434	962	1,030	899
19	69	296	307	2,750	980	755	1,290	510	431	707	1,020	959
20	77	356	329	3,430	902	688	1,190	293	368	471	1,040	2,860
21	63	390	340	6,130	834	665	1,380	295	300	366	984	4,450
22	62	406	366	9,270	815	587	1,610	183	258	366	930	3,960
23	63	406	486	8,860	812	424	1,730	139	241	340	873	3,210
24	62	392	775	6,760	782	437	1,590	108	241	1,560	838	2,620
25	63	378	918	5,150	727	479	1,370	120	249	1,580	777	2,310
26	65	393	907	4,440	795	513	1,280	268	244	1,410	724	2,050
27	62	405	845	4,070	1,270	547	1,120	323	484	1,260	977	1,770
28	58	385	687	3,450	1,450	544	747	292	527	1,510	2,150	1,590
29	58	372		3,020	1,440	520	588	291	400	1,710	3,220	1,930
30	58	369		3,230	1,360	493	468	316	484	1,670	5,350	2,170
31	59	359		3,210		500		320	323		4,720	
Total	2,122	6,247	12,694	70,772	45,137	23,974	33,756	8,443	11,359	33,314	40,549	56,728
Mean	68.5	202	453	2,283	1,505	773	1,125	272	366	1,110	1,308	1,891

Year total 345,095 (ft³/s)-d

Mean 945 ft³/s

46

Table 13. Daily mean discharge, Neversink River at Neversink, New York (station number 01436000), for year ending November 30, 2003

[All values except total in cubic feet per second, ft³/s; total in cubic feet per second days, (ft³/s)-d]

DAY	DEC	JAN	FEB	MAR	APR	MAY	JUN	JUL	AUG	SEP	OCT	NOV
1	24	23	27	27	583	37	1,050	53	67	58	75	590
2	25	24	26	26	475	49	903	53	56	60	60	468
3	24	24	26	25	456	52	479	62	57	60	31	400
4	25	24	26	26	425	52	378	75	65	60	88	347
5	24	24	26	26	401	52	334	75	64	58	196	357
6	24	24	26	26	336	52	282	75	57	58	34	422
7	24	23	25	26	309	52	157	82	66	58	27	346
8	24	24	26	26	285	53	54	90	71	58	27	199
9	24	25	26	25	257	53	54	73	56	58	27	29
10	24	25	26	25	247	53	55	54	57	58	27	29
11	24	24	26	26	304	53	53	55	57	58	27	30
12	24	24	26	26	417	53	53	55	63	58	27	31
13	24	24	26	25	387	52	154	54	86	58	27	35
14	25	24	26	25	259	52	435	55	74	58	27	28
15	24	24	27	26	28	53	375	65	62	58	27	25
16	23	25	27	26	30	53	189	77	73	58	27	27
17	24	25	27	26	27	53	71	65	73	58	27	27
18	24	25	27	26	27	53	53	55	74	58	27	27
19	24	25	27	26	27	53	53	55	74	59	28	27
20	24	26	27	26	27	53	53	61	73	58	28	26
21	24	26	27	27	27	53	53	63	74	58	28	26
22	24	26	27	27	27	53	55	57	67	58	28	27
23	23	26	27	27	26	53	83	55	56	60	27	27
24	23	26	27	27	26	53	66	55	56	60	27	27
25	23	26	27	27	27	53	55	65	57	60	28	26
26	23	26	27	27	27	53	53	85	57	60	28	27
27	23	27	27	124	26	53	68	90	57	60	30	27
28	23	27	27	459	26	53	84	75	57	137	28	27
29	23	26		967	23	53	84	57	57	680	710	55
30	23	26		1,670	21	55	70	56	57	188	1,500	28
31	23	27		854		90		69	58		846	
Total	737	775	742	4,752	5,563	1,655	5,906	2,016	1,978	2,588	4,144	3,767
Mean	23.8	25.0	26.5	153	185	53.4	197	65.0	63.8	86.3	134	126

Year total 34,623 (ft³/s)-d

Mean 94.9 ft³/s

Table 14. Daily mean discharge, Wallenpaupack Creek at Wilsonville, Pennsylvania (station number 01432000), for year ending November 30, 2003 (Record furnished by PPL Corporation)

[All values except total in cubic feet per second, ft^3/s; total in cubic feet per second days, (ft^3/s)-d]

DAY	DEC	JAN	FEB	MAR	APR	MAY	JUN	JUL	AUG	SEP	OCT	NOV
1	277	1,500	635	189	1,020	158	1,170	1,700	445	0	0	0
2	636	1,670	543	127	996	0	1,600	1,610	0	502	0	0
3	807	1,340	653	458	1,100	0	1,720	1,290	0	579	0	696
4	647	1,050	544	627	1,010	0	1,690	1,110	250	510	0	643
5	625	1,050	687	413	1,010	0	1,720	1,160	185	543	0	972
6	626	952	717	496	1,550	0	1,360	1,270	245	327	0	1,040
7	283	820	690	589	1,120	0	1,120	724	283	399	0	1,070
8	238	780	560	168	1,300	0	1,090	754	440	637	0	1,040
9	663	887	512	176	1,370	97	735	315	232	562	0	1,060
10	645	763	583	603	1,320	0	700	426	367	630	0	1,090
11	686	765	565	386	1,290	0	952	562	0	597	12	1,070
12	684	790	579	385	2	0	1,200	0	0	721	0	1,060
13	736	800	655	440	0	0	1,050	0	354	361	672	1,100
14	1,060	852	562	459	525	2	815	627	649	333	611	1,070
15	440	831	662	0	703	0	741	524	588	563	526	1,040
16	753	688	574	12	793	1	617	467	382	1,400	556	1,080
17	810	707	817	12	672	0	430	511	271	1,580	466	638
18	735	628	669	0	651	0	598	462	392	1,570	0	695
19	749	512	502	0	0	126	557	0	533	1,580	0	625
20	679	659	552	276	0	348	576	0	410	1,570	481	872
21	270	620	687	84	493	179	617	529	447	1,580	508	647
22	261	925	726	436	527	146	1,690	431	514	1,420	529	576
23	736	1,020	754	448	543	204	1,720	687	2	1,270	430	500
24	811	974	828	381	550	0	1,720	499	0	1,430	587	460
25	614	970	444	598	657	0	1,720	602	685	1,430	0	488
26	1,270	985	491	789	0	0	1,720	348	573	1,430	0	476
27	1,460	830	519	744	0	136	1,720	556	623	564	705	0
28	1,050	906	553	588	0	197	1,700	847	20	0	761	519
29	1,350	974		851	0	271	1,690	953	394	0	796	823
30	727	870		996	0	260	1,680	1,000	0	0	654	588
31	877	856		1,030		0		981	0		685	
Total	22,205	27,974	17,263	12,761	19,202	2,125	36,418	20,945	9,284	24,088	8,979	21,938
Mean	716	902	617	412	640	68.5	1214	676	299	803	290	731

Year total 223,182 (ft^3/s)-d

Mean 611 ft^3/s

Table 15. Daily mean discharge, Delaware River at Montague, New Jersey (station number 01438500), for year ending November 30, 2003 (U.S. Geological Survey published record)

[All values except total in cubic feet per second, ft³/s; total in cubic feet per second days, (ft³/s)-d; e, estimated]

DAY	DEC	JAN	FEB	MAR	APR	MAY	JUN	JUL	AUG	SEP	OCT	NOV
1	4,960	6,760	e3,440	e5,150	18,700	5,720	9,560	5,600	2,630	2,120	12,400	24,200
2	5,100	14,500	e3,120	e4,470	16,300	5,450	19,700	5,140	3,040	10,700	10,600	18,400
3	4,790	17,600	e3,260	e4,720	15,500	8,600	15,000	4,500	3,680	26,400	9,250	15,600
4	4,260	13,500	e3,710	e5,200	14,400	9,800	12,800	3,930	3,690	28,500	7,750	13,500
5	3,990	11,300	e3,650	e4,990	14,000	8,530	11,900	3,710	5,640	34,100	8,140	12,200
6	3,860	9,810	e4,190	e4,790	14,000	7,510	10,700	3,630	7,140	21,300	8,710	12,900
7	3,750	8,810	e4,470	e4,940	13,400	6,760	9,590	3,490	7,330	15,200	7,360	12,000
8	3,250	8,130	e3,990	e4,650	12,800	6,030	11,100	3,190	5,720	11,800	6,830	10,100
9	3,210	7,820	e3,740	e4,140	12,000	5,710	9,860	3,070	5,590	9,530	6,100	8,810
10	e2,910	7,400	e3,650	4,360	11,300	4,990	8,410	2,910	6,120	7,850	5,620	8,120
11	3,510	6,730	e3,570	4,390	11,300	4,450	7,340	2,800	6,340	6,910	5,210	7,780
12	4,250	6,310	e3,300	3,930	12,100	4,540	7,440	4,080	12,200	5,720	4,760	7,690
13	4,770	e5,680	e2,960	4,030	11,500	5,960	9,440	3,180	11,000	4,570	4,450	8,190
14	6,520	e5,160	e3,090	3,990	10,400	5,640	11,300	2,470	9,510	4,030	4,450	7,450
15	8,780	e4,540	e3,010	3,880	9,550	5,400	15,300	e2,770	8,560	4,560	7,390	6,830
16	8,700	e4,530	e2,270	3,980	8,640	5,030	12,100	2,500	7,100	12,500	11,500	6,520
17	7,590	e3,880	e1,940	7,180	7,930	4,740	9,790	2,400	5,360	11,400	9,310	6,020
18	6,590	e3,380	e2,240	13,800	7,230	4,280	8,530	2,640	4,730	9,020	7,790	5,710
19	5,730	e3,480	e2,860	24,800	6,530	3,930	7,970	2,500	4,350	8,510	6,700	5,930
20	6,310	e3,390	e3,100	23,200	5,740	3,780	7,020	2,000	3,960	8,260	6,850	21,900
21	10,500	e3,360	e2,740	38,000	5,450	3,710	11,200	2,030	3,600	6,820	6,920	30,700
22	11,000	e3,040	e3,060	49,900	5,750	3,530	20,500	2,850	3,320	5,660	6,520	22,900
23	9,350	e3,120	e4,550	46,400	5,720	3,420	21,600	4,690	2,980	11,700	6,190	18,200
24	8,350	e3,360	e6,230	34,400	5,510	3,260	16,600	5,260	2,250	26,200	5,800	14,900
25	7,690	e3,410	e6,810	26,700	4,950	3,190	12,300	4,260	2,040	17,400	5,260	13,500
26	7,120	e3,160	e6,220	23,700	4,720	4,300	10,300	3,460	2,680	13,600	4,500	12,500
27	7,330	e3,420	e6,050	21,700	6,160	6,100	8,840	2,980	2,500	11,200	6,950	10,700
28	7,060	e3,090	e5,930	18,400	7,820	5,620	7,970	3,350	2,460	12,100	28,500	10,000
29	6,810	e3,330		16,700	6,880	5,250	6,750	3,460	1,960	18,600	36,000	17,700
30	5,930	e3,530		22,400	6,190	4,840	6,100	3,210	2,410	15,300	49,900	19,300
31	5,940	e3,500		22,200		4,400		3,090	2,150		34,300	
Total	189,910	189,480	107,150	461,090	292,470	164,470	337,010	105,150	152,040	381,560	342,010	390,250
Mean	6,126	6,112	3,827	14,870	9,749	5,305	11,230	3,392	4,905	12,720	11,030	13,010

Year total 3,112,590 (ft³/s)-d

Mean 8,528 ft³/s

Table 16. Diversions by New Jersey; daily mean discharge, Delaware and Raritan Canal at Port Mercer, New Jersey (station number 01460440), for year ending November 30, 2003
(U.S. Geological Survey published record)

[All data except total in million gallons per day, Mgal/d; total in Million gallons, Mgal; e, estimated]

DAY	DEC	JAN	FEB	MAR	APR	MAY	JUN	JUL	AUG	SEP	OCT	NOV
1	95	78	e99	97	94	102	77	95	98	93	95	95
2	95	82	e98	68	100	104	87	95	95	97	94	97
3	96	89	e98	64	104	102	92	96	94	95	93	97
4	95	84	e98	79	103	101	27	95	96	98	93	96
5	100	86	e98	71	101	99	65	95	93	96	95	87
6	102	89	e98	56	103	102	88	95	91	97	96	68
7	102	90	e98	74	102	104	77	95	93	96	96	83
8	104	90	e98	78	100	103	76	96	95	97	95	88
9	103	90	e98	76	91	99	88	94	97	95	97	92
10	100	91	e98	79	90	104	89	94	88	94	98	92
11	97	91	e98	80	93	106	90	94	90	94	96	93
12	82	91	103	81	80	104	90	94	95	95	94	90
13	88	91	102	87	97	100	82	95	97	97	94	90
14	69	92	e100	86	99	103	81	94	97	96	94	90
15	85	93	e99	84	99	100	85	95	97	94	86	92
16	93	97	e94	86	100	97	86	95	98	83	92	93
17	94	100	e89	88	100	98	81	95	97	92	94	93
18	93	97	96	89	102	96	79	93	97	93	92	95
19	93	e100	100	89	102	98	79	87	97	94	91	86
20	91	e100	105	92	102	96	84	90	96	96	92	e26
21	88	e100	104	71	102	94	74	e90	e92	95	94	79
22	92	e100	e26	82	102	95	79	88	e92	96	93	89
23	93	e100	33	88	99	95	85	e87	e93	85	91	91
24	95	e100	65	102	101	95	86	e90	e90	94	92	92
25	83	e100	83	99	102	93	90	e97	e90	95	92	92
26	74	e99	92	101	101	68	93	e94	e90	98	94	92
27	86	e99	95	99	102	78	95	e94	e94	91	78	94
28	89	e99	97	101	101	88	94	95	e94	79	77	90
29	91	e99		100	103	91	94	96	92	90	65	76
30	93	e99		94	103	93	95	95	95	91	77	83
31	93	e99		93		94		97	93		92	
Total	2,854	2,915	2,562	2,634	2,978	3,002	2,488	2,905	2,916	2,806	2,822	2,621
Mean	92.1	94.0	91.5	85.0	99.3	96.8	82.9	93.7	94.1	93.5	91.0	87.4

Year total 33,503 Mgal

Mean 91.8 Mgal/d

QUALITY OF WATER IN THE DELAWARE ESTUARY

Introduction

This section describes the water-quality monitoring program for the Delaware Estuary during the River Master 2003 report year, December 1, 2002, to November 30, 2003. This program is conducted by the USGS, in cooperation with the Delaware River Basin Commission (DRBC). Selected data collected for this program are presented and water-quality conditions are summarized. The DRBC and others use these data to assess water-quality conditions and track the movement of the "salt front" in the Delaware Estuary.

Water-Quality Monitoring Program

As part of a long-term program, the quality of water in the Delaware Estuary between Trenton, New Jersey, and Reedy Island Jetty, Delaware, is monitored at various locations (fig. 5). Data on water temperature, specific conductance, dissolved oxygen, and pH were collected by electronic instruments at four sites—Trenton, Benjamin Franklin Bridge (Philadelphia), Chester, and Reedy Island Jetty. Water-quality monitors at Trenton and Reedy Island Jetty were operated continuously throughout the report year, whereas monitors at the Benjamin Franklin Bridge and Chester were operated from April to November 2003.

Water-quality data were collected on a monthly basis in March, June, July, and October, and on a semi-monthly basis in April, May, August, and September 2003 at 19 sites between Biles Channel and Mahon River (sites A–T on fig. 5). These data were collected by the State of Delaware for the DRBC. At each site, water samples were collected at a single point near the center of the channel and analyzed for selected physical properties and chemical constituents including temperature, chloride, alkalinity, specific conductance, dissolved oxygen, pH, nutrients, and trace metals. These analyses consist of field measurements and laboratory determinations.

From March to October, water-quality data were obtained on a monthly basis at three additional sites in lower Delaware Bay (sites U–W on fig. 5). Water samples were analyzed for selected physical properties and chemical constituents.

Data obtained from the water-quality monitors are processed and stored in the USGS National Water Information System data base. These data are published annually by the USGS in water resources data reports for New Jersey and Pennsylvania. Water-quality data for the other sampling sites are not presented in this report but are available from DRBC and STORET, an environmental quality database operated by the U.S. Environmental Protection Agency.

Water Quality During the 2003 Report Year

Streamflow

Streamflow has a major effect on the quality of water in the Delaware Estuary. High freshwater flows commonly result in improved water quality by limiting the upstream movement of seawater and reducing the concentration of dissolved substances. High flows also aid in maintaining lower water temperatures during warm weather and in supporting higher concentrations of dissolved oxygen. Under certain conditions, however, high streamflows can transport large quantities of nutrients to the estuary, which may result in algal blooms.

Streamflow from the Delaware River Basin above Trenton, New Jersey, is the major source of freshwater inflow to the Delaware Estuary. During the report year, monthly mean streamflow measured at the USGS gaging station Delaware River at Trenton, New Jersey, was highest during June 2003 (31,200 ft^3/s) and lowest during July (9,224 ft^3/s; table 17). Monthly mean streamflows were greater than long-term

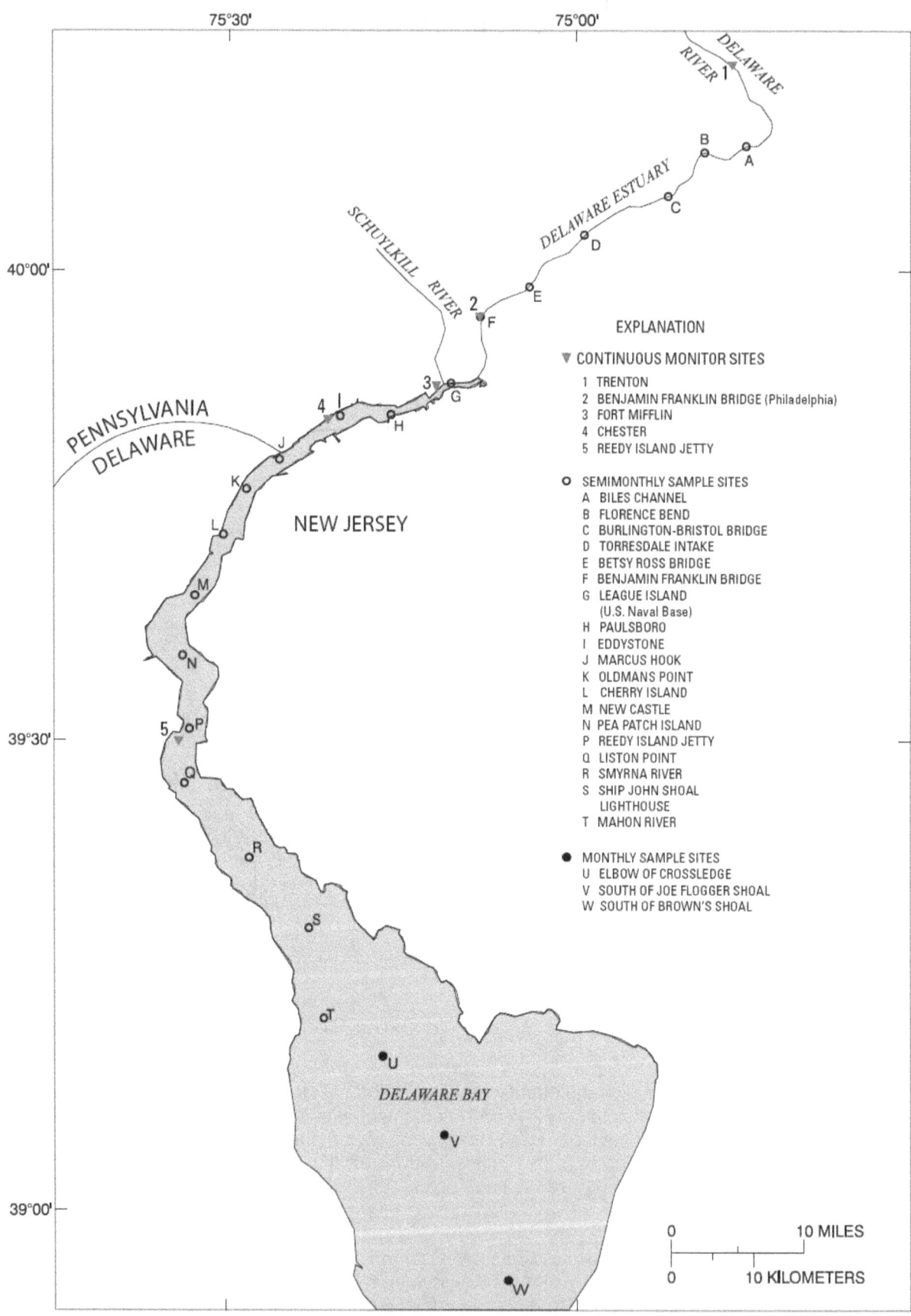

75°30'

75°00'

40°00'

39°30'

39°00'

DELAWARE RIVER

DELAWARE ESTUARY

SCHUYLKILL RIVER

PENNSYLVANIA
DELAWARE

NEW JERSEY

DELAWARE BAY

1

B
A

C

D

2
E
F

3
G

4
H

J

K

L

M

N

5
P

Q

R

S

T

U

V

W

EXPLANATION

▼ CONTINUOUS MONITOR SITES

1 TRENTON
2 BENJAMIN FRANKLIN BRIDGE (Philadelphia)
3 FORT MIFFLIN
4 CHESTER
5 REEDY ISLAND JETTY

○ SEMIMONTHLY SAMPLE SITES

A BILES CHANNEL
B FLORENCE BEND
C BURLINGTON-BRISTOL BRIDGE
D TORRESDALE INTAKE
E BETSY ROSS BRIDGE
F BENJAMIN FRANKLIN BRIDGE
G LEAGUE ISLAND
    (U.S. Naval Base)
H PAULSBORO
I EDDYSTONE
J MARCUS HOOK
K OLDMANS POINT
L CHERRY ISLAND
M NEW CASTLE
N PEA PATCH ISLAND
P REEDY ISLAND JETTY
Q LISTON POINT
R SMYRNA RIVER
S SHIP JOHN SHOAL
    LIGHTHOUSE
T MAHON RIVER

● MONTHLY SAMPLE SITES
U ELBOW OF CROSSLEDGE
V SOUTH OF JOE FLOGGER SHOAL
W SOUTH OF BROWN'S SHOAL

0   10 MILES

0   10 KILOMETERS

Figure 5. Location of water-quality monitoring sites on the Delaware Estuary.

mean monthly flows in all months except February, April, and May 2003. The monthly mean streamflow for September set a new high for the month. The greatest percentage flow deficiency was in May 2003, when monthly mean streamflow was 74 percent of the long-term mean monthly flow. Long-term mean monthly streamflow was computed on the basis of data for the period from 1913 to 2002. The highest daily mean streamflow during the report year was 79,000 ft^3/s on March 23, 2003. The lowest daily mean streamflow was 5,350 ft^3/s on July 21, 2003.

Water Temperature

Water temperature has an important influence on water quality because it affects various physical, chemical, and biological properties of water. Generally, increases in water temperature have detrimental effects on water quality by decreasing the saturation level of dissolved oxygen and increasing the biological activity of aquatic organisms. Although the primary factors that affect water temperature in the Delaware Estuary are climatic, various kinds of water use, especially powerplant cooling, also can have important effects.

At the Benjamin Franklin Bridge, Philadelphia, Pennsylvania, monthly mean water temperatures during the report year were less than the long-term mean monthly temperatures in all months of monitor operation—April to November 2003. Long-term mean water temperatures were computed using data for the period from 1964 to 2002 (fig. 6). The maximum daily mean water temperature of 26.5° C was recorded on August 6 and 7, 2003.

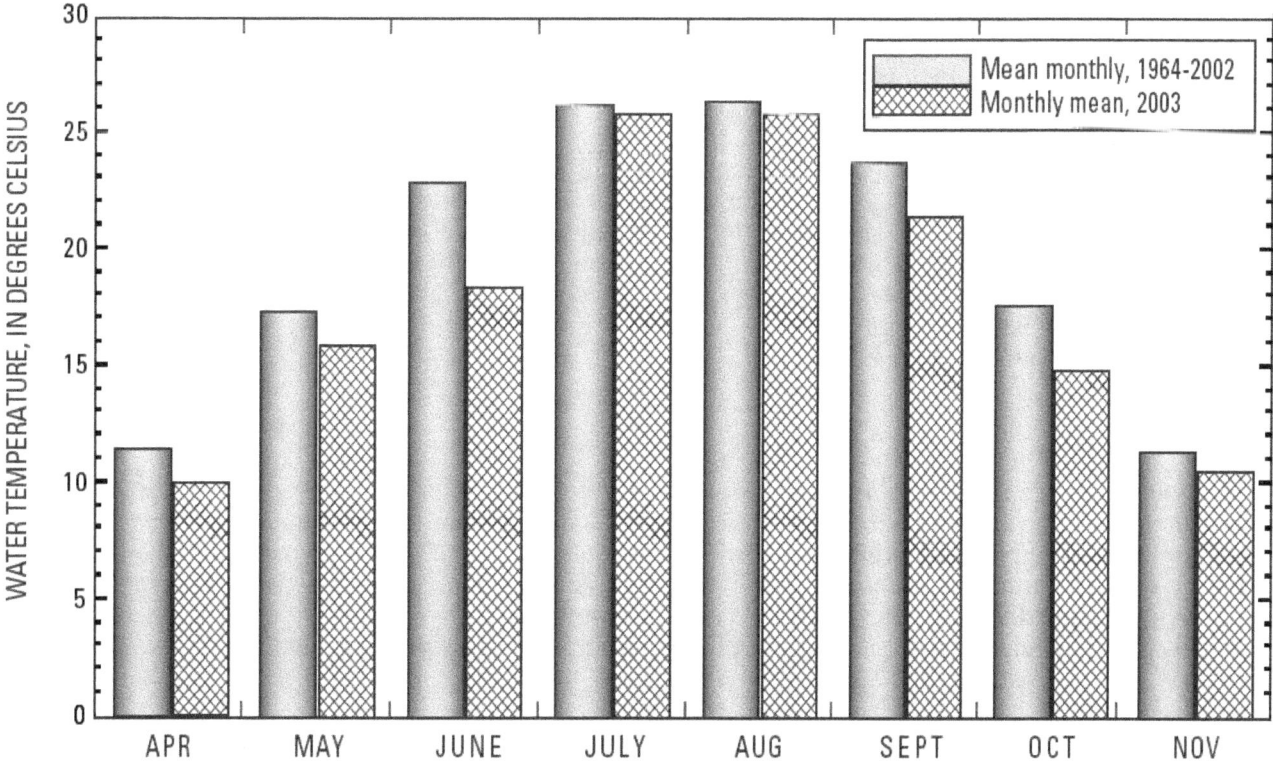

Figure 6. Water temperature in the Delaware Estuary at Benjamin Franklin Bridge at Philadelphia, Pennsylvania, April to November.

Specific Conductance and Chloride

Specific conductance is a measure of the capacity of water to conduct an electrical current and is a function of the types and quantities of dissolved substances in water. As concentrations of dissolved ions increase, specific conductance of the water increases. Specific conductance measurements are good indicators of dissolved solids content and total ion concentrations. Seawater and some man-made constituents can cause the specific conductance of estuary water to increase substantially. Dilution associated with high streamflows results in decreased levels of dissolved solids and lower specific conductance whereas low streamflows have the opposite effect.

The upstream movement of seawater and the accompanying increase in chloride concentrations is an important concern for water supplies obtained from the Delaware Estuary. Water with chloride concentrations greater than 250 mg/L (milligrams per liter) is considered undesirable for domestic use, and water with concentrations exceeding 50 mg/L is unsatisfactory for some industrial processes. Chloride concentrations in the estuary increase in a downstream direction, with proximity to the Atlantic Ocean.

Chloride concentration was not measured directly at the Reedy Island Jetty, Delaware, monitor site. Instead, a mathematical relation between specific conductance and chloride concentration has been developed on the basis of long-term field measurements of specific conductance and laboratory analyses of chloride; this relation can be used to estimate chloride concentrations from specific conductance values. Chloride concentrations estimated from the relation are presented in table 18. The specific conductance-chloride relation is less reliable when chloride concentrations are less than 30 mg/L, because other dissolved substances may be present in amounts large enough to affect the relation. Therefore, chloride concentrations estimated from specific conductance data are not presented when concentrations of less than 30 mg/L would result from the relation. Instead, estimated values less than 30 mg/L are reported as < 30 mg/L. Chloride concentrations at Chester, Pennsylvania (table 19), were measured directly by Kimberly Clark Chester Operations and are not derived from specific conductance data.

At Chester, the highest daily maximum chloride concentration was 91 mg/L on February 22, 2003 (table 19). During the report year, daily maximum concentrations exceeded 50 mg/L on 13 percent of the days. The lowest daily minimum chloride concentration was 21 mg/L on December 1–2, 2002. Daily minimum concentrations exceeded 50 mg/L on nearly 12 percent of the days. Chloride concentrations were persistently high from mid-February to mid-March 2003, when daily minimum concentrations exceeded 50 mg/L on all days.

At Reedy Island Jetty, the highest daily maximum chloride concentration was 7,400 mg/L on February 18, 2003 (table 18). Daily maximum chloride concentrations during the report year exceeded 1,000 mg/L on 84 percent of the days. The lowest daily minimum chloride concentration for the report year was <30 mg/L on several days in March, April, June, and November. Daily minimum chloride concentrations exceeded 1,000 mg/L on 21 percent of the days. From December to May, daily maximum chloride concentrations at Reedy Island Jetty ranged from 56 to 7,400 mg/L. From June to November, daily maximum chloride concentrations ranged from <30 to 5,700 mg/L.

Dissolved Oxygen

Dissolved oxygen in water is necessary for the respiratory processes of aquatic organisms and in chemical reactions in aquatic environments. Fish and many other clean-water species require relatively high dissolved oxygen concentrations at all times. The major source of dissolved oxygen in the Delaware Estuary is diffusion from the atmosphere, and, to a lesser extent, photosynthetic activity of aquatic plants. The principal factors that affect dissolved oxygen concentrations in the Estuary are water temperature, biochemical oxygen demand, freshwater inflow, phytoplankton, turbidity, salinity, and tidal and wind-driven mixing.

Concentrations of dissolved oxygen at several sites on the Delaware Estuary have been measured since 1962 by the USGS. Two of these sites, Delaware River at Benjamin Franklin Bridge at Philadelphia, Pennsylvania, and Delaware River at Chester, Pennsylvania, have nearly continuous records and are in the reach of the estuary most affected by wastewater discharges. For these two stations, the mean and minimum daily mean dissolved oxygen concentrations for the three-month period of July to September during each of the 1965–2003 report years is shown in figure 7. An increasing trend in concentration is evident. Although concentrations have increased considerably over this 39-year period, mean concentrations can vary substantially from year to year.

Concentrations of dissolved oxygen in the Delaware Estuary generally are greatest near Trenton and decrease in a downstream direction. In an area just downstream of Benjamin Franklin Bridge, concentrations usually reach minimum levels. During the report year, daily mean concentrations of dissolved oxygen at the Benjamin Franklin Bridge monitor site were lowest in mid-July, early August, and early September, and the lowest recorded daily mean concentration was 4.4 mg/L on August 2 and September 3 (table 20). Daily mean concentrations of dissolved oxygen were consistently 6.0 mg/L or greater on most days from April 1 to July 9 and September 6 to November 30, 2003. At Chester, daily mean dissolved oxygen concentrations were lowest during early September and the lowest recorded daily mean concentration was 3.8 mg/L on September 5 and 6, 2003 (table 21).

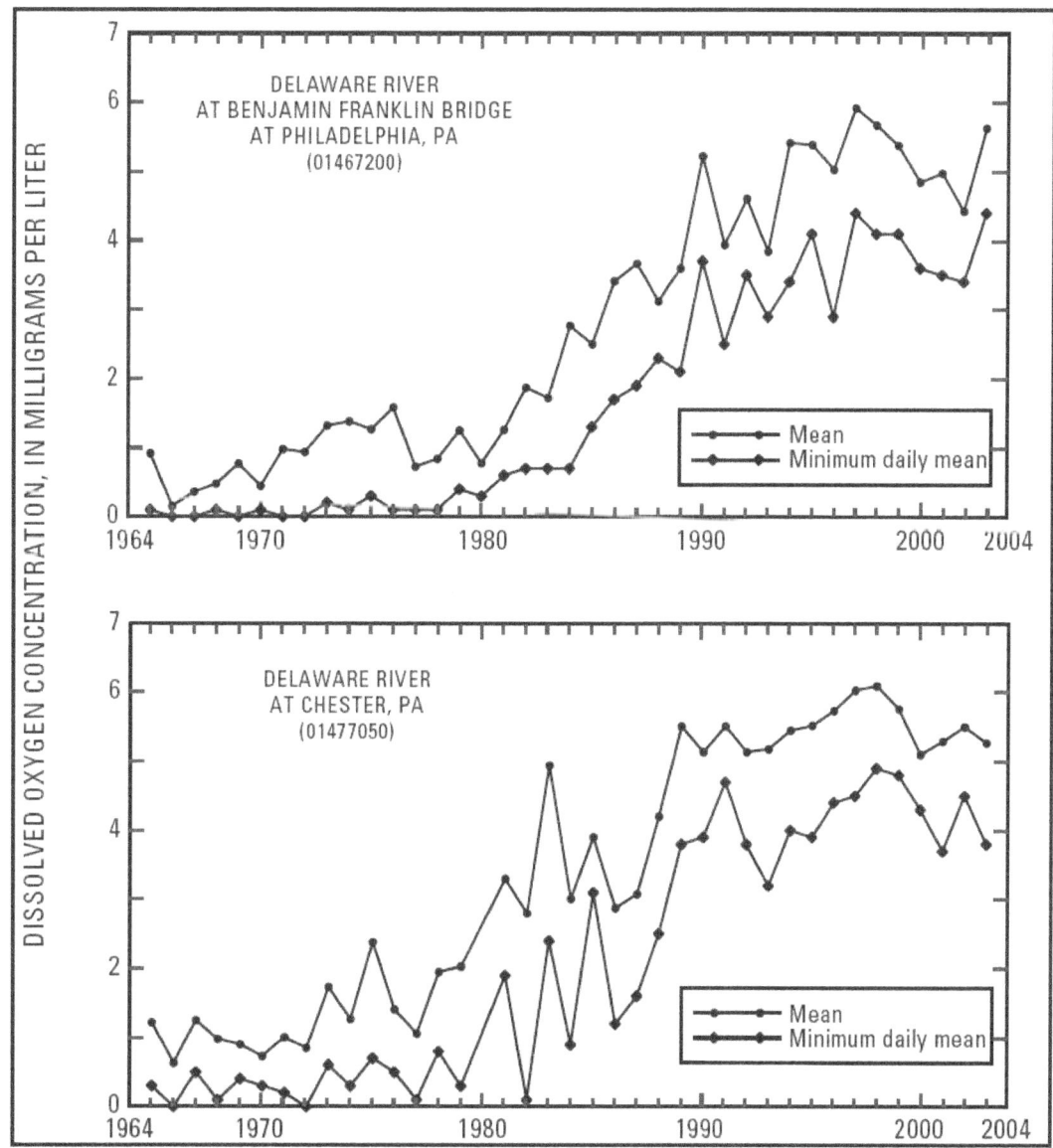

Figure 7. Mean and minimum daily mean dissolved oxygen concentrations from July to September at two monitor sites on the Delaware Estuary, 1965–2003.

Histograms of hourly dissolved oxygen concentrations at the Benjamin Franklin Bridge and Chester monitor sites during the critical summer period—July to September 2003—are presented in figure 8. Hourly concentrations at the Benjamin Franklin Bridge were 4 mg/L or less during 5.5 percent of this period. At Chester, hourly dissolved oxygen concentrations were 4 mg/L or less during 19 percent of the 2003 critical summer period. Dissolved oxygen concentrations less than 4 mg/L can have adverse, and possibly lethal, effects on fish and other aquatic organisms.

Hydrogen-Ion Activity (pH)

The pH of a solution is a measure of the effective concentration (activity) of dissolved hydrogen ions. Solutions having pH less than 7 are characterized as acidic, whereas solutions with pH greater than 7 are considered basic or alkaline. The pH of uncontaminated surface water generally ranges from 6.5 to 8.5. Major factors affecting the pH of surface water include the geologic composition of the drainage basin and human inputs, including wastewater discharges. In addition, photosynthetic activity, and dissolved gases including carbon dioxide, hydrogen sulfide, and ammonia can have a considerable effect on pH. During the report year, pH was measured seasonally at the Benjamin Franklin Bridge and Chester monitor sites, and continuously at the Reedy Island Jetty site. The range of daily median pH for these stations was as follows: Benjamin Franklin Bridge, 6.9 to 7.5; Chester, 6.8 to 7.5; and Reedy Island Jetty, 6.9 to 7.9. Generally, the pH of water in the Delaware Estuary is lowest near Trenton, New Jersey, and increases (that is, becomes more alkaline) in a downstream direction. The pH of water in the Delaware Estuary between the Benjamin Franklin Bridge and Reedy Island Jetty is not a limiting factor for aquatic health and other beneficial uses of the water.

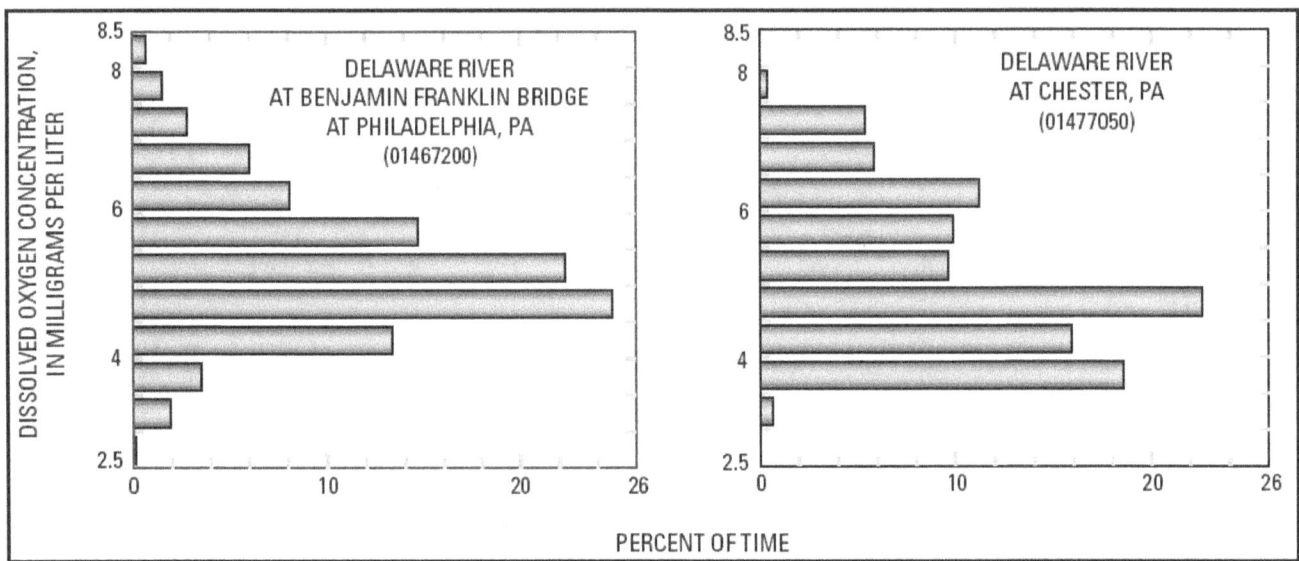

Figure 8. Distribution of hourly dissolved oxygen concentrations at two monitor sites on the Delaware Estuary, July to September 2003.

Table 17. Daily mean discharge, Delaware River at Trenton, New Jersey (station number 01463500), for year ending November 30, 2003 (U.S. Geological Survey published record)

[All values, except total, in cubic feet per second ft³/s; total in cubic feet per second days, (ft³/s)-d; e, estimated]

DAY	DEC	JAN	FEB	MAR	APR	MAY	JUN	JUL	AUG	SEP	OCT	NOV
1	12,000	15,600	e8,700	12,400	37,100	11,700	15,500	14,800	6,550	5,740	27,800	54,700
2	11,400	29,000	e8,400	13,600	32,800	11,000	34,000	13,300	7,200	6,950	23,000	41,700
3	11,000	38,200	8,770	17,500	30,000	10,500	38,000	12,300	6,760	15,600	19,800	32,900
4	10,600	36,500	8,180	14,100	28,300	12,600	43,700	11,400	8,490	33,700	17,500	28,600
5	9,450	29,000	8,610	14,100	26,400	14,500	39,300	10,400	16,800	39,100	16,200	25,600
6	9,070	24,800	8,630	17,600	25,500	13,300	30,700	9,420	27,800	38,400	15,800	25,300
7	8,620	22,100	9,020	14,900	24,700	12,300	26,400	8,790	24,500	27,000	16,300	25,100
8	8,420	20,000	9,300	13,000	23,700	11,800	31,500	8,830	21,000	20,300	14,400	22,900
9	7,690	18,600	8,230	14,000	23,500	11,100	28,700	8,290	16,800	16,500	13,300	19,700
10	7,130	17,900	7,780	15,400	24,300	10,500	25,500	8,050	19,800	13,800	12,200	17,700
11	7,270	16,900	7,700	12,500	23,400	9,840	22,700	7,640	19,200	11,800	11,400	16,500
12	15,100	15,500	7,050	11,600	25,400	9,140	21,400	7,420	23,100	10,800	10,800	16,500
13	18,100	14,000	6,590	11,800	24,700	9,000	26,200	7,720	27,400	9,840	10,100	16,600
14	22,500	13,200	6,290	13,900	22,500	9,930	29,800	8,160	24,000	9,710	9,620	16,600
15	25,300	11,900	6,160	12,900	20,300	9,870	28,500	6,660	19,300	10,400	13,500	15,600
16	25,000	10,900	6,720	13,300	18,700	9,580	29,900	6,320	16,600	20,900	17,600	13,700
17	22,400	10,300	e5,500	15,500	17,100	9,160	25,200	6,040	15,500	27,400	19,900	13,200
18	19,200	10,300	e6,100	22,700	16,100	8,650	22,300	5,550	14,300	23,500	17,300	12,700
19	16,400	8,880	e7,500	36,200	15,100	8,240	21,000	5,820	12,200	21,000	15,400	13,000
20	17,400	8,970	e8,800	46,500	14,100	7,490	22,300	6,010	10,800	19,200	14,100	30,200
21	24,500	9,460	e9,600	60,300	12,900	7,170	45,200	5,350	9,670	17,300	13,500	45,300
22	25,900	8,990	13,900	78,100	12,400	7,330	52,800	11,500	8,740	15,600	13,700	45,900
23	23,700	e8,700	23,800	79,000	12,500	7,110	58,700	18,600	8,160	21,200	12,400	36,600
24	21,000	e8,400	23,200	67,700	12,200	7,100	51,400	15,000	7,490	51,100	11,700	30,600
25	20,600	e8,600	17,900	52,900	11,700	7,320	41,700	13,300	6,550	48,400	11,600	26,800
26	20,700	e8,900	15,900	43,600	11,200	10,700	33,900	11,000	5,950	37,200	11,200	25,100
27	18,200	e8,800	14,200	40,400	11,300	15,200	29,400	8,940	5,890	30,100	16,200	22,800
28	16,600	e8,400	12,800	36,400	11,400	14,700	24,200	7,900	6,010	29,300	40,100	20,500
29	15,900	e8,300		31,600	13,600	14,500	19,400	7,360	5,730	30,800	68,600	32,400
30	15,200	e8,600		34,800	12,700	13,100	16,600	7,220	5,620	33,200	78,900	39,300
31	14,200	e8,800		40,400		11,800		6,840	5,490		74,400	
Total	500,550	468,500	285,330	908,700	595,600	326,230	935,900	285,930	413,400	695,840	668,320	784,100
Mean	16,150	15,110	10,190	29,310	19,850	10,520	31,200	9,224	13,340	23,190	21,560	26,140

Year total 6,868,400 (ft³/s)-d

Mean 18,820 ft³/s

Table 18. Daily maximum and minimum chloride concentrations estimated from values of specific conductance, Delaware River at Reedy Island Jetty, Delaware (station number 01482800), for year ending November 30, 2003

[Concentrations in milligrams per liter; Max, maximum value; Min, minimum value; <, less than; n.d., not determined]

DAY	DEC Max	DEC Min	JAN Max	JAN Min	FEB Max	FEB Min	MAR Max	MAR Min	APR Max	APR Min	MAY Max	MAY Min	JUN Max	JUN Min	JUL Max	JUL Min	AUG Max	AUG Min	SEP Max	SEP Min	OCT Max	OCT Min	NOV Max	NOV Min
1	1,800	350	2,700	430	6,600	2,600	3,600	840	950	<30	2,700	730	3,500	690	2,100	280	3,100	940	4,500	2,100	1,000	120	170	46
2	2,600	350	2,900	430	5,900	2,900	3,300	880	520	<30	2,700	750	3,400	660	2,400	330	3,100	970	4,200	2,100	910	120	150	45
3	2,100	330	2,600	400	4,800	2,700	1,900	510	320	<30	2,400	730	3,000	530	2,500	370	3,000	890	4,800	2,200	2,000	110	290	43
4	3,200	390	2,100	160	5,500	2,900	2,100	420	590	<30	3,100	770	2,500	350	1,800	370	2,600	860	4,100	2,100	1,700	250	380	43
5	3,400	550	1,600	190	3,800	2,200	1,400	380	720	41	2,700	730	1,700	160	1,900	410	2,400	770	3,800	1,500	1,400	360	670	48
6	4,100	930	1,200	190	3,600	2,100	1,500	340	760	<30	2,300	720	1,300	100	1,900	400	2,500	590	3,900	1,100	2,000	370	590	39
7	4,000	950	610	120	4,300	2,200	1,300	200	210	<30	2,500	610	920	120	2,100	430	1,800	520	3,400	960	2,500	400	270	34
8	3,100	920	1,000	130	4,400	2,300	1,600	210	870	39	2,400	640	480	84	2,300	450	2,100	400	3,600	910	2,500	370	270	<30
9	2,700	750	1,400	140	4,600	2,000	1,400	220	1,000	130	2,500	650	760	53	3,100	480	1,900	400	3,800	1,100	1,800	380	1,000	<30
10	3,200	890	2,000	180	4,700	1,700	1,200	220	1,500	270	2,500	650	570	76	3,200	530	1,900	330	4,300	1,100	1,800	400	920	<30
11	4,200	1,100	2,100	380	4,700	1,800	1,500	280	2,700	950	3,100	670	520	56	3,200	700	1,200	280	4,000	1,100	2,800	620	1,400	44
12	4,000	1,500	2,600	410	5,500	2,000	2,200	410	3,300	790	3,200	770	690	90	3,200	700	790	220	3,900	1,200	3,200	760	1,300	52
13	3,400	940	3,600	950	4,500	1,800	2,300	590	3,800	750	2,700	650	690	62	2,900	690	720	190	4,300	1,300	2,700	680	1,100	50
14	4,400	1,200	3,800	840	5,300	1,400	3,100	990	3,000	660	3,200	640	740	54	2,700	710	410	170	3,500	1,400	3,100	630	1,500	91
15	2,900	800	4,900	1,300	4,900	2,000	3,700	1,200	3,000	530	2,500	680	200	43	2,600	760	370	160	3,500	1,200	2,900	480	2,700	370
16	3,000	560	4,400	1,500	5,000	2,100	4,000	880	1,800	500	3,100	840	170	40	2,800	780	1,200	160	2,600	810	1,400	400	3,300	620
17	3,200	660	5,100	1,600	7,100	3,700	3,500	1,100	2,500	540	3,600	1,000	120	31	2,300	770	1,400	140	2,500	630	1,800	330	4,300	1,200
18	3,700	660	4,800	1,700	7,400	3,400	3,100	1,000	3,100	730	4,000	1,000	55	32	2,800	770	2,200	170	3,200	890	3,100	400	4,600	1,700
19	3,300	820	5,200	1,900	6,300	3,500	3,500	950	2,700	680	3,300	1,200	45	32	2,300	830	2,100	210	5,000	1,900	3,800	700	5,300	2,000
20	3,200	790	3,400	1,300	6,300	3,400	2,600	660	2,600	640	3,200	990	45	<30	2,900	840	2,200	270	3,100	710	3,700	1,100	3,900	1,600
21	2,600	520	3,500	1,100	5,800	3,200	2,000	360	2,600	680	3,000	960	40	<30	3,000	960	2,500	290	3,700	810	3,800	1,300	3,300	810
22	1,600	490	3,200	960	6,000	3,100	660	220	2,500	680	2,600	960	<30	<30	2,500	790	3,200	390	4,400	800	4,400	810	3,000	640
23	1,700	320	2,600	840	5,700	2,100	350	150	1,800	620	3,400	1,000	570	<30	2,400	630	3,700	540	3,400	880	4,500	1,300	2,500	480
24	1,300	280	4,000	820	2,500	1,400	180	59	2,000	510	3,100	1,200	1,100	<30	2,200	510	4,500	790	3,200	580	4,200	1,300	2,600	400
25	2,600	280	5,200	1,800	1,900	940	120	47	2,400	600	3,200	1,300	1,700	<30	2,400	400	5,100	1,200	2,200	330	3,900	1,300	1,700	320
26	750	230	6,000	1,900	2,400	790	110	46	2,600	700	3,100	1,200	1,800	35	2,800	440	5,400	1,500	1,700	290	3,800	1,300	1,600	280
27	2,200	190	4,400	1,400	3,300	780	130	50	3,100	750	3,200	950	2,100	110	2,800	360	5,700	1,700	1,100	230	3,900	1,300	1,400	260
28	2,300	250	5,700	2,400	3,300	750	94	45	2,900	720	3,200	880	2,500	160	3,000	370	5,300	1,900	1,200	190	3,000	750	1,300	260
29	2,900	250	5,300	2,100			59	41	2,900	700	3,000	810	2,700	190	3,200	490	5,300	2,100	1,200	160	2,300	350	390	79
30	2,900	310	5,800	2,500			56	30	2,600	660	3,100	790	2,400	280	3,900	720	5,000	2,100	980	110	500	180	120	<30
31	3,000	430	6,200	2,800			710	<30			3,300	810			3,400	860	4,700	2,000			280	120		
Mean	2,900	610	3,500	1,100	4,900	2,200	1,700		n.d.	n.d.	3,000	840	n.d.	n.d.	2,700	580	2,800	750	3,300	1,000	2,600	610	1,734	n.d.
Max	4,400	1,500	6,200	2,800	7,400	3,700	4,000	1,200	3,800	950	4,000	1,300	3,500	690	3,900	960	5,700	2,100	5,000	2,200	4,500	1,300	5,300	2,000
Min	750	190	610	120	1,900	750	56	<30	210	<30	2,300	610	<30	<30	1,800	280	370	140	980	110	280	110	120	<30

Table 19. Daily maximum and minimum chloride concentrations, Delaware River at Chester, Pennsylvania (station number 01477050), for year ending November 30, 2003
(Record furnished by Kimberly Clark Chester Operations)

[Concentrations in milligrams per liter; Max, maximum value; Min, minimum value]

DAY	DEC Max	DEC Min	JAN Max	JAN Min	FEB Max	FEB Min	MAR Max	MAR Min	APR Max	APR Min	MAY Max	MAY Min	JUN Max	JUN Min	JUL Max	JUL Min	AUG Max	AUG Min	SEP Max	SEP Min	OCT Max	OCT Min	NOV Max	NOV Min
1	22	21	42	42	51	49	70	66	26	25	37	35	37	33	31	25	44	37	37	31	31	25	25	25
2	22	21	42	38	54	52	84	68	27	27	43	33	34	32	37	31	44	37	37	31	31	25	25	25
3	23	22	43	42	52	52	77	68	30	27	39	37	32	32	37	25	44	37	37	37	25	25	25	25
4	24	23	42	40	54	54	72	67	29	29	42	38	31	28	31	31	51	37	37	27	25	25	25	25
5	24	23	40	37	58	53	78	68	29	27	37	36	32	28	31	31	37	37	44	31	25	25	25	25
6	26	26	40	39	54	51	70	64	28	27	36	36	24	23	37	31	44	44	31	25	25	25	25	25
7	30	27	45	45	52	48	66	60	26	25	36	35	25	25	37	25	44	37	31	31	25	25	31	25
8	31	30	45	39	54	51	65	63	27	26	38	35	23	23	37	31	37	31	31	31	25	25	31	25
9	32	30	46	43	55	53	63	63	29	28	37	36	31	31	37	31	44	37	31	31	25	25	31	25
10	29	28	50	43	54	48	60	59	32	29	36	36	37	31	37	31	44	25	37	31	31	25	31	25
11	42	28	48	45	50	48	60	59	28	27	38	37	37	31	37	31	41	37	31	31	31	25	25	25
12	49	40	47	47	61	48	58	56	34	31	37	37	37	31	37	37	44	31	37	31	31	25	25	25
13	55	49	45	45	51	51	57	56	32	30	37	35	31	31	44	37	44	31	37	31	25	25	31	25
14	49	45	47	45	60	56	53	53	35	34	36	35	31	31	44	37	37	31	37	31	25	25	31	25
15	49	43	45	44	57	56	57	52	35	34	37	37	31	31	44	37	31	31	37	31	25	25	31	25
16	46	45	43	43	59	59	53	51	33	31	39	37	31	31	37	31	31	25	37	31	25	25	25	25
17	40	35	44	43	58	57	53	52	34	33	37	36	31	31	44	37	31	25	25	25	31	25	25	25
18	44	40	50	44	59	59	54	52	33	32	38	37	31	31	37	31	31	31	31	25	31	25	31	25
19	44	41	46	45	66	64	49	49	34	33	38	37	37	37	37	31	31	25	31	31	31	25	31	31
20	42	41	48	46	66	64	49	48	37	36	40	38	37	31	37	31	31	25	31	25	25	25	31	25
21	42	41	47	47	67	65	47	44	38	37	37	37	37	31	37	31	37	37	31	25	31	25	31	25
22	39	39	46	43	91	71	45	42	37	37	39	35	37	31	37	31	31	25	31	25	31	25	31	25
23	40	38	45	44	78	77	39	37	37	37	44	37	37	25	37	31	31	25	31	25	31	25	31	25
24	37	36	45	45	89	73	32	27	37	37	38	36	31	31	37	31	31	31	31	31	31	25	31	25
25	39	35	46	45	73	72	30	30	35	34	40	37	31	25	37	31	31	31	31	25	25	25	25	25
26	38	36	45	43	72	69	27	26	38	36	37	37	31	25	37	31	31	31	31	25	31	31	31	25
27	38	34	44	44	71	66	26	24	35	35	35	35	31	25	44	31	31	27	25	25	31	25	31	25
28	41	40	44	44	66	62	25	24	36	34	37	35	31	25	44	37	37	31	31	25	58	31	25	25
29	40	40	46	45			24	23	35	34	41	37	37	31	44	41	37	31	31	25	31	25	31	25
30	40	40	45	44			26	23	37	34	35	34	37	31	44	41	37	31	31	25	31	25	31	25
31	64	51	50	46			26	25			35	31			44	31	37	31			31	25		
Mean	38	35	45	43	62	58	51	48	33	32	38	36	33	30	38	32	37	32	33	28	30	25	29	25
Max	64	51	50	47	91	77	84	68	38	37	44	38	37	33	44	41	51	44	44	37	58	31	31	34
Min	22	21	40	37	50	48	24	23	26	25	35	31	23	23	31	25	31	25	25	25	25	25	25	25

Table 20. Daily mean dissolved oxygen concentration, Delaware River at Benjamin Franklin Bridge at Philadelphia, Pennsylvania (station number 01467200), April 1 to November 30, 2003 (U.S. Geological Survey published record)

[Concentrations in milligrams per liter; Max, maximum value; Min, minimum value; --, missing data]

DAY	APR	MAY	JUN	JUL	AUG	SEP	OCT	NOV
1	10.5	10.0	6.9	7.2	4.6	4.8	6.7	9.5
2	10.6	9.7	7.0	7.0	4.4	4.5	7.5	9.6
3	10.7	9.5	7.5	--	4.6	4.4	7.7	9.4
4	11.0	9.2	7.7	--	4.7	4.6	7.9	9.3
5	11.1	8.7	8.5	--	4.5	5.2	8.1	9.4
6	--	--	8.5	--	4.6	6.4	8.3	9.1
7	--	--	8.4	--	5.1	6.8	8.3	8.9
8	--	--	8.3	6.5	5.2	6.8	8.5	8.9
9	11.3	--	8.3	6.3	5.3	6.8	8.5	9.0
10	11.6	--	8.2	5.8	5.2	6.9	8.6	9.1
11	11.8	--	8.1	5.3	5.4	6.9	8.7	9.2
12	11.8	--	7.9	5.1	5.4	6.9	8.7	9.2
13	--	7.0	7.7	5.0	5.5	6.7	8.8	9.6
14	--	7.4	7.5	4.9	5.6	6.6	8.7	10.3
15	11.1	7.7	7.2	4.9	5.7	6.5	8.7	10.4
16	10.6	8.0	7.2	4.8	5.6	6.2	8.8	10.3
17	10.5	8.2	7.2	4.8	5.6	6.8	8.7	10.3
18	10.4	8.4	7.2	4.7	5.7	6.9	8.5	10.2
19	10.2	8.4	7.1	4.7	5.6	7.0	8.4	10.0
20	10.0	8.3	7.0	4.7	5.7	6.9	8.2	9.9
21	9.8	8.1	7.0	4.8	5.7	6.6	8.2	10.1
22	9.6	7.8	7.4	5.0	5.9	6.4	8.3	9.6
23	9.8	7.7	7.6	5.3	6.2	6.0	8.4	9.7
24	10.2	7.7	7.9	5.6	6.4	6.1	8.6	9.9
25	10.5	7.6	7.9	5.5	6.4	6.6	8.7	10.1
26	10.5	7.8	7.8	5.5	6.1	6.0	8.7	10.3
27	10.5	7.9	7.4	5.5	5.4	5.8	8.5	10.3
28	10.5	7.8	7.2	5.1	4.9	5.8	8.8	10.3
29	10.3	7.6	6.9	4.9	5.4	5.2	9.1	10.3
30	10.3	7.5	7.0	4.8	5.2	5.4	8.9	10.8
31		7.4		5.0	5.0		9.2	
Mean	10.6	8.1	7.6	5.3	5.4	6.2	8.4	9.8
Max	11.8	10.0	8.5	7.2	6.4	7.0	9.2	10.8
Min	9.6	7.0	6.9	4.7	4.4	4.4	6.7	8.9

Table 21. Daily mean dissolved oxygen concentration, Delaware River at Chester, Pennsylvania (station number 01477050), April 1 to November 30, 2003 (U.S. Geological Survey published record)

[Concentrations in milligrams per liter; Max, maximum value; Min, minimum value; --, missing data]

DAY	APR	MAY	JUN	JUL	AUG	SEP	OCT	NOV
1	10.2	8.7	6.9	7.2	5.2	4.5	6.6	8.9
2	10.1	8.5	7.1	7.3	5.1	4.5	6.6	8.9
3	10.0	8.1	7.2	7.1	5.1	4.6	7.0	8.8
4	9.9	7.5	7.2	6.9	5.1	4.4	7.3	8.7
5	10.0	7.6	7.3	7.0	5.0	3.8	7.5	8.6
6	10.1	7.3	7.4	7.0	4.8	3.8	7.5	8.5
7	10.3	6.8	7.4	7.3	4.6	4.1	7.5	8.3
8	10.5	6.5	7.5	7.2	4.5	4.6	7.4	8.3
9	10.5	6.1	7.5	6.5	4.2	5.2	7.4	8.4
10	10.7	5.5	7.4	5.6	4.4	5.6	7.3	8.3
11	10.8	--	7.2	5.1	4.5	5.8	7.4	8.3
12	10.9	--	7.0	4.8	4.5	6.1	7.4	8.2
13	10.9	--	6.8	4.8	4.3	6.4	7.5	8.5
14	11.0	--	6.5	4.6	4.2	6.1	7.4	9.2
15	11.0	--	6.4	4.6	4.2	5.8	8.0	9.4
16	10.9	--	6.6	4.7	4.3	5.7	8.2	9.3
17	10.9	7.5	6.8	4.6	4.3	5.5	8.1	9.1
18	10.9	7.2	6.7	4.5	4.4	5.9	7.8	9.0
19	10.8	7.0	6.3	4.6	4.5	7.0	7.7	9.1
20	10.6	6.7	6.1	4.7	4.5	6.5	7.6	9.2
21	10.4	6.4	6.6	5.0	4.6	6.1	7.8	9.5
22	10.0	6.2	6.4	5.3	4.7	5.9	7.7	9.3
23	9.7	6.3	6.7	5.1	4.7	6.0	7.8	9.4
24	9.8	6.7	7.0	5.0	4.8	6.0	7.9	9.3
25	9.7	6.6	7.0	5.0	5.0	6.1	7.8	9.2
26	9.6	6.9	6.9	5.1	5.0	6.2	7.8	9.1
27	9.4	6.9	6.8	5.4	4.9	6.2	7.8	9.1
28	9.3	6.6	6.8	5.3	4.7	6.3	8.0	9.1
29	9.1	7.2	6.9	5.2	4.7	6.4	8.3	9.7
30	9.0	7.2	7.1	5.4	4.7	6.6	9.1	10.3
31		7.0		5.6	4.6		9.0	
Mean	10.2	7.0	6.9	5.6	4.6	5.6	7.7	9.0
Max	11.00	8.7	7.5	7.3	5.2	7.0	9.1	10.3
Min	9.0	5.5	6.1	4.5	4.2	3.8	6.6	8.2

Appendix A

DOCKET NO. D-77-20 CP (Revision 6)

DELAWARE RIVER BASIN COMMISSION

A RESOLUTION to extend Docket No. D-77-20 CP (Revision 5) (Amended) for one year to continue the experimental augmented conservation release program for the New York City Delaware Basin Reservoirs.

WHEREAS, Document No. 77-20 CP (Revision 5) (Amended) specified it would expire on April 30, 2003; and

WHEREAS, the Parties to the 1954 Supreme Court Decree are in the process of negotiating a permanent fisheries release program more responsive to the water conditions downstream of the New York City Delaware Basin Reservoirs; and

WHEREAS, the Parties in the 1954 Supreme Court Decree desire to develop a program for protecting tail water fisheries below the New York City Delaware Basin Reservoirs, based upon sustainable sources of water, including consideration of other down-basin needs; and

WHEREAS, the Delaware River Basin Commission (DRBC), through its Flow Management Technical Advisory Committee (FMTAC) and its Comprehensive Plan update process, is considering several approaches to assess overall needs in the tailwaters below the New York City Delaware Basin Reservoirs and in the main stem and bay; and

WHEREAS, the New York City Department of Environmental Protection (NYCDEP) and the New York State Department of Environmental Conservation (NYSDEC) have funded a modeling analysis of alternatives for a fisheries protection program for the reservoir tailwaters, and based on the results of this analysis, the NYSDEC will submit a formal proposal for an interim fisheries protection program for consideration by the parties to the 1954 Supreme Court Decree and the Commission; and

WHEREAS, the NYCDEP and NYSDEC have agreed to make their best efforts to complete updating the OASIS model, to complete analysis of alternatives for an interim fisheries protection program for the reservoir tailwaters, and to submit, by September 30, 2003, a formal proposal for consideration by the parties to the 1954 Supreme Court Decree and the Commission for interim fisheries protection while discussions continue toward development of a long-term flexible reservoir releases program; and

WHEREAS, agreement on the interim fisheries release program is not expected prior to April 30, 2003, the date upon which the current program will automatically terminate; and

WHEREAS, the State of New York has proposed a revision and extension to Docket No. D-77-20 CP (Revision 5) (Amended) for one calendar year ending April 30, 2004; and

WHEREAS, the requested revision and extension has been agreed to by all parties to the 1954 Supreme Court Decree; now therefore,

BE IT RESOLVED by the undersigned Commissioners and Parties to the Decree:

1. The Parties to the 1954 Supreme Court Decree agree that development of a viable permanent fisheries release program requires consideration of other related issues, including interbasin transfer policy, Good Faith operations, the DRBC Comprehensive Plan currently being developed, New York City participation, and procedures for computing the Excess Release Quantity.

2. The Parties to the 1954 Supreme Court decree commit to continuing discussions with the aid of one or more approaches being considered by the FMTAC and in the Comprehensive Plan update, with the goal of developing a long-term, flexible program to manage releases from the NYC Delaware Basin reservoirs.

3. Docket No. D-77-20 CP (Revision 5) (Amended) is hereby extended for one year to April 30, 2004, with the following modifications.

A. A "Habitat Bank" is established, which shall consist of 4,567 cfs-days that shall be contributed for one year only from the Excess Release Quantity (ERQ) as the ERQ is currently computed and such quantity of water as may be transferred from the Thermal Release Bank (TRB) from time to time as may be necessary. The 4,567 cfs-days from the ERQ shall be credited on June 15, 2003, and any water remaining from that quantity shall expire on March 15, 2004. The 9,200 cfs-days TRB shall be credited on May 1, 2003, and shall expire on April 30, 2004. Waters from the ERQ not contributed to the Habitat Bank shall be utilized to provide a proportionally-reduced increase in the Montague flow objective according to the current procedures, or may be banked in accordance with the procedures outlined in the Lower Basin Drought Management Plan.

B. Upon entry into "Drought Watch," the remaining TRB shall be reduced by 15 percent.

C. Upon entry into "Drought Warning," the remaining TRB shall be suspended until storage in the New York City Delaware River Basin Reservoirs is 25 billion gallons (bg) above the drought watch line for 15 consecutive days.

D. The Habitat Bank may be used to meet the following targets in the West Branch Delaware River at Hale Eddy:

> During Normal Conditions – 225 cfs
> During Watch Conditions – 190 cfs
> During Warning Conditions – 150 cfs
> The Habitat Bank also may be used for augmenting flows in the West Branch, Delaware River at Hale Eddy, and contingent on the prior approval of the New York City, the East Branch Delaware River at Harvard and the Neversink River at Bridgeville, during normal, Drought Watch and Drought Warning conditions. In addition, the Habitat Bank may be used as needed for augmenting flows during Drought Warning conditions to maintain summer baseline releases as stipulated in Docket No. D-77-20 CP (Revision 4).

E. Upon entry into Drought Emergency, the Habitat Bank shall be suspended until storage in the New York City Delaware River Basin Reservoirs is 25 bg above the drought watch line for 15 consecutive days.

F. Conservation releases from Cannonsville Reservoir shall be:

> During Normal conditions – 45 cfs
> During Drought Watch Conditions – 35 cfs
> During Drought Warning Conditions – 23 cfs
> During Drought Emergency Conditions – 8 – 23 cfs

However, all thermal release charges shall be calculated using the augmented release rates stipulated in Docket No. D-77-20 CP (Revision 4).

G. Comparison of the difference between releases from the Habitat Bank and the conservation releases under D-77-20 CP (Revision 4) will be made and the difference debited or credited to the Habitat Bank. However, a negative balance in the Habitat Bank is not allowed.

H. All other conditions shall continue as specified in Docket No. D-77-20 CP (Revision 4).

I. This resolution takes effect immediately and will expire on April 30, 2003.

4. These specific conservation releases are not available when coming out of Drought Emergency until storage is 25 bg above the Drought Watch line for 15 consecutive days.

5. By April 30, 2004, NYSDEC shall submit to the Commission and to the Parties to the 1954 Supreme Court decree a report, including an executive summary, describing experience with implementation of this resolution and the progress of any negotiations leading toward further amendments to this resolution. Discussion of such reports shall be included as an agenda item on the annual meeting of the Delaware River Master's Advisory Committee.

6. This resolution shall take effect immediately and shall expire on April 30, 2004, or earlier, when an alternative release program, unanimously approved by the 1954 Supreme Court Decree parties, is implemented.

/S/ John Hines
John Hines, Chairman pro tem

/S/ Pamela M. Bush
Pamela M. Bush, Esq., Commission Secretary

ADOPTED: March 19, 2003

<u>Consent to Action by</u>

<u>Delaware River Basin Commission</u>

Consent of the parties to the U.S. Supreme Court Decree in New Jersey v. New York, 347 U.S. 995 (1954) to the action of the Delaware River Basin Commission approving and extending Docket No. D-77-20 CP (Revision 5) (Amended)*, amending the Comprehensive Plan with respect to experimental modifications to the schedule of release rates from Cannonsville, Pepacton and Neversink Reservoirs.

/S/ Ernest P. Hahn	3/19/03	/S/ Warren T. Lavery	3/19/03
State of New Jersey	Date	State of New York	Date

/S/ John H. Talley	3/24/03	/S/ John Hines	3/19/03
State of Delaware	Date	Commonwealth of Pennsylvania	Date

/S/ Kevin C. Donnelly	3/19/03	/S/ Michael A. Principe	4/23/03
State of Delaware	Date	City of New York	Date

The consent of the City of New York to the above action is hereby granted.

*Although the resolution was originally titled "Extension of Docket No. D-77-20 CP (Revision 5) (Amended)," the Commission Secretary has re-named it "Docket No. D-77-20 CP (Revision 6)" for ease of reference.

Appendix B

AGREEMENT

Temporary Bottom Release Program from Cannonsville and Pepacton Reservoirs

Given the unusually high storage levels of Pepacton and Cannonsville Reservoirs, the persistent wet weather, and existing high runoff patterns, without action both reservoirs are likely to spill beginning on or around August 9, 2003. Spilling would result in warm Reservoir surface water to be discharged down stream. Surface water temperatures in the reservoirs on August 8, 2003 ranged from 72°F to 76°F. In order to avoid warm water spillage, the program described below will be implemented.

Bottom releases will be made in following manner:

1. Establishment of an emergency fisheries protection program designed to allow special stream releases designed by the NYSDEC within the terms specified by this Agreement. The emergency program includes the following provisions:

2. Upon reaching the 1.5 Bgal threshold, the bottom release quantity for the day will be computed in the following manner using data from the 8:00 a.m. New York City Department of Environmental Protection (NYCDEP) Water Supply Report:

   a. Case 1: Void less than 1.5 Bgal and greater than 0.5 Bgal:

      i. Available Program Release Volume=runoff minus diversion minus 200 million gallons (Mgal) or the normal conservation release, whichever is greater

      ii. Actual release rates will be determined by the New York State Department of Environmental Conservation (NYSDEC) based on the available program release volume

      iii. Goal is to allow reservoir storage to increase at the rate of 200 million gallons per day (Mgal/d).

   b. Case 2: Void less than 0.5 Bgal:

      i. Available Program Release Volume=Runoff minus diversion, or the normal conservation release, whichever is greater

      ii. Actual release rates will be determined by NYSDEC based on the available program release volume

      iii. Goal is to maintain a 0.5 Bgal void in each reservoir.

3. Release rates are subject to the approval of NYSDEC.

4. Release rates will be stepped up and stepped down in accordance with the standard NYCDEP protocol of no more than 200 Mgal/d in a three-hour period.

5. Releases will not be charged to existing NYSDEC thermal or habitat banks.

6. Parties to this agreement will reconvene as needed by meeting or telephone conference to reconsider this program, should any party request it.

7. This agreement takes effect on August 8, 2003 and will continue unless it is modified by unanimous agreement of the Decree Parties or terminated by any one of these Parties, but in any case it will be terminated automatically on September 30, 2003.

/S/ John H. Talley
/S/ Kevin C. Donnelly
State of Delaware

/S/ Samuel Wolfe
State of New Jersey

/S/ Fred Nuffer
State of New York

/S/ Cathleen Curran Myers
Commonwealth of Pennsylvania

/S/ Kurt Rieke
City of New York

OCS Study
MMS 2002-025

Socioeconomic Baseline and Projections of the Impact of an OCS Onshore Base for Selected Florida Panhandle Communities

Volume II: Technical Description of the MMS Florida Panhandle Model

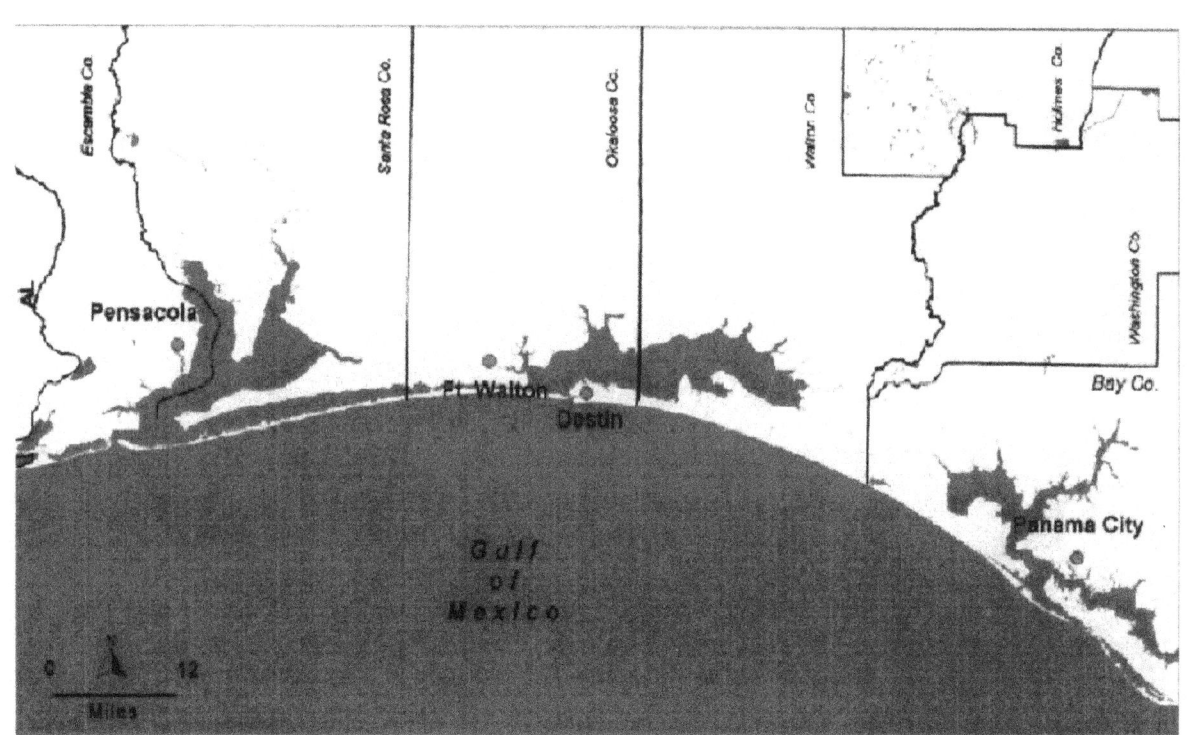

U.S. Department of the Interior
Minerals Management Service
Gulf of Mexico OCS Region

DISCLAIMER

This model and user's guide were prepared under contract between the Minerals Management Service (MMS) and Research and Planning Consultants, Inc. This report has been technically reviewed by the MMS, and it has been approved for publication. Approval does not signify that the contents necessarily reflect the views and policies of the MMS, nor does mention of trade names or commercial products constitute endorsement or recommendation for use. It is, however, exempt from review and compliance with the MMS editorial standards.

REPORT AVAILABILITY

Extra copies of this model and user guide may be obtained from the Public Information Unit (Mail Stop 5034) at the following address:

> U.S. Department of the Interior
> Minerals Management Service
> Gulf of Mexico OCS Region
> Public Information Unit (MS 5034)
> 1201 Elmwood Park Boulevard
> New Orleans, Louisiana 70123-2394
>
> Telephone: (504) 736-2519 or
> 1-800-200-GULF

CITATION

Suggested citation:

Luke, R. T., E.S. Schubert, G. Olsson, and F.L. Leistritz. 2002. Socioeconomic Baseline and Projection Model for Selected Florida Panhandle Communities, Volume II: Technical Description of the MMS Florida Panhandle Model. U.S. Dept. of the Interior, Minerals Management Service, Gulf of Mexico OCS Region, New Orleans, LA. OCS Study MMS 2002-025. 87 pp.

TABLE OF CONTENTS

List of Tables vii

Overview of Methodology 1

Demographic Module 1

Economic Module 15

Labor Market (Economic-Demographic Interaction) Modul 25

Baseline Projections 33

Public Services and Fiscal Impact Module 58

References 72

LIST OF TABLES

Table   Page

1.1   Estimated Distribution of the Population of Bay County by Age, Sex,
      and Race in 1995 3
1.2   Estimated Distribution of the Population of Escambia County by Age,
      Sex, and Race in 1995 4
1.3   Estimated Distribution of the Population of Okaloosa County by Age,
      Sex, and Race in 1995 5
1.4   Estimated Distribution of the Population of Santa Rosa County by Age,
      Sex, and Race in 1995 6
1.5   Estimated Distribution of the Population of Walton County by Age,
      Sex, and Race in 1995 7
2   Survival Rates by Age, Sex, and Race in 1995 8
3   Adjustments to Survival Rates from 2000 to 2045 9
4.1   Five-Year Fertility Rates by Age, Sex, and Race in Bay County 10
4.2   Five-Year Fertility Rates by Age, Sex, and Race in Escambia
      County 10
4.3   Five-Year Fertility Rates by Age, Sex, and Race in Okaloosa County 11
4.4   Five-Year Fertility Rates by Age, Sex, and Race in Santa Rosa County 11
4.5   Five-Year Fertility Rates by Age, Sex, and Race in Walton County 12
5.1   Inmigration and Outmigration Rates of People Over 65 Years Old
      (Bay County) 12
5.2   Inmigration and Outmigration Rates of People Over 65 Years Old
      (Escambia County) 13
5.3   Inmigration and Outmigration Rates of People Over 65 Years Old
      (Okaloosa County) 13
5.4   Inmigration and Outmigration Rates of People Over 65 Years Old
      (Santa Rosa County) 14
5.5   Inmigration and Outmigration Rates of People Over 65 Years Old
      (Walton County) 14
6   Labor Participation in Rates by Age, Sex, and Race 15
7   Industrial Sectors Used in MMS Florida Panhandle Model 17
8.1   Impact Multiplier Matrix for the Fort Walton Beach Area 18
8.2   Impact Multiplier Matrix for the Panama City Area 20
8.3   Impact Multiplier Matrix for the Pensacola Area 22
8.4   Industries Associated with Operation and Maintenance of Offshore Oil and
      Gas Platforms Adjusted for Commuting Patterns of Offshore Workers. 24
9   Unemployment Rates in the Florida Panhandle (1990-1997) 26
10   Inmigration into the Florida Panhandle for Selected MSAs (1970-1990) 27
11.1 Inmigration and Outmigration Rates of Workers and Their Families
      (Bay County) 28
11.2 Inmigration and Outmigration Rates of Workers and Their Families
      (Escambia County) 29

Table   Page

11.3   Inmigration and Outmigration Rates of Workers and Their Families
       (Okaloosa County) 30
11.4   Inmigration and Outmigration Rates of Workers and Their Families
       (Santa Rosa County) 31
11.5   Inmigration and Outmigration Rates of Workers and Their Families
       (Walton County) 32
12   Comparison of Census Bureau U.S. Population Projections 34
13   Population in the Florida Panhandle Baseline Scenario 35
14.1   Output and Employment per $1 Million of Output by Sector in 1994
       (Fort Walton Beach Area) 37
14.2   Output and Employment per $1 Million of Output by Sector in 1994
       (Panama City Area) 38
14.3   Output and Employment per $1 Million of Output by Sector in 1994
       (Pensacola Area) 39
15.1   Comparison of IMPLAN and BEA Employment by Sector in 1994
       (Fort Walton Beach Area) 40
15.2   Comparison of IMPLAN and BEA Employment by Sector in 1994
       (Panama City Area) 41
15.3   Comparison of IMPLAN and BEA Employment by Sector in 1994
       (Pensacola Area) 42
16   Adjustment Factor - Jobs per Worker 1995-2045 43
17.1   Baseline Employment by Major Non-Farm Industry for the Florida
       Panhandle - (Fort Walton Beach) 44
17.2   Baseline Employment by Major Non-Farm Industry for the Florida
       Panhandle - (Panama City) 45
17.3   Baseline Employment by Major Non-Farm Industry for the Florida
       Panhandle - (Pensacola) 46
18.1   Baseline Output by Major Non-Farm Industry for the Florida Panhandle
       (Fort Walton Beach) 47
18.2   Baseline Output by Major Non-Farm Industry for the Florida Panhandle
       (Panama City) 48
18.3   Baseline Output by Major Non-Farm Industry for the Florida Panhandle
       (Pensacola) 49
19   Allocation of Economic Migration Between Counties in a Metropolitan
       Area 50
20   Annual Migration in the Florida Panhandle Baseline Scenario 51
21.1   Distribution of Expenditures by Tourists in the Fort Walton Beach Area 53
21.2   Distribution of Expenditures by Tourists in the Panama City Area 54
21.3   Distribution of Expenditures by Tourists in the Pensacola Area 55
22.1   Projected Expenditures by Tourists in the Fort Walton Beach Area 56
22.2   Projected Expenditures by Tourists in the Panama City Area 56
22.3   Projected Expenditures by Tourists in the Pensacola Area 57
23.1   County Government Revenues of Bay County 59
23.2   County Government Revenues of Escambia County 59

Table   Page

23.3   County Government Revenues of Okaloosa County 60
23.4   County Government Revenues of Santa Rosa County 60
23.5   County Government Revenues of Walton County 61
23.6   County Government Expenditures 61
24.1   Combined Municipal Government Revenues of Bay County 62
24.2   Combined Municipal Government Revenues of Escambia County 62
24.3   Combined Municipal Government Revenues of Okaloosa County 63
24.4   Combined Municipal Government Revenues of Santa Rosa County 63
24.5   Combined Municipal Government Revenues of Walton County 64
24.6   Combined Municipal Government Expenditures 64
25   Population of Florida Panhandle Living in Unincorporated Areasin 1996 65
26   Per Capita Expenditures for County Governments and for Municipal
       Governments in the Florida Panhandle 65
27   Millage Rates for County Governments and Selected Special Districts
       in the Florida Panhandle 67
28   Municipal Taxation in the Florida Panhandle in 1997 67
29   Average Taxable Value of Residential Property in 1997 68
30   Value of Taxable Commercial and Industrial Property in 1997 68
31   Per Capita Revenues (direct taxes, fees, and licenses) 69
32   School District Expenditures per Full-Time Equivalent (FTE) Student 69
33   Millage Rates for School Districts in the Florida Panhandle 70
34   School District Revenues per Full-Time Equivalent (FTE) by Source 70
35   Baseline Community Service Multipliers for Counties in the Florida
       Panhandle 71

ix

Technical Description of the MMS Florida Panhandle Model

Overview of Methodology

RPC has developed a set of economic-demographic models in which population, labor force, output, final demand, unemployment, and economic and retiree migration are all linked in five-year periods. This economic-demographic model projects both baseline and impact-related economic activity through the interaction of output, labor force, and migration from 1995 through 2045.

For purposes of this study, the RPC team defined the Florida Panhandle as the five counties of Escambia, Santa Rosa, Okaloosa, Walton, and Bay. Within the Panhandle are three metropolitan areas, Fort Walton Beach, Panama City, and Pensacola. The three areas of the Florida Panhandle are defined as follows:

Fort Walton Beach: Okaloosa and Walton Counties
Panama City: Bay County
Pensacola: Escambia and Santa Rosa Counties

The definitions of the Panama City and Pensacola areas are identical to their metropolitan statistical areas (MSAs). The Fort Walton Beach MSA is defined as Okaloosa County. Since Walton County is not part of an MSA, RPC had to decide whether to include Walton County as part of the Fort Walton Beach area or the Panama City area. A review of data on commuter movements across counties indicated that Walton County's workforce had closer ties to Okaloosa County than to Bay County, so RPC chose to include Walton County as part of the Fort Walton Beach area for this project. (BEA, 1998)

Discussion of the model will be divided into the following parts:
Demographic Module
Economic Module
Labor Market Module
Baseline Projections
Public Services and Fiscal Impact Module

Demographic Module

RPC based its demographic module on a cohort-component model that many demographers use. The cohort-component module uses information about the existing age, sex, and racial composition of the population in an area to project the population of an area over time. The Florida Bureau of Economic and Business Research (BEBR) uses this approach to generate detailed population projections at the county level.

RPC used data supplied by BEBR to construct its demographic module. The starting point for projecting the population and labor force before economic migration in each county is the 1995 Age, Sex, Ratio cohorts (persons of the same sex and race born in the same five-year period) for each county (Tables 1.1-1.5). The model applies five-year survival rates for each cohort (Tables 2 and 3). The module then applies age- and race-specific fertility rates to the number of women in childbearing ages (10-44) to determine births by current residents (Tables 4.1-4.5). The model determines migration for people over 65 years old by applying outmigration rates to the surviving population and inmigration rates to the population of the U.S. excluding the county in question (Tables 5.1-5.5). The demographic module also estimates the labor supply for each period by applying labor participation rates by age, sex, and race cohort that the Bureau of Labor Statistics publishes (Table 6). The labor supply comes from the area's pool of people ages 16 through 64.

The model then compares the area's available labor supply with the projections of labor demand (from the economic model) for the county for the relevant period. The supply of and demand for labor is balanced through migration of workers (and associated household members). If local labor supply exceeds projected demand (after allowing for unemployment), some of the area's working age population out-migrates. On the other hand, if the projected labor demand exceeds the estimated local labor supply (as is typical in the Florida Panhandle counties), workers are assumed to immigrate from other areas. (For a detailed discussion of the rationale and procedures associated with this economic-demographic interface, see Leistritz et al. 1990).

Table 1.1

Estimated Distribution of the Population of Bay County
by Age, Sex, and Race in 1995

Age Cohort	White Male	White Female	Non-White Male	Non-White Female	Total
0-4	4,139	3,982	946	911	9,978
5-9	4,331	4,189	961	925	10,406
10-14	4,068	3,798	895	849	9,610
15-19	3,902	3,604	797	814	9,117
20-24	4,006	3,749	749	795	9,299
25-29	4,175	3,981	717	782	9,655
30-34	5,031	4,806	784	868	11,489
35-39	5,105	4,985	703	895	11,688
40-44	4,558	4,527	574	718	10,377
45-49	4,228	4,211	409	457	9,305
50-54	3,299	3,349	222	351	7,221
55-59	2,876	3,147	202	320	6,545
60-64	2,816	2,991	186	278	6,271
65-69	2,664	3,088	166	265	6,183
70-74	2,116	2,578	142	227	5,063
75-79	1,370	1,770	110	174	3,424
80-84	744	1,239	65	114	2,162
85+	373	870	40	97	1,380
Total	59,801	60,864	8,668	9,840	139,173

Source: Florida Bureau of Economic and Business Research, personal communication, June Nogle, 1996-1999.

Table 1.2

Estimated Distribution of the Population of Escambia County
by Age, Sex, and Race in 1995

Age Cohort	White Male	White Female	Non-White Male	Non-White Female	Total
0-4	7,061	6,795	3,513	3,382	20,751
5-9	6,776	6,465	3,407	3,296	19,944
10-14	6,637	6,373	3,224	3,128	19,362
15-19	7,507	6,798	2,943	2,871	20,119
20-24	8,636	7,727	2,760	2,637	21,760
25-29	9,554	8,372	2,577	2,718	23,221
30-34	9,200	8,581	2,437	2,749	22,967
35-39	8,662	8,348	2,200	2,806	22,016
40-44	7,706	7,972	1,800	2,323	19,801
45-49	7,305	7,577	1,431	1,877	18,190
50-54	5,808	6,118	1,063	1,473	14,462
55-59	4,904	5,263	985	1,331	12,483
60-64	4,469	4,975	812	1,186	11,442
65-69	4,240	5,107	730	1,050	11,127
70-74	3,842	4,965	549	893	10,249
75-79	2,480	3,489	395	629	6,993
80-84	1,400	2,466	217	506	4,589
85+	758	1,931	156	421	3,266
Total	106,945	109,322	31,199	35,276	282,742

Source: Florida Bureau of Economic and Business Research, personal communication, June Nogle, 1996-1999.

Table 1.3

Estimated Distribution of the Population of Okaloosa County
by Age, Sex, and Race in 1995

Age Cohort	White Male	White Female	Non-White Male	Non-White Female	Total
0-4	5,098	4,905	977	940	11,920
5-9	5,483	5,273	1,118	1,098	12,972
10-14	5,015	4,797	1,009	946	11,767
15-19	4,247	4,109	895	872	10,123
20-24	5,083	4,786	888	863	11,620
25-29	5,916	5,232	1,021	984	13,153
30-34	7,192	6,425	1,080	1,042	15,739
35-39	6,513	5,934	868	986	14,301
40-44	5,406	5,160	741	919	12,226
45-49	4,712	4,496	471	656	10,335
50-54	3,519	3,516	259	403	7,697
55-59	3,051	3,385	196	311	6,943
60-64	3,139	3,141	162	250	6,692
65-69	2,602	3,019	116	197	5,934
70-74	2,188	2,650	75	127	5,040
75-79	1,448	1,671	49	59	3,227
80-84	616	1,058	23	46	1,743
85+	347	861	14	53	1,275
Total	71,575	70,418	9,962	10,752	162,707

Source: Florida Bureau of Economic and Business Research, personal communication, June Nogle, 1996-1999.

Table 1.4

Estimated Distribution of the Population of Santa Rosa County
by Age, Sex, and Race in 1995

Age Cohort	White Male	White Female	Non-White Male	Non-White Female	Total
0-4	3,259	3,136	258	249	6,902
5-9	3,604	3,354	278	259	7,495
10-14	3,310	3,105	265	229	6,909
15-19	3,021	2,809	243	250	6,323
20-24	2,819	2,572	284	242	5,917
25-29	3,502	3,329	301	242	7,374
30-34	3,973	3,923	297	283	8,476
35-39	3,887	3,904	233	243	8,267
40-44	3,424	3,541	208	263	7,436
45-49	3,071	3,037	158	188	6,454
50-54	2,499	2,618	105	129	5,351
55-59	2,143	2,183	87	132	4,545
60-64	1,879	1,949	72	109	4,009
65-69	1,725	1,954	58	76	3,813
70-74	1,347	1,601	41	76	3,065
75-79	778	965	22	36	1,801
80-84	430	705	13	40	1,188
85+	213	496	16	41	766
Total	44,884	45,181	2,939	3,087	96,091

Source: Florida Bureau of Economic and Business Research, personal communication, June Nogle, 1996-1999.

Table 1.5

Estimated Distribution of the Population of Walton County
by Age, Sex, and Race in 1995

Age Cohort	White Male	White Female	Non-White Male	Non-White Female	Total
0-4	857	825	110	106	1,898
5-9	972	906	108	95	2,081
10-14	974	903	106	119	2,102
15-19	1,002	921	139	106	2,168
20-24	1,021	852	180	90	2,143
25-29	841	726	208	79	1,854
30-34	1,184	1,134	221	95	2,634
35-39	1,137	1,099	190	100	2,526
40-44	1,017	977	147	99	2,240
45-49	1,122	1,052	93	88	2,355
50-54	964	960	59	72	2,055
55-59	826	929	57	65	1,877
60-64	917	965	47	70	1,999
65-69	831	943	44	51	1,869
70-74	666	763	33	47	1,509
75-79	418	531	23	35	1,007
80-84	258	368	16	20	662
85+	131	266	12	27	436
Total	15,138	15,120	1,793	1,364	33,415

Source: Florida Bureau of Economic and Business Research, personal communication, June Nogle, 1996-1999.

Table 2

Survival Rates by Age, Sex, and Race in 1995

From	To	Surviving White Male	White Female	Non-White Male	Non-White Female
Birth	1-4	0.99455	0.99608	0.98940	0.99150
1-4	5-9	0.99379	0.99566	0.98821	0.99064
5-9	10-14	0.99838	0.99910	0.99782	0.99854
10-14	15-19	0.99628	0.99824	0.99403	0.99780
15-19	20-24	0.99369	0.99740	0.98724	0.99611
20-24	25-29	0.99189	0.99713	0.98217	0.99329
25-29	30-34	0.98989	0.99629	0.97849	0.98967
30-34	35-39	0.98686	0.99508	0.97367	0.98720
35-39	40-44	0.98342	0.99375	0.96731	0.98439
40-44	45-49	0.97910	0.99047	0.96076	0.98074
45-49	50-54	0.96990	0.98501	0.94510	0.97116
50-54	55-59	0.95332	0.97661	0.91853	0.95762
55-59	60-64	0.93138	0.96419	0.88689	0.93864
60-64	65-69	0.90589	0.94788	0.84374	0.90788
65-69	70-74	0.86749	0.92337	0.78712	0.87553
70-74	75-79	0.80893	0.88199	0.72039	0.82700
75-79	80-84	0.71888	0.81223	0.64231	0.75010
80-84	85+	0.50228	0.57733	0.50871	0.58450

Source: Florida Bureau of Business and Economic Research, personal communication, June Nogle, 1996-1999.

Table 3

Adjustments to Survival Rates from 2000 to 2045

Age Cohort	Years 2000-2005 Male	Years 2000-2005 Female	Years 2010-2015 Male	Years 2010-2015 Female	Year 2020 and Later Male	Year 2020 and Later Female
Birth	1.00138	1.00112	1.00263	1.00213	1.00388	1.00314
1-4	1.00020	1.00013	1.00037	1.00025	1.00055	1.00037
5-9	1.00015	1.00010	1.00028	1.00019	1.00042	1.00028
10-14	1.00030	1.00020	1.00058	1.00037	1.00086	1.00055
15-19	1.00055	1.00025	1.00104	1.00047	1.00154	1.00070
20-24	1.00054	1.00019	1.00103	1.00036	1.00152	1.00053
25-29	1.00020	1.00012	1.00038	1.00023	1.00057	1.00034
30-34	0.99977	1.00011	0.99956	1.00022	0.99934	1.00032
35-39	0.99973	1.00040	0.99949	1.00077	0.99925	1.00113
40-44	1.00055	1.00093	1.00105	1.00177	1.00155	1.00261
45-49	1.00267	1.00173	1.00511	1.00330	1.00754	1.00488
50-54	1.00535	1.00248	1.01022	1.00474	1.01509	1.00700
55-59	1.00837	1.00310	1.01598	1.00592	1.02359	1.00873
60-64	1.01226	1.00289	1.02340	1.00552	1.03454	1.00815
65-69	1.01889	1.00332	1.03606	1.00633	1.05323	1.00934
70-74	1.02861	1.00729	1.05462	1.01391	1.08063	1.02053
75-79	1.03940	1.01699	1.07522	1.03243	1.11104	1.04788
80-84	1.03435	1.03087	1.06559	1.05893	1.09682	1.08700

Source: Florida Bureau of Business and Economic Research, personal communication, June Nogle, 1996-1999.

Table 4.1

Five-Year Fertility Rates by Age, Sex, and Race in Bay County

Age Cohort	White Fertility Rates	Non-White Fertility Rates	Non-White Adjustment Factor
10-14	0.00139	0.00435	0.90
15-19	0.06808	0.11031	0.90
20-24	0.14293	0.18274	0.90
25-29	0.10837	0.12495	0.90
30-34	0.06064	0.06560	0.90
35-39	0.01896	0.02889	0.90
40-44	0.00250	0.00335	0.90

Source: Florida Bureau of Business and Economic Research, personal communication, June Nogle, 1996-1999.

Table 4.2

Five-Year Fertility Rates by Age, Sex, and Race in Escambia County

Age Cohort	White Fertility Rates	Non-White Fertility Rates	Non-White Adjustment Factor
10-14	0.00064	0.00584	0.90
15-19	0.05117	0.12746	0.90
20-24	0.10979	0.20213	0.90
25-29	0.10966	0.14216	0.90
30-34	0.06331	0.06598	0.90
35-39	0.02471	0.02674	0.90
40-44	0.00219	0.00548	0.90

Source: Florida Bureau of Business and Economic Research, personal communication, June Nogle, 1996-1999.

Table 4.3

Five-Year Fertility Rates by Age, Sex, and Race in Okaloosa County

Age Cohort	White Fertility Rates	Non-White Fertility Rates	Non-White Adjustment Factor
10-14	0.00059	0.00342	0.90
15-19	0.05519	0.10166	0.90
20-24	0.14211	0.17961	0.90
25-29	0.11388	0.12416	0.90
30-34	0.06363	0.06239	0.90
35-39	0.02089	0.02813	0.90
40-44	0.00394	0.00392	0.90

Source: Florida Bureau of Business and Economic Research, personal communication, June Nogle, 1996-1999.

Table 4.4

Five-Year Fertility Rates by Age, Sex, and Race in Santa Rosa County

Age Cohort	White Fertility Rates	Non-White Fertility Rates	Non-White Adjustment Factor
10-14	0.00063	0.00126	0.95
15-19	0.05936	0.07132	0.95
20-24	0.13773	0.18213	0.95
25-29	0.11536	0.13360	0.95
30-34	0.05956	0.06614	0.95
35-39	0.02127	0.01444	0.95
40-44	0.00298	0.00775	0.95

Source: Florida Bureau of Business and Economic Research, personal communication, June Nogle, 1996-1999.

Table 4.5

Five-Year Fertility Rates by Age, Sex, and Race in Walton County

Age Cohort	White Fertility Rates	Non-White Fertility Rates	Non-White Adjustment Factor
10-14	0.00083	0.00672	0.90
15-19	0.07503	0.09297	0.90
20-24	0.14136	0.14050	0.90
25-29	0.08833	0.16024	0.90
30-34	0.05305	0.07125	0.90
35-39	0.02134	0.02073	0.90
40-44	0.00280	0.00951	0.90

Source: Florida Bureau of Business and Economic Research, personal communication, June Nogle, 1996-1999.

Table 5.1

Inmigration and Outmigration Rates of People Over 65 Years Old (Bay County)

Age Cohort	Inmigration Rates				Outmigration Rates			
	White Male	White Female	Non-White Male	Non-White Female	White Male	White Female	Non-White Male	Non-White Female
65-69	0.00006	0.00006	0.00002	0.00002	0.10939	0.10939	0.05882	0.05882
70-74	0.00004	0.00004	0.00002	0.00002	0.08228	0.08228	0.04159	0.04159
75-79	0.00004	0.00004	0.00002	0.00002	0.09269	0.09269	0.04193	0.04193
80-84	0.00003	0.00003	0.00002	0.00002	0.12186	0.12186	0.06361	0.06361

Source: Florida Bureau of Business and Economic Research, personal communication, June Nogle, 1996-1999.

Table 5.2

Inmigration and Outmigration Rates of People Over 65 Years Old
(Escambia County)

Age Cohort	Inmigration Rates				Outmigration Rates			
	White Male	White Female	Non-White Male	Non-White Female	White Male	White Female	Non-White Male	Non-White Female
65-69	0.00010	0.00010	0.00008	0.00008	0.06565	0.06565	0.05348	0.05348
70-74	0.00007	0.00007	0.00005	0.00005	0.05841	0.05841	0.03781	0.03781
75-79	0.00009	0.00009	0.00005	0.00005	0.06539	0.06539	0.03812	0.03812
80-84	0.00007	0.00007	0.00007	0.00007	0.09734	0.09734	0.05782	0.05783

Source: Florida Bureau of Business and Economic Research, personal communication, June Nogle, 1996-1999.

Table 5.3

Inmigration and Outmigration Rates of People Over 65 Years Old
(Okaloosa County)

Age Cohart	Inmigration Rates				Outmigration Rates			
	White Male	White Female	Non-White Male	Non-White Female	White Male	White Female	Non-White Male	Non-White Female
65-69	0.00006	0.00006	0.00004	0.00004	0.07448	0.07448	0.06952	0.06952
70-74	0.00005	0.00005	0.00002	0.00002	0.05885	0.05885	0.04916	0.04916
75-79	0.00004	0.00004	0.00001	0.00001	0.06928	0.06928	0.04955	0.04955
80-84	0.00003	0.00003	0.00002	0.00001	0.06260	0.06260	0.07517	0.07517

Source: Florida Bureau of Business and Economic Research, personal communication, June Nogle, 1996-1999.

Table 5.4

Inmigration and Outmigration Rates of People Over 65 Years Old
(Santa Rosa County)

Age Cohort	Inmigration Rates				Outmigration Rates			
	White Male	White Female	Non-White Male	Non-White Female	White Male	White Female	Non-White Male	Non-White Female
65-69	0.00004	0.00004	0.00001	0.00001	0.09131	0.09131	0.06952	0.06952
70-74	0.00002	0.00002	0.00001	0.00001	0.08313	0.08313	0.04916	0.04916
75-79	0.00002	0.00002	0.00001	0.00001	0.06473	0.06473	0.04955	0.04955
80-84	0.00002	0.00002	0.00001	0.00001	0.10000	0.10000	0.07517	0.07517

Source: Florida Bureau of Business and Economic Research, personal communication, June Nogle, 1996-1999.

Table 5.5

Inmigration and Outmigration Rates of People Over 65 Years Old
(Walton County)

Age Cohort	Inmigration Rates				Outmigration Rates			
	White Male	White Female	Non-White Male	Non-White Female	White Male	White Female	Non-White Male	Non-White Female
65-69	0.00002	0.00002	0.00001	0.00001	0.05418	0.05418	0.08021	0.08021
70-74	0.00002	0.00002	0.00000	0.00000	0.04638	0.04638	0.05672	0.05672
75-79	0.00001	0.00001	0.00000	0.00000	0.04315	0.04315	0.05718	0.05718
80-84	0.00001	0.00001	0.00000	0.00000	0.05779	0.05779	0.08674	0.08674

Source: Florida Bureau of Business and Economic Research, personal communication, June Nogle, 1996-1999.

Table 6

Labor Participation Rates by Age, Sex, and Race
(in percent)

Age	2000					2005				2010-2045		
	White Male	White Female	Black Male	Black Female	White Male	White Female	Black Male	Black Female	White Male	White Female	Black Male	Black Female
16-19	56.7	54.7	39.2	39.5	55.9	54.4	38.0	39.8	55.6	54.3	37.9	39.9
20-24	84.2	73.6	72.2	65.6	84.0	73.8	71.3	66.7	83.9	73.8	70.9	66.9
25-29	93.9	77.3	87.7	74.9	93.8	78.5	87.1	75.0	93.8	78.8	87.0	75.1
30-34	94.5	76.3	85.9	77.5	94.3	77.5	84.7	78.4	94.2	77.7	84.5	78.6
35-39	93.3	77.8	83.4	79.7	92.8	79.1	81.9	80.8	92.7	79.4	81.7	81.0
40-44	93.0	80.3	81.9	78.3	92.2	81.8	80.3	79.0	92.0	82.0	80.1	79.1
45-49	92.0	81.5	80.0	75.8	91.3	84.0	78.3	76.7	91.2	84.5	78.1	76.9
50-54	87.6	74.6	72.6	68.4	87.2	77.4	71.5	69.7	87.1	77.9	71.3	69.9
55-59	80.3	63.7	65.9	61.1	80.4	66.9	65.2	64.3	80.4	67.5	65.1	65.0
60-64	55.3	40.4	41.8	34.2	55.3	42.2	40.5	34.6	55.0	42.4	40.2	34.5

Source: U.S. Bureau of Labor Statistics website, http://www.bls.gov/emplab1.htm

Economic Module

The economic module is representative of the economic relationships in the study area. The economic module uses an "input / output" approach to estimate the level of output for each economic sector and regional employment by sector.[1] Like other input-output models, the MMS Florida Panhandle module assumed that economic activity in the Florida Panhandle is largely dependent on the basic industries of the area. The basic industries are those that earn income for the region by generating income from goods and services sold to people or institutions outside the region.

In the case of the Florida Panhandle, tourism and the operation of military bases are two basic industries. Spending on tourism comes from people who live outside the Florida Panhandle who visit the area to enjoy the area's scenic beauty and to fish. The military spends taxpayer dollars in the Florida Panhandle generated from all U.S. residents. When the demands for any of the basic sectors increase, then the demands for the sector's outputs increase. For instance, an increase in tourism increases spending on hotels, restaurants, and boat rentals. Other sectors within the regional economy provide goods and services that are consumed primarily by residents of the

---

[1]For an introduction on the topic of input/output models and their use in regional economics, see Hoover and Giarratani (1984), Leontief (1953), and Miller and Blair (1985).

15

Florida Panhandle (e.g., retail trade and service sectors). Because these sectors primarily serve a local market, they are often referred to as nonbasic sectors. In addition, some firms and/or sectors market their products or services primarily to other business and industrial customers within the region, rather than exporting (i.e., selling to customers outside the region) or selling directly to final consumers (e.g., households).

The logic of input-output analysis is that an increase in demand for an area's exports or other final products (collectively referred to as sales to final demand) results in successive rounds of spending and respending, as the firm/sector than initially receives payment for the sale must in turn purchase additional inputs (or intermediate products), hire more labor, etc. Input-output (I-O) analysis is essentially a technique for tabulating and describing the linkages between sectors (groups of similar economic units) within an economy. I-O models thus provide a means of measuring the effect of an initial stimulus (i.e., additional sales to final demand) to a given sector on all other sectors of the regional economy (Miller and Blair 1985, Leistritz and Murdock 1981).

The economic model used IMPLAN software and data to generate detailed employment, output, and input-output matrices for 1994, the year for which most recent data was available when RPC built the economic module.[2] While IMPLAN can generate modeling information for as many as 528 industries or sectors of the study area, RPC structured the economic module into 23 industries that represented the broad industrial groupings the Bureau of Economic Analysis uses in its employment projections for metropolitan statistical areas and the subsectors involved in the impact portion of the model: the tourism industry, the military, commercial fishing, and Outer Continental Shelf (OCS) oil and natural gas activity.[3] (see Table 7).

The model generates a variety of scenarios described in the User's Guide. RPC developed a set of input / output matrices know as Type II multipliers and the associated Leontief-inverse matrices for projecting the impacts that changes in OCS, tourism, or military expenditures would have on the economy of the three metropolitan areas of the Florida Panhandle over time. The Leontief-inverse matrices measure the direct, indirect, and induced effects of these impacts based on the size and type of interrelationships among the 23 sectors of the study areas. Type II multipliers are closed with respect to households, already incorporates the economic impacts of additional spending and any net migration (see Tables 8.1 - 8.3).

---

[2]In 1998 MMS concluded a contract with the Minnesota Implan Group, the maker of IMPLAN, to provide software and data for future modeling projects that the MMS plans to undertake.

[3]The MMS Florida Panhandle model uses two counties, Okaloosa and Walton, to represent the Fort Walton Beach area. Okaloosa is the Fort Walton Beach MSA. Therefore, to project employment and population in both counties, RPC used BEA projections of the Pensacola Economic Area (which includes the Pensacola MSA, the FWB MSA, and Walton County) and subtracted the projection from the Pensacola MSA.

commuting patterns of offshore workers in the Gulf of Mexico. Gramling and Brabant (1986) estimate that 70 percent of offshore workers live more than 100 miles from where they meet to go offshore (i.e., an onshore support base). If an onshore base were located in Panama City or Pensacola, these commuting workers and their families would not spend their incomes in the Florida Panhandle. As shown in Table 8.4, RPC adjusted for these commuting workers by lowering projected expenditures in SIC category 1389 "Other Oil and Gas Services" by half when compared to Table 2.6 in the Final Report.[4]

Table 7
Industrial Sectors Used in MMS Florida Panhandle Model

Agriculture (excluding Commercial Fishing)

Commercial Fishing

Mining (excluding Maintenance and Repairs of Oil and Gas Wells)

Maintenance and Repair of Oil and Gas Wells

Construction

Non-Durable Manufacturing

Durable Manufacturing

Transportation, Communications, & Utilities (excluding Air & Water Transportation)

Water Transportation

Air Transportation

Wholesale Trade

Retail Trade (excluding Eating & Drinking Places)

Eating & Drinking Places

Finance, Insurance, and Real Estate

Services (excluding the six service categories listed below)

Hotel and Lodging Places

Equipment Rental and Leasing Services

Amusement and Recreation Services, N.E.C.

Engineering, Architectural Services

Accounting, Auditing and Bookkeeping Services

Research, Development & Testing Services

Government (excluding Federal Government - Military)

Federal Government - Military

Sources: Minnesota IMPLAN Group, Inc. 1997.
　　　　IMPLAN professional version 1.1 Software, User's Guide, Analysis Guide, and Data Guide. Stillwater, Mn. and RPC

---

[4]In its impact study on Destin Dome, Chevron (1997) does not appear to adjust for commuting offshore workers or assumes that all offshore workers are local. This assumption might be consistent with an effort to show the maximum potential economic impact of the project on Mobile, Alabama.

Table 8.1

Impact Multiplier Matrix for the Fort Walton Beach Area
(direct, indirect, and induced effects)

Sector	1	25	28	48	57	58	133	433	436	437	447	448
1	1.021927	2.27E-03	7.42E-04	3.08E-03	3.05E-03	2.19E-02	2.86E-03	1.77E-03	1.94E-03	2.14E-03	2.32E-03	2.31E-03
25	1.65E-04	1.0007778	5.68E-05	1.47E-04	2.66E-04	4.77E-04	1.25E-04	1.26E-04	1.43E-04	1.58E-04	1.73E-04	2.02E-04
28	2.56E-04	2.94E-04	1.001253	6.32E-04	4.36E-04	2.67E-03	6.28E-04	2.61E-03	6.11E-04	5.96E-04	3.88E-04	3.58E-04
48	1.47E-02	1.66E-02	1.17E-02	1.015247	1.96E-02	1.81E-02	2.51E-02	8.56E-02	3.74E-02	3.56E-02	3.62E-02	3.61E-02
57	9.62E-06	1.10E-05	3.76E-02	2.38E-05	1.000016	1.00E-04	2.36E-05	9.79E-05	2.30E-05	2.24E-05	1.46E-05	1.35E-05
58	2.92E-02	4.22E-02	1.09E-02	0.029978	4.68E-02	1.07337	3.08E-02	2.49E-02	3.19E-02	0.038936	3.49E-02	3.13E-02
133	7.94E-03	1.32E-02	6.54E-03	3.92E-02	2.03E-02	1.05E-02	1.051725	1.40E-02	2.81E-02	1.40E-02	1.18E-02	1.08E-02
433	3.93E-02	3.80E-02	2.89E-02	5.01E-02	6.45E-02	6.03E-02	5.68E-02	1.171789	0.131819	1.25E-01	7.03E-02	6.56E-02
436	1.55E-03	6.05E-03	1.15E-03	1.80E-03	2.57E-03	2.42E-03	1.82E-03	2.45E-03	1.124539	4.19E-03	1.86E-03	1.83E-03
437	3.22E-03	3.00E-03	1.53E-03	3.35E-03	8.34E-03	3.37E-03	4.59E-03	4.35E-03	4.86E-03	1.035498	9.70E-03	4.36E-03
447	2.43E-02	3.68E-02	1.27E-02	3.98E-02	3.89E-02	4.35E-02	5.21E-02	2.65E-02	3.98E-02	4.85E-02	1.044537	2.65E-02
448	6.11E-02	6.01E-02	2.16E-02	1.03E-01	9.71E-02	4.23E-02	4.67E-02	7.16E-02	4.35E-02	5.40E-02	6.67E-02	1.07774
454	2.72E-02	2.56E-02	9.49E-03	2.46E-02	4.38E-02	1.89E-02	2.09E-02	2.17E-02	1.89E-02	3.39E-02	3.23E-02	3.54E-02
456	8.42E-02	8.41E-02	3.33E-02	8.52E-02	1.33E-01	6.19E-02	0.069686	8.32E-02	0.131221	9.52E-02	1.08E-01	1.08E-01
463	5.26E-02	4.56E-02	5.00E-02	4.92E-02	7.23E-02	4.06E-02	4.57E-02	6.23E-02	9.72E-02	6.82E-02	1.03E-01	1.03E-01
464	1.44E-01	1.56E-01	5.89E-02	0.154351	2.29E-01	1.32E-01	1.46E-01	1.73E-01	0.331808	0.231357	0.278185	2.44E-01
473	1.13E-03	1.86E-03	6.37E-04	5.90E-03	3.50E-02	2.33E-03	2.89E-03	2.33E-03	8.11E-03	9.20E-03	4.87E-03	2.93E-03
488	3.97E-03	3.67E-03	1.34E-03	3.47E-03	6.40E-03	2.64E-03	2.89E-03	2.91E-03	2.50E-03	3.11E-03	3.84E-03	4.75E-03
506	5.12E-04	7.01E-04	2.31E-03	0.022139	7.33E-04	1.90E-03	1.47E-03	2.43E-03	1.33E-03	1.12E-03	1.47E-03	1.08E-03
507	2.31E-03	2.29E-03	1.14E-03	3.78E-03	4.12E-03	4.37E-03	3.24E-03	3.67E-03	4.53E-03	3.95E-03	6.71E-03	4.80E-03
509	4.06E-04	6.44E-04	2.57E-04	7.33E-04	6.88E-04	7.24E-04	6.98E-04	1.09E-03	9.02E-03	1.10E-03	1.89E-03	1.20E-03
510	1.47E-02	1.47E-02	8.22E-03	1.65E-02	2.37E-02	1.75E-02	1.72E-02	3.71E-02	3.02E-02	2.97E-02	0.02452	2.41E-02
519	0.00E+00	0.00E+00	0.00E+00	0.00E+00	0.00E+00	0.00E+00	0.00E+00	0.00E+00	0.00E+00	0.00E+00	0.00E+00	0.00E+00

Table 8.1 (continued)
Impact Multiplier Matrix for the Fort Walton Beach Area
(direct, indirect, and induced effects)

Sector	454	456	463	464	473	488	506	507	509	510	519
1	5.13E-03	2.05E-03	2.39E-03	2.92E-03	1.95E-03	4.18E-03	2.63E-03	2.53E-03	2.96E-03	3.33E-03	3.53E-03
25	2.00E-03	7.71E-05	8.25E-05	2.25E-04	1.61E-04	2.18E-04	2.30E-04	2.16E-04	2.58E-04	3.06E-04	3.37E-04
28	5.21E-04	1.83E-04	2.10E-04	4.16E-04	3.10E-04	3.47E-04	3.57E-04	3.58E-04	4.06E-04	5.92E-04	4.27E-04
48	3.70E-02	3.37E-02	8.01E-02	4.00E-02	2.68E-02	4.12E-02	2.53E-02	2.51E-02	2.69E-02	0.057824	2.35E-02
57	1.96E-05	6.88E-06	7.89E-06	1.56E-05	1.17E-05	1.30E-05	1.34E-05	1.35E-05	1.53E-05	2.23E-05	1.61E-05
58	7.18E-02	1.40E-02	0.016312	4.49E-02	2.82E-02	3.52E-02	3.65E-02	3.70E-02	4.22E-02	4.39E-02	4.62E-02
133	1.05E-02	5.60E-03	7.39E-03	1.79E-02	1.36E-02	1.30E-02	1.26E-02	1.43E-02	1.80E-02	1.55E-02	1.50E-02
433	7.05E-02	3.39E-02	3.48E-02	6.72E-02	5.63E-02	5.79E-02	6.22E-02	6.26E-02	6.87E-02	7.92E-02	7.10E-02
436	1.86E-03	7.28E-04	8.00E-04	2.17E-03	1.48E-03	2.50E-03	2.09E-03	1.93E-03	2.37E-03	3.18E-03	2.88E-03
437	3.84E-03	3.09E-03	2.44E-03	7.21E-03	4.85E-03	4.55E-03	6.44E-03	6.48E-03	1.34E-02	6.67E-03	5.89E-03
447	5.88E-02	1.18E-02	1.38E-02	3.69E-02	2.62E-02	2.92E-02	3.00E-02	3.34E-02	3.56E-02	3.87E-02	3.91E-02
448	6.02E-02	3.06E-02	3.36E-02	8.52E-02	5.98E-02	7.26E-02	8.53E-02	7.88E-02	9.59E-02	1.14E-01	1.25E-01
454	1.027655	1.41E-02	1.60E-02	3.68E-02	2.80E-02	3.33E-02	3.88E-02	3.74E-02	4.43E-02	5.05E-02	5.62E-02
456	0.095459	1.151266	8.04E-02	1.18E-01	1.00E-01	1.06E-01	1.31E-01	1.14E-01	1.37E-01	1.53E-01	1.68E-01
463	1.04E-01	7.84E-02	1.152447	1.16E-01	8.73E-02	1.26E-01	1.12E-01	1.10E-01	1.00E-01	8.47E-02	8.96E-02
464	2.15E-01	1.29E-01	0.133023	1.283711	0.332419	0.264122	0.362818	0.424157	2.93E-01	2.67E-01	2.87E-01
473	2.65E-03	2.56E-03	1.45E-03	3.61E-03	1.007211	3.12E-03	1.87E-03	1.95E-03	3.72E-03	2.11E-03	2.05E-03
488	3.77E-03	1.74E-03	1.76E-03	5.23E-03	3.75E-03	1.00453	5.50E-03	5.04E-03	6.12E-03	7.38E-03	8.24E-03
506	1.13E-03	1.32E-03	2.05E-03	1.64E-03	1.00E-03	1.19E-03	1.032285	1.33E-03	4.18E-03	3.09E-03	8.63E-04
507	5.15E-03	6.27E-03	3.86E-03	8.59E-03	1.15E-02	4.64E-03	4.93E-02	1.075543	0.006886	3.52E-03	3.45E-03
509	1.61E-03	1.22E-03	1.20E-03	1.57E-03	1.40E-03	1.88E-03	1.09E-03	1.82E-03	1.011012	7.95E-04	7.51E-04
510	2.17E-02	2.02E-02	1.41E-02	2.84E-02	2.81E-02	2.44E-02	2.30E-02	2.26E-02	2.83E-02	1.028742	2.82E-02
519	0.00E+00	0.00E+00	0.00E+00	0.00E+00	0.00E+00	0.00E+00	0.00E+00	0.00E+00	0.00E+00	0.00E+00	1.00E+00

Sources: RPC. Minnesota IMPLAN Group, Inc. 1997. IMPLAN professional version 1.1 Software, User's Guide, Analysis Guide, and Data Guide. Stillwater, MN.

19

Table 8.2
Impact Multiplier Matrix for the Panama City Area
(direct, indirect, and induced effects)

Sector	1	25	28	48	57	58	133	433	436	437	447	448
1	1.018056	1.31E-03	2.55E-04	1.52E-03	1.63E-03	1.10E-02	1.39E-03	9.16E-04	1.04E-03	1.13E-03	1.25E-03	1.22E-03
25	5.49E-05	1.000178	9.02E-06	3.54E-05	6.25E-05	1.13E-04	2.75E-05	3.02E-05	3.53E-05	3.59E-05	4.24E-05	4.73E-05
28	2.21E-04	1.87E-04	1.00035	3.21E-04	2.52E-04	1.45E-03	3.20E-04	1.30E-03	3.12E-04	3.32E-04	2.18E-04	2.00E-04
48	2.26E-02	1.81E-02	7.06E-03	1.01551	2.03E-02	1.92E-02	2.47E-02	8.69E-02	3.67E-02	3.80E-02	3.62E-02	3.65E-02
57	5.84E-06	4.94E-06	2.65E-02	8.50E-06	1.000006	3.83E-05	8.46E-06	3.45E-05	8.27E-06	8.78E-06	5.77E-06	5.30E-06
58	6.86E-02	6.89E-02	1.10E-02	0.046558	7.38E-02	1.117922	4.56E-02	3.96E-02	5.01E-02	0.061587	5.54E-02	4.94E-02
133	8.75E-03	1.06E-02	3.02E-03	2.84E-02	1.55E-02	8.10E-03	1.038578	1.07E-02	2.06E-02	1.09E-02	8.97E-03	8.21E-03
433	6.29E-02	4.52E-02	1.87E-02	5.36E-02	7.10E-02	6.68E-02	5.84E-02	1.181191	0.134881	1.39E-01	7.62E-02	7.11E-02
436	2.30E-03	6.22E-03	7.02E-04	1.83E-03	2.64E-03	2.54E-03	1.76E-03	2.50E-03	1.118582	4.43E-03	1.95E-03	1.88E-03
437	4.68E-03	3.26E-03	9.84E-04	3.35E-03	8.31E-03	3.44E-03	4.40E-03	4.36E-03	4.84E-03	1.037759	9.46E-03	4.32E-03
447	5.36E-02	5.64E-02	1.15E-02	5.60E-02	5.75E-02	6.62E-02	7.25E-02	3.90E-02	5.67E-02	7.32E-02	1.064529	3.91E-02
448	8.80E-02	6.61E-02	1.47E-02	1.02E-01	9.92E-02	4.10E-02	4.37E-02	7.33E-02	4.71E-02	5.18E-02	7.02E-02	1.079291
454	3.87E-02	2.80E-02	6.47E-03	2.52E-02	4.43E-02	1.82E-02	1.94E-02	2.24E-02	2.05E-02	3.36E-02	3.35E-02	3.58E-02
456	1.22E-01	9.22E-02	2.22E-02	8.70E-02	1.35E-01	6.07E-02	0.065749	8.57E-02	0.13276	9.44E-02	1.12E-01	1.10E-01
463	7.93E-02	5.05E-02	2.96E-02	5.02E-02	7.45E-02	4.10E-02	4.39E-02	6.35E-02	9.54E-02	6.91E-02	1.03E-01	1.04E-01
464	1.89E-01	1.55E-01	3.55E-02	0.142499	2.13E-01	1.21E-01	1.27E-01	1.61E-01	0.296639	0.214246	0.25507	2.24E-01
473	1.72E-03	2.02E-03	4.16E-04	5.64E-03	3.58E-03	2.51E-03	2.85E-03	2.37E-03	7.80E-03	9.96E-03	4.80E-03	2.95E-03
488	5.77E-03	4.12E-03	9.44E-04	3.66E-03	6.63E-03	2.57E-03	2.73E-03	3.07E-03	2.80E-03	2.96E-03	4.16E-03	4.94E-03
506	5.84E-04	5.73E-04	9.68E-04	0.015683	5.70E-04	1.53E-03	1.07E-03	1.77E-03	9.71E-04	8.68E-04	1.08E-03	7.99E-04
507	4.62E-03	3.24E-03	9.15E-04	4.55E-03	5.44E-03	6.07E-03	4.11E-03	4.79E-03	5.68E-03	5.33E-03	8.54E-03	6.21E-03
509	1.12E-03	1.27E-03	2.95E-04	1.33E-03	1.30E-03	1.42E-03	1.26E-03	2.03E-03	1.58E-02	2.14E-03	3.41E-03	2.20E-03
510	1.99E-02	1.50E-02	4.67E-03	1.53E-02	2.23E-02	1.61E-02	1.48E-02	3.21E-02	2.58E-02	2.68E-02	0.022907	2.25E-02
519	0.00E+00	0.00E+00	0.00E+00	0.00E+00	0.00E+00	0.00E+00	0.00E+00	0.00E+00	0.00E+00	0.00E+00	0.00E+00	0.00E+00

Table 8.2 (continued)
Impact Multiplier Matrix for the Panama City Area
(direct, indirect, and induced effects)

Sector	454	456	463	464	473	488	506	507	509	510	519
1	2.70E-03	1.11E-03	1.21E-03	1.53E-03	1.04E-03	2.10E-03	1.38E-03	1.37E-03	1.53E-03	1.77E-03	1.86E-03
25	4.44E-04	2.03E-05	2.08E-05	5.29E-05	3.84E-05	5.08E-05	5.33E-05	5.24E-05	5.77E-05	7.25E-05	7.84E-05
28	3.12E-04	1.11E-04	1.19E-04	2.33E-04	1.74E-04	1.97E-04	2.04E-04	2.07E-04	2.33E-04	3.25E-04	2.47E-04
48	3.83E-02	3.73E-02	8.18E-02	3.86E-02	2.65E-02	4.17E-02	2.55E-02	2.49E-02	2.86E-02	0.057338	2.42E-02
57	8.27E-06	2.93E-06	3.15E-06	6.16E-06	4.60E-06	5.22E-06	5.39E-06	5.48E-06	6.18E-06	8.60E-06	6.55E-06
58	1.12E-01	2.44E-02	0.026813	6.87E-02	4.45E-02	5.52E-02	5.73E-02	5.89E-02	6.62E-02	7.03E-02	7.29E-02
133	8.16E-03	4.65E-03	5.72E-03	1.31E-02	1.02E-02	9.81E-03	9.48E-03	1.07E-02	1.45E-02	1.19E-02	1.14E-02
433	7.80E-02	4.04E-02	3.90E-02	7.17E-02	6.11E-02	6.31E-02	6.81E-02	6.92E-02	7.60E-02	8.67E-02	7.81E-02
436	1.97E-03	8.34E-04	8.70E-04	2.20E-03	1.54E-03	2.55E-03	2.13E-03	2.04E-03	2.36E-03	3.26E-03	2.95E-03
437	4.01E-03	3.37E-03	2.52E-03	6.90E-03	4.73E-03	4.50E-03	6.35E-03	6.29E-03	1.51E-02	6.65E-03	5.86E-03
447	8.69E-02	1.91E-02	2.10E-02	5.30E-02	3.82E-02	4.28E-02	4.38E-02	4.91E-02	5.22E-02	5.78E-02	5.78E-02
448	6.32E-02	3.48E-02	3.61E-02	8.64E-02	6.19E-02	7.38E-02	8.61E-02	8.32E-02	9.31E-02	1.18E-01	1.27E-01
454	1.028805	1.59E-02	1.71E-02	3.72E-02	2.87E-02	3.36E-02	3.88E-02	3.90E-02	4.30E-02	5.19E-02	5.66E-02
456	0.099699	1.166747	8.45E-02	1.19E-01	1.02E-01	1.07E-01	1.32E-01	1.19E-01	1.35E-01	1.58E-01	1.71E-01
463	1.07E-01	8.61E-02	1.154683	1.13E-01	8.61E-02	1.26E-01	1.13E-01	1.08E-01	1.05E-01	8.80E-02	9.18E-02
464	2.03E-01	1.30E-01	0.126432	1.253814	0.298423	0.241711	0.33336	0.375976	2.74E-01	2.50E-01	2.65E-01
473	2.79E-03	2.81E-03	1.49E-03	3.48E-03	1.007016	3.15E-03	1.88E-03	1.95E-03	4.20E-03	2.19E-03	2.12E-03
488	4.02E-03	2.03E-03	1.97E-03	5.43E-03	3.96E-03	1.004683	5.64E-03	5.44E-03	5.98E-03	7.76E-03	8.51E-03
506	8.80E-04	1.07E-03	1.50E-03	1.16E-03	7.25E-04	8.84E-04	1.024924	9.60E-04	3.75E-03	2.23E-03	6.62E-04
507	6.91E-03	8.92E-03	5.09E-03	1.06E-02	1.45E-02	6.00E-03	6.54E-03	1.090855	0.010029	4.62E-03	4.51E-03
509	3.03E-03	2.44E-03	2.25E-03	2.74E-03	2.50E-03	3.46E-03	2.02E-03	3.16E-03	1.024414	1.50E-03	1.40E-03
510	2.05E-02	2.12E-02	1.38E-02	2.61E-02	2.64E-02	2.30E-02	2.14E-02	2.13E-02	2.72E-02	1.027143	2.66E-02
519	0.00E+00	0.00E+00	0.00E+00	0.00E+00	0.00E+00	0.00E+00	0.00E+00	0.00E+00	0.00E+00	0.00E+00	1.00E+00

Sources: RPC.
Minnesota IMPLAN Group, Inc. 1997.
IMPLAN professional version 1.1 Software, User's Guide, Analysis Guide, and Data Guide. Stillwater, MN.

21

Table 8.3
Impact Multiplier Matrix for the Pensacola Area
(direct, indirect, and induced effects)

Sector	1	25	28	48	57	58	133	433	436	437	447	448
1	1.042142	3.66E-03	1.98E-03	3.88E-03	4.31E-03	2.30E-02	3.82E-03	2.31E-03	2.95E-03	3.23E-03	3.38E-03	3.21E-03
25	5.89E-05	1.000275	4.28E-05	5.76E-05	9.87E-05	1.71E-04	4.98E-05	4.58E-05	5.90E-05	6.22E-05	6.89E-05	7.55E-05
28	9.47E-04	1.10E-03	1.005929	1.83E-03	1.39E-03	7.65E-03	1.91E-03	6.48E-03	1.59E-03	1.62E-03	1.18E-03	1.07E-03
48	1.79E-02	1.88E-02	2.11E-02	1.015999	2.03E-02	1.98E-02	2.69E-02	7.95E-02	3.75E-02	3.67E-02	3.65E-02	3.64E-02
57	1.42E-05	1.64E-05	1.50E-02	2.73E-05	1.000021	1.14E-04	2.85E-05	9.69E-05	2.38E-05	2.42E-05	1.76E-05	1.60E-05
58	8.88E-02	1.16E-01	5.32E-02	0.07903	1.21E-01	1.184163	8.30E-02	6.21E-02	8.79E-02	0.10307	9.40E-02	8.33E-02
133	6.70E-03	1.17E-02	9.41E-03	3.16E-02	1.68E-02	8.97E-03	1.045098	1.08E-02	2.29E-02	1.17E-02	9.78E-03	8.91E-03
433	4.68E-02	4.80E-02	5.61E-02	5.57E-02	7.18E-02	6.91E-02	6.47E-02	1.167543	0.139536	1.35E-01	7.78E-02	7.22E-02
436	1.71E-03	6.35E-03	2.13E-03	1.92E-03	2.72E-03	2.65E-03	1.99E-03	2.37E-03	1.121075	4.38E-03	2.04E-03	1.96E-03
437	3.68E-03	3.68E-03	2.93E-03	3.73E-03	8.89E-03	3.92E-03	5.16E-03	4.37E-03	5.46E-03	1.037744	1.02E-02	4.71E-03
447	4.16E-02	5.69E-02	3.33E-02	5.63E-02	5.70E-02	6.48E-02	7.69E-02	3.61E-02	5.77E-02	7.07E-02	1.064026	3.92E-02
448	5.91E-02	6.91E-02	4.44E-02	1.05E-01	9.95E-02	4.77E-02	4.94E-02	6.91E-02	4.95E-02	5.67E-02	7.20E-02	1.080538
454	2.54E-02	2.91E-02	1.93E-02	2.57E-02	4.40E-02	2.10E-02	2.18E-02	2.12E-02	2.14E-02	3.48E-02	3.40E-02	3.60E-02
456	8.33E-02	9.66E-02	6.69E-02	8.98E-02	1.36E-01	6.96E-02	0.074124	8.12E-02	0.13742	9.96E-02	1.15E-01	1.12E-01
463	5.88E-02	5.13E-02	8.71E-02	5.07E-02	7.25E-02	4.45E-02	4.77E-02	5.83E-02	9.68E-02	6.91E-02	1.02E-01	1.02E-01
464	1.48E-01	1.85E-01	1.23E-01	0.169384	2.44E-01	1.52E-01	1.62E-01	1.74E-01	0.351285	0.249491	0.296153	2.58E-01
473	1.31E-03	2.13E-03	1.16E-03	5.82E-03	3.65E-03	2.56E-03	3.14E-03	2.24E-03	8.07E-03	9.51E-03	4.90E-03	3.01E-03
488	2.33E-03	2.65E-03	1.74E-03	2.30E-03	4.07E-03	1.85E-03	1.90E-03	1.81E-03	1.81E-03	2.04E-03	2.62E-03	3.07E-03
506	8.45E-04	1.11E-03	5.11E-03	0.027763	1.08E-03	2.67E-03	2.09E-03	2.93E-03	1.85E-03	1.56E-03	1.98E-03	1.47E-03
507	1.05E-03	9.48E-04	7.61E-04	1.47E-03	1.51E-03	1.66E-03	1.25E-03	1.24E-03	1.64E-03	1.46E-03	2.36E-03	1.71E-03
509	1.04E-03	1.67E-03	1.11E-03	1.75E-03	1.67E-03	1.83E-03	1.76E-03	2.38E-03	2.04E-02	2.65E-03	4.35E-03	2.80E-03
510	1.48E-02	1.64E-02	1.50E-02	1.63E-02	2.33E-02	1.74E-02	1.68E-02	2.94E-02	2.72E-02	2.61E-02	0.024393	2.40E-02
519	0.00E+00	0.00E+00	0.00E+00	0.00E+00	0.00E+00	0.00E+00	0.00E+00	0.00E+00	0.00E+00	0.00E+00	0.00E+00	0.00E+00

Table 8.3 (continued)
Impact Multiplier Matrix for the Pensacola Area
(direct, indirect, and induced effects)

Sector	454	456	463	464	473	488	506	507	509	510	519
1	7.13E-03	2.57E-03	2.70E-03	4.16E-03	2.84E-03	5.16E-03	3.62E-03	3.52E-03	4.02E-03	4.52E-03	4.79E-03
25	6.88E-04	3.19E-05	2.77E-05	8.83E-05	6.29E-05	8.11E-05	8.42E-05	7.95E-05	8.83E-05	1.11E-04	1.22E-04
28	1.81E-03	5.62E-04	5.78E-04	1.30E-03	9.61E-04	1.09E-03	1.11E-03	1.11E-03	1.29E-03	1.83E-03	1.35E-03
48	3.93E-02	3.51E-02	8.09E-02	3.81E-02	2.69E-02	4.19E-02	2.54E-02	2.45E-02	3.01E-02	0.063354	2.41E-02
57	2.70E-05	8.40E-06	8.64E-06	1.94E-05	1.44E-05	1.63E-05	1.66E-05	1.65E-05	1.93E-05	2.74E-05	2.01E-05
58	1.87E-01	4.01E-02	0.039582	1.16E-01	7.74E-02	9.31E-02	9.60E-02	9.65E-02	1.11E-01	1.15E-01	1.21E-01
133	8.97E-03	4.86E-03	5.66E-03	1.42E-02	1.11E-02	1.07E-02	1.01E-02	1.12E-02	1.65E-02	1.29E-02	1.23E-02
433	8.15E-02	3.91E-02	3.59E-02	7.41E-02	6.29E-02	6.46E-02	6.85E-02	6.79E-02	7.81E-02	8.87E-02	7.87E-02
436	2.12E-03	8.51E-04	7.67E-04	2.37E-03	1.64E-03	2.63E-03	2.19E-03	2.03E-03	2.40E-03	3.38E-03	3.02E-03
437	4.48E-03	3.47E-03	2.44E-03	7.41E-03	5.19E-03	4.93E-03	6.78E-03	6.63E-03	1.81E-02	7.28E-03	6.32E-03
447	8.75E-02	1.86E-02	1.84E-02	5.37E-02	3.88E-02	4.30E-02	4.33E-02	4.73E-02	5.23E-02	5.68E-02	5.72E-02
448	6.53E-02	3.45E-02	3.07E-02	9.12E-02	6.42E-02	7.51E-02	8.65E-02	8.00E-02	9.04E-02	1.16E-01	1.27E-01
454	1.029437	1.56E-02	1.45E-02	3.90E-02	2.94E-02	3.38E-02	3.86E-02	3.72E-02	4.16E-02	5.03E-02	5.61E-02
456	0.103051	1.158221	7.70E-02	1.26E-01	1.05E-01	1.09E-01	1.33E-01	1.16E-01	1.34E-01	1.55E-01	1.71E-01
463	1.07E-01	7.98E-02	1.147671	1.10E-01	8.56E-02	1.24E-01	1.10E-01	1.04E-01	1.08E-01	8.45E-02	8.91E-02
464	2.39E-01	1.43E-01	0.131536	1.295952	0.345466	0.280011	0.376838	0.424518	3.25E-01	2.83E-01	3.04E-01
473	2.95E-03	2.69E-03	1.44E-03	3.49E-03	1.007102	3.23E-03	1.95E-03	1.98E-03	4.73E-03	2.27E-03	2.18E-03
488	2.54E-03	1.24E-03	9.84E-04	3.53E-03	2.52E-03	1.002919	3.47E-03	3.19E-03	3.52E-03	4.65E-03	5.21E-03
506	1.70E-03	1.80E-03	2.63E-03	2.08E-03	1.35E-03	1.64E-03	1.043208	1.74E-03	7.62E-03	4.48E-03	1.24E-03
507	1.97E-03	2.28E-03	1.35E-03	2.80E-03	3.95E-03	1.67E-03	1.78E-02	1.025868	0.003101	1.31E-03	1.26E-03
509	3.95E-03	2.90E-03	2.77E-03	3.39E-03	3.19E-03	4.41E-03	2.49E-03	4.00E-03	1.036055	1.93E-03	1.79E-03
510	2.25E-02	2.12E-02	1.48E-02	2.80E-02	2.79E-02	2.50E-02	2.29E-02	2.21E-02	2.92E-02	1.028129	2.79E-02
519	0.00E+00	0.00E+00	0.00E+00	0.00E+00	0.00E+00	0.00E+00	0.00E+00	0.00E+00	0.00E+00	0.00E+00	1.00E+00

Sources: RPC.
Minnesota IMPLAN Group, Inc. 1997.
IMPLAN professional version 1.1 Software, User's Guide, Analysis Guide, and Data Guide. Stillwater, MN.

Table 8.4
Industries Associated with Operation and Maintenance
of Offshore Oil and Gas Platforms
Adjusted for Commuting Patterns of Offshore Workers

Code Number		Industry	Typical Supply Base	Operation and Maintenance Spending Percent of Total	Florida Panhandle Supply Base	Percent of Total
132	39	Oil & gas operations	X	36.3%		0.0%
1389	57	Other oil and gas services excl. commuting workers	X	9.2%	X	17.5%
1389	57	Other oil and gas services: commuting offshore workers only		9.2%		17.5%
2899	209	Chemical, not elsewhere classified	X	0.9%		0.0%
291	210	Petroleum fuel	X	4.4%		0.0%
324	232	Hydraulic cement	X	0.7%		0.0%
3559	331	Special industry machinery, not elsewhere classified	X	5.1%		0.0%
44	436	Water transportation	X	4.0%	X	7.6%
45	437	Air transportation	X	3.8%	X	7.2%
58	454	Eating and drinking places	X	1.7%	X	3.2%
7359	473	Miscellaneous equipment rent / lease	X	1.4%	X	2.7%
871	506	Environmental and engineering services	X	14.7%	X	27.9%
872	507	Accounting / miscellaneous business services	X	4.2%	X	8.0%
873	509	Test / research services	X	4.5%	X	8.6%
		Total for a typical onshore base		100.0%		100.0%
		Total for Florida Panhandle onshore base		**52.6%**		

* Assumes no more than 30% of offshore workers are locals
Sources: RPC

Chevron, *Destine Dome Unit 56, Development and Production Plan*, July, 1997.

The model generates impacts of OCS-related activity on the Florida Panhandle by multiplying a final demand vector of projected OCS expenditures that would occur in the Florida Panhandle by the Type II multiplier matrix.

To examine the impact of OCS activity or a decline in tourism or military expenditures within the Florida Panhandle, the model multiplies these expenditures by sector by a Type II multiplier to generate the change in total output by sector resulting from the scenario inputs chosen. The model would generate change in labor demand by multiplying output per sector by output per employee by sector.

Labor Market (Economic-Demographic Interaction) Module

The Economic-Demographic interface is the component of the model that links the projections of required employment from the economic module (labor demand) with projections of people in the workforce generated by the demographic module (labor supply). In the MMS Florida Panhandle model, interaction is at the metropolitan area rather than at the county level. For instance, in the Pensacola submodel, output is projected for the entire Pensacola area rather than for Escambia and Santa Rosa Counties individually.

The purpose of this module is to ensure that the size of the labor force rises or falls to the level that ensures equilibrium in the labor market over time. When the labor force in any given year is too small (large) for the underlying labor demand, the model will increase (decrease) the number of workers in the area through migration to restore market equilibrium. This type of migration is called economic migration, which affects age cohorts under 65 years of age. Economic migration differs from the retiree migration discussed above in that the availability of work in the area is the primary motivation for economic migration, whereas the state of the job market has little or no impact on the movement of retirees.

The triggering mechanism in the model is the unemployment rate.[5] If the unemployment rate in a given year is less than four percent, then the model will inmigrate workers and their families. Four percent figure is based on recent trends in unemployment and makes the economic model more consistent with BEBR's population projections. These low unemployment rates are also consistent with the area's net inmigration of recent years (Tables 9,10). If the unemployment rate in a given year is more than thirteen percent, the model will outmigrate workers and their families.[6] If the unemployment rate in a given year is between four percent and thirteen percent, no economic migration occurs. The module distributes economic migrants (1) by the proportion for each county within a metropolitan area that is consistent with baseline economic inmigration, and (2) using the age, sex, and race distribution of economic migration (working-age people and their families) developed based on information that BEBR provided (Tables 11.1 - 11.5). These changes are injected back into the demographic module for use in projecting population and labor supply for the next five-year period.

---

[5]This approach was adapted from Murdock and Leistritz, et al (1979)
[6]RPC based the 13 percent for the outmigration rate from TAMS.

Table 9

Unemployment Rates in the Florida Panhandle
(1990 - 1997)

County	1990	1991	1992	1993	1994	1995	1996	1997
Bay	8.9%	7.9%	9.1%	9.2%	8.5%	6.7%	6.0%	6.6%
Escambia	5.6%	5.7%	5.6%	5.0%	4.7%	4.3%	4.1%	4.2%
Okaloosa	5.7%	6.1%	6.1%	6.1%	5.2%	4.4%	3.8%	3.6%
Santa Rosa	5.3%	5.3%	5.3%	4.5%	4.2%	4.1%	3.5%	3.6%
Walton	6.2%	6.7%	5.3%	5.4%	5.0%	4.4%	4.3%	4.3%
Florida	6.0%	7.4%	8.2%	7.0%	6.6%	5.5%	5.1%	4.8%
United States	5.6%	6.8%	7.4%	6.8%	6.1%	5.6%	5.4%	4.9%

Source: Florida Department of Labor and Employment Security, personal communication.

Table 10

Inmigration into the Florida Panhandle for selected MSA's
(1970 - 1990)

Year	Fort Walton Beach: Okaloosa County only	Pensacola: Escambia and Santa Rosa Counties	Panama City: Bay County
1970	2780	1842	854
1971	302	2860	1125
1972	3571	6613	770
1973	282	641	1245
1974	-204	596	3922
1975	5481	5497	1824
1976	-1537	4071	1843
1977	897	434	707
1978	-8	-1532	568
1979	1115	215	1870
1980	-1997	-821	76
1981	1489	2573	1610
1982	1566	2359	2468
1983	1476	3082	1355
1984	2050	3520	4233
1985	2907	2479	6601
1986	1684	952	2789
1987	1795	3385	961
1988	2200	2764	494
1989	1697	3319	-30
1990	1686	1434	-1157

Source: Bureau of Economic and Business Research, University of Florida, personal communication, June Nogle, 1996-1999.

Table 11.1

Inmigration and Outmigration Rates of Workers and Their Families
(Bay County)

Distribution of Inmigrating Children

	White		Non-White	
Age	Male	Female	Male	Female
0-4	8%	8%	4%	4%
5-9	8%	8%	4%	4%
10-14	5%	5%	6%	6%
15-19	12%	12%	3%	3%

Distribution of Inmigrating Adults

	White		Non-White	
Age	Male	Female	Male	Female
20-24	5%	5%	1%	1%
25-29	3%	3%	2%	2%
30-34	3%	3%	2%	2%
35-39	4%	4%	2%	2%
40-44	7%	7%	1%	1%
45-49	7%	7%	0%	0%
50-54	3%	3%	0%	0%
55-59	5%	5%	0%	0%
60-64	5%	5%	0%	0%

Sources: RPC.
Florida Bureau of Business and Economic Research, personal communication, June Nogle, 1996-1999.

Table 11.2

Inmigration and Outmigration Rates of Workers and Their Families
(Escambia County)

Distribution of Inmigrating Children

Inmigrating

	White		Non-White	
Age	Male	Female	Male	Female
0-4	0%	0%	8%	8%
5-9	0%	0%	8%	8%
10-14	9%	9%	9%	9%
15-19	8%	8%	8%	8%

Distribution of Inmigrating Adults

	White		Non-White	
Age	Male	Female	Male	Female
15-19	15%	15%	0%	0%
20-24	9%	9%	0%	0%
25-29	3%	3%	2%	2%
30-34	0%	0%	0%	0%
35-39	0%	0%	1%	1%
40-44	5%	5%	1%	1%
45-49	6%	6%	1%	1%
50-54	3%	3%	0%	0%
55-59	3%	3%	0%	0%
60-64	1%	1%	0%	0%

Sources: RPC.
Florida Bureau of Business and Economic Research, personal communication, June Nogle, 1996-1999.

Table 11.3

Inmigration and Outmigration Rates of Workers and Their Families
(Okaloosa County)

Distribution of Inmigrating Children

	White		Non-White	
Age	Male	Female	Male	Female
0-4	7%	7%	5%	5%
5-9	10%	10%	5%	5%
10-14	10%	10%	3%	3%
15-19	7%	7%	3%	3%

Distribution of Inmigrating Adults

	White		Non-White	
Age	Male	Female	Male	Female
20-24	10%	10%	2%	2%
25-29	6%	6%	2%	2%
30-34	6%	6%	1%	1%
35-39	4%	4%	1%	1%
40-44	6%	6%	2%	2%
45-49	4%	4%	0%	0%
50-54	2%	3%	0%	0%
55-59	2%	3%	0%	0%
60-64	1%	1%	0%	0%

Sources: RPC.
Florida Bureau of Business and Economic Research, personal communication, June Nogle, 1996-1999.

Table 11.4

Inmigration and Outmigration Rates of Workers and Their Families
(Santa Rosa County)

Distribution of Inmigrating Children

	White		Non-White	
Age	Male	Female	Male	Female
0-4	13%	13%	3%	3%
5-9	12%	12%	3%	3%
10-14	7%	7%	3%	3%
15-19	7%	7%	2%	2%

Distribution of Inmigrating Adults

	White		Non-White	
Age	Male	Female	Male	Female
20-24	0%	0%	1%	1%
25-29	14%	14%	1%	1%
30-34	5%	5%	1%	1%
35-39	4%	4%	1%	1%
40-44	7%	7%	1%	1%
45-49	4%	4%	1%	1%
50-54	4%	4%	0%	0%
55-59	3%	3%	0%	0%
60-64	3%	3%	0%	0%

Sources: RPC.
Florida Bureau of Business and Economic Research, personal communication, June Nogle, 1996-1999.

Table 11.5

Inmigration and Outmigration Rates of Workers and Their Families
(Walton County)

Distribution of Inmigrating Children

	White		Non-White	
Age	Male	Female	Male	Female
0-4	10%	10%	0%	0%
5-9	10%	10%	0%	0%
10-14	10%	10%	0%	0%
15-19	20%	20%	0%	0%

Distribution of Inmigrating Adults

	White		Non-White	
Age	Male	Female	Male	Female
20-24	0%	0%	0%	0%
25-29	0%	0%	0%	0%
30-34	10%	10%	0%	0%
35-39	0%	0%	0%	0%
40-44	0%	0%	0%	0%
45-49	10%	10%	0%	0%
50-54	10%	10%	0%	0%
55-59	10%	10%	0%	0%
60-64	10%	10%	0%	0%

Sources: RPC.
Florida Bureau of Business and Economic Research, personal communication, June Nogle, 1996-1999.

Baseline Projections

The MMS Florida Panhandle Model baseline projections (1995 - 2045) are the levels of economic activity and population that would likely occur with a continuation of present activity and trends in the area's basic industries prior to any impacts of an onshore support base located in the Port of Panama City or the Port of Penascola that would support OCS activity in the Eastern Gulf of Mexico.

Working from a target population projection, RPC calibrated the model's employment, population, and final demand projections to be consistent with federal and state employment and population projections as well as IMPLAN's output per employee ratios. RPC took the following steps to calibrate the baselines for the three metropolitan areas:

Created a Baseline Population Consistent with BEBR / BEA Population Projections

In preparing the model's baseline projections, the RPC team gathered historical and projected baselines from two sources: Bureau of Economic and Business Research at the University of Florida at Gainesville (BEBR) and the U.S. Bureau of Economic Analysis (BEA). The two baselines used two different approaches and two projection periods - the BEBR projections went to 2020, while the BEA projections went to 2045. (See Appendices A and B)

BEBR uses a cohort-component model to project population without the direct interaction with an economic module.[7] Migration for working-age people and their children are based on historical inmigration and outmigation rates, rather than projected economic conditions such as output and labor demand and supply.

In 1995, the BEA published projections of employment and earnings from 1995 to 2045. This set of projections is commonly known as the "OBERS" projections, which have been used by the Army Corps of Engineers and other agencies and firms working on long-term water development projects. In these projections, the BEA started with U.S. Census population projections on a national level and used long-term shares in employment by industry group to allocate employment and population among states and MSAs across the United States.

Because local and state government officials use BEBR and BEA figures in making long-term planning decisions, RPC calibrated its model so that the population baselines of the model were consistent with the population projections of these sources. The BEA and BEBR numbers for the Panama City and Fort Walton Beach areas were consistent, after adjusting for more recent U.S. Census projections (Table 12). After consulting with Dr. June Nogle, a demographer at BEBR, RPC adjusted the BEA's Pensacola MSA population projections to make them consistent with the BEBR's projections. Table 13 shows the baseline population projections of the model.

---

[7] BEBR (1997), pp. 1-4 describes BEBR's methodology in detail.

Table 12

Comparison of Census Bureau U.S. Population Projections
(millions of people)

| Year | Projections | | Difference | |
	Published in 1996	Published in 1993	People	%
2000	274.63	276.24	-1.61	-0.58%
2005	285.98	288.29	-2.31	-0.80%
2010	297.72	300.43	-2.71	-0.90%
2015	310.13	313.12	-2.98	-0.95%
2025	335.05	338.34	-3.29	-0.97%
2045	381.71	381.78	-0.07	-0.02%

Source: U.S. Bureau of the Census, *Population of the United States by Age, Sex and Hispanic Origin*, P25-1104 (November 1993) and P25-1130 (February 1996).

Table 13
Population in the Florida Panhandle
Baseline Scenario

Area	1995	2000	2005	2010	2015	2020	2025	2030	2035	2040	2045
Fort Walton Beach	196,122	216,005	235,159	254,195	274,218	292,374	311,399	329,090	343,428	355,713	367,255
Okaloosa County	162,707	178,803	194,199	209,523	225,720	240,693	256,235	270,726	282,836	293,458	303,489
Walton County	33,415	37,202	40,959	44,672	48,498	51,681	55,165	58,364	60,592	62,255	63,766
Panama City	139,173	150,277	162,188	174,575	187,536	198,341	210,054	218,838	227,033	234,538	241,999
Bay County	139,173	150,277	162,188	174,575	187,536	198,341	210,054	218,838	227,033	234,538	241,999
Pensacola	377,822	410,086	441,204	469,488	502,482	526,239	547,200	567,029	584,973	601,966	618,202
Escambia County	281,162	296,578	316,849	334,339	352,894	366,819	379,386	390,820	400,920	410,113	418,437
Santa Rosa County	96,660	113,508	124,354	135,149	149,589	159,420	167,814	176,209	184,053	191,853	199,765
Total	713,117	776,368	838,550	898,258	964,236	1,016,954	1,068,653	1,114,957	1,155,434	1,192,217	1,227,456

Sources: RPC.
Florida Bureau of Business and Economic Research, personal communication, June Nogle, 1996-1999.

35

Adjusted BEA Employment Projections to be Consistent with 1994 IMPLAN Employment Data

To create a baseline for the time frame involved with development and production of oil and gas from Lease Sale 181, RPC combined the sectoral detail of a single year that IMPLAN provides with the 50-year time frame of the less-detailed OBERS projections from 1995 to 2045. Tables 14.1-14.3 show the 1994 employment and output figures IMPLAN generated for the three study areas under this sectoring scheme, and Tables 15.1-15.3 show the reconciliation of IMPLAN and BEA employment by subsector in 1994 After reconciling the sectors and subsectors, RPC used adjustment factors that reconciled the different classification of employment that IMPLAN and the BEA used. IMPLAN used number of jobs, and the BEA figures projected the number of workers, assuming that a number of people held more than of one job and that the number of jobs per worker changed over time (Table 16). The MMS Florida Panhandle model measures employment as the number of people employed. RPC projected subsectors as a constant percentage of a sector over time.

Table 14.1

**Output and Employment per $1 Million of Output by Sector in 1994
(Fort Walton Beach Area)**

Description	Output ($ Millions)	Employment	Employees per $1 Million
Agriculture	61.95	1,512	24.408
Commercial Fishing	3.80	172	45.257
Mining	5.94	53	8.927
Construction	496.95	7,469	15.030
Maintenance and Repair Oil & Gas Wells	0.22	22	98.576
Non-Durable Manufacturing	184.84	2,090	11.307
Durable Manufacturing	435.26	3,397	7.805
TCPU	315.56	2,297	7.279
Water Transportation	16.74	95	5.675
Air Transportation	28.42	209	7.354
Wholesale Trade	208.09	2,689	12.922
Trade	420.70	13,429	31.921
Eating & Drinking	272.02	7,997	29.398
FIRE Excluding Rentals	549.54	2,307	4.198
Hotels, Lodging, & Rentals	821.41	6,469	7.875
Services	999.17	22,746	22.765
Equipment Rental and Leasing	16.01	240	14.987
Amusement and Recreation Services	32.27	810	25.097
Engineering, Architectural Services	54.24	881	16.242
Accounting, Auditing and Bookkeeping	18.60	382	20.543
Research, Development & Testing Services	71.38	1,085	15.200
Government	583.45	18,019	30.884
Federal Government - Military	479.58	15,808	32.962
Total	6,076.16	110,178	18.133

Sources: RPC.
     Minnesota IMPLAN Group, Inc. 1997.
     IMPLAN professional version 1.1 Software, User's Guide, Analysis Guide, and Data Guide. Stillwater, MN.

Table 14.2

Output and Employment per $1 Million of Output by Sector in 1994
(Panama City Area)

Description	Output ($ Millions)	Employment	Employees per $1 Million
Agriculture	12.28	532	43.332
Commercial Fishing	0.67	34	51.004
Mining	2.56	21	8.214
Construction	468.37	6,061	12.941
Maintenance and Repair Oil & Gas Wells	0.12	12	100.231
Non-Durable Manufacturing	246.20	1,390	5.646
Durable Manufacturing	239.14	1,658	6.933
TCPU	322.10	2,183	6.778
Water Transportation	66.42	358	5.390
Air Transportation	21.27	177	8.323
Wholesale Trade	234.93	2,764	11.765
Trade	351.64	10,977	31.216
Eating & Drinking	241.59	7,034	29.116
FIRE Excluding Rentals	448.68	2,048	4.565
Hotels, Lodging, & Rentals	584.61	5,695	9.742
Services	664.98	14,552	21.883
Equipment Rental and Leasing	14.88	182	12.230
Amusement and Recreation Services	48.57	1,192	24.544
Engineering, Architectural Services	40.50	679	16.764
Accounting, Auditing and Bookkeeping	22.90	412	17.989
Research, Development & Testing Services	25.66	522	20.342
Government	457.13	13,334	29.169
Federal Government - Military	169.03	5,802	34.325
Total	4,684.21	77,619	16.570

Sources: RPC.
        Minnesota IMPLAN Group, Inc. 1997.
        MPLAN professional version 1.1 Software, User's Guide, Analysis Guide, and Data Guide. Stillwater, MN.

Table 14.3

Output and Employment per $1 Million of Output by Sector in 1994
(Pensacola Area)

Description	Output ($ Millions)	Employment	Employees per $1 Million
Agriculture	128.85	2,552	19.806
Commercial Fishing	2.42	129	53.388
Mining	18.19	376	20.670
Construction	1,162.96	15,786	13.574
Maintenance and Repair Oil & Gas Wells	0.27	46	169.142
Non-Durable Manufacturing	1,529.74	7,766	5.077
Durable Manufacturing	499.45	4,318	8.646
TCPU	904.97	5,392	5.958
Water Transportation	84.90	468	5.512
Air Transportation	142.10	1,071	7.537
Wholesale Trade	623.40	7,358	11.803
Trade	730.41	22,212	30.410
Eating & Drinking	369.04	10,988	29.775
FIRE Excluding Rentals	1,065.00	4,971	4.668
Hotels, Lodging, & Rentals	643.50	4,723	7.340
Services	2,181.26	50,180	23.005
Equipment Rental and Leasing	44.61	536	12.016
Amusement and Recreation Services	25.14	735	29.231
Engineering, Architectural Services	119.21	2,003	16.802
Accounting, Auditing and Bookkeeping	50.36	995	19.756
Research, Development & Testing Services	19.95	508	25.470
Government	1,189.59	31,142	26.179
Federal Government - Military	336.43	10,127	30.101
Total	11,871.76	184,382	15.531

Sources: RPC.
   Minnesota IMPLAN Group, Inc. 1997.
   IMPLAN professional version 1.1 Software, User's Guide, Analysis Guide, and Data Guide. Stillwater, MN.

Table 15.1

Comparison of IMPLAN and BEA Employment by Sector in 1994
(Fort Walton Beach Area)
(in thousands)

Sector	IMPLAN	BEA
All-Industry Total Jobs	110.178	101.368
Farm, Ag Services, Forestry	1.684	1.943
Mining	0.053	0.114
Construction	7.491	5.581
Manufacturing	5.487	5.449
Durables	3.397	3.373
Nondurables	2.090	2.076
Transportation, Communications, and Utilities	2.601	2.599
Wholesale Trade	2.689	1.557
Retail Trade	21.426	20.048
Finance, Insurance and Real Estate	2.307	6.126
Services	32.613	26.650
Government	33.827	31.301
Military	15.808	16.087
Other Government	18.019	15.214

Sources: Minnesota IMPLAN Group, Inc. 1997. IMPLAN professional version 1.1 Software, User's Guide, Analysis Guide, and Data Guide. Stillwater, MN.
RPC.
U.S. Bureau of Economic Analysis 1998. Regional economic information system 1969-1996. U.S. Department of Commerce. Washington, DC.

Table 15.2

Comparison of IMPLAN and BEA Employment by Sector in 1994
(Panama City Area)
(in thousands)

Sector	IMPLAN	BEA
All-Industry Total Jobs	77.619	77.619
Farm, Ag Services, Forestry	0.566	1.068
Mining	0.021	0.043
Construction	6.073	5.269
Manufacturing	3.048	3.111
Durables	1.658	1.692
Nondurables	1.390	1.419
Transportation, Communications, and Utilities	2.718	2.605
Wholesale Trade	2.764	2.573
Retail Trade	18.011	18.762
Finance, Insurance and Real Estate	2.048	5.354
Services	23.234	21.213
Government	19.136	17.623
Military	5.802	5.831
Other Government	13.334	11.792

Sources. Minnesota IMPLAN Group, Inc. 1997. IMPLAN professional version 1.1Software, User's Guide, Analysis Guide, and Data Guide. Stillwater, MN.
RPC.
U.S. Bureau of Economic Analysis 1998. Regional economic information system 1969-1996.
U.S. Department of Commerce. Washington, DC.

Table 15.3

Comparison of IMPLAN and BEA Employment by Sector in 1994
(Pensacola Area) (in thousands)

Sector	IMPLAN	BEA
All-Industry Total Jobs	184.382	179.826
Farm, Ag Services, Forestry	2.681	3.161
Mining	0.376	0.600
Construction	15.832	12.475
Manufacturing	12.084	11.961
Durables	4.318	4.274
Nondurables	7.766	7.687
Transportation, Communications, and Utilities	6.931	7.940
Wholesale Trade	7.358	6.308
Retail Trade	33.200	33.398
Finance, Insurance and Real Estate	4.971	9.962
Services	59.680	55.492
Government	41.269	38.529
Military	10.127	10.794
Other Government	31.142	27.735

Sources: Minnesota IMPLAN Group, Inc. 1997. IMPLAN professional version 1.1Software, User's Guide, Analysis Guide, and Data Guide. Stillwater, MN.
RPC.
U.S. Bureau of Economic Analysis 1998. Regional economic information system 1969-1996. U.S. Department of Commerce. Washington, DC.

Table 16

Adjustment Factor - Jobs per Worker
(1995-2045)

	Adjustment
Year	Factor
1995	1.1580
2000	1.1598
2005	1.1616
2010	1.1634
2015	1.1652
2020	1.1670
2025	1.1688
2030	1.1706
2035	1.1724
2040	1.1742
2045	1.1760

Source: Bureau of Economic and Business Research 1995.
OBERS Projections, Population Estimates and Projections. University Press of Florida, FL.

Using the Model to Calibrate Employment, Modifying to the Adjusted BEA Employment Projections to bring the Model's Baseline Population Figures Close to BEBR / BEA Population Projections

RPC made a final adjustment to make the model's baseline populations within a few percent of the BEBR / BEA population baseline in each year of the projection period. The Fort Walton Beach and Panama City baselines needed a simple 3.5 to 4.0 percent decrease from the adjusted BEA numbers. The Pensacola baseline required a much larger adjustment that varied over time (15 percent around 2000 rising to 19-20 percent by 2030).

Divide RPC Baseline Employment Projections Among 23 Sectors

After RPC calibrated employment so that the model's baseline population would approximate BEBR / BEA population projections, RPC subdivided employment among sectors based on the reconciliation of IMPLAN and BEA employment by subsector in 1994 (Tables 17.1-17.3). Having established baseline employment by sector, RPC used output by worker by sector (Tables 14.1-14.3), to convert baseline employment into baseline output (Tables 18.1-18.3).

Table 17.1
Baseline Employment by Major Non-Farm Industry for the Florida Panhandle
(Fort Walton Beach) (in thousands of workers)

Sector	1995	2000	2005	2010	2015	2020	2025	2030	2035	2040	2045
Agriculture	1.265	1.394	1.574	1.634	1.752	1.748	1.743	1.804	1.867	1.931	1.998
Commercial Fishing	0.144	0.159	0.179	0.186	0.199	0.199	0.198	0.205	0.212	0.220	0.227
Mining	0.035	0.027	0.027	0.027	0.026	0.026	0.026	0.026	0.026	0.026	0.026
Construction	6.619	7.327	8.149	8.784	9.285	9.582	9.885	10.227	10.578	10.941	11.314
Maintenance and Repair Oil & Gas Wells	0.015	0.011	0.011	0.011	0.011	0.011	0.011	0.011	0.011	0.011	0.011
Non-Durable Manufacturing	1.686	2.052	2.201	2.279	2.349	2.424	2.499	2.560	2.622	2.685	2.749
Durable Manufacturing	2.740	2.708	2.690	2.685	2.674	2.585	2.499	2.541	2.583	2.626	2.668
TCPU	1.941	2.233	2.433	2.571	2.702	2.766	2.831	2.918	3.007	3.099	3.193
Water Transportation	0.080	0.092	0.101	0.106	0.112	0.114	0.117	0.121	0.124	0.128	0.132
Air Transportation	0.177	0.203	0.221	0.234	0.246	0.252	0.258	0.265	0.274	0.282	0.291
Wholesale Trade	2.260	2.674	3.216	3.349	3.474	3.602	3.733	3.868	4.007	4.151	4.299
Retail Trade	11.510	13.318	14.696	15.914	16.759	17.225	17.698	18.301	18.922	19.563	20.222
Eating & Drinking	6.855	7.931	8.752	9.477	9.980	10.258	10.539	10.899	11.268	11.650	12.042
FIRE Excluding Real Estate Rentals	2.038	2.401	2.730	3.023	3.249	3.394	3.545	3.687	3.833	3.985	4.142
Hotels, Lodging Places, and Rentals	5.716	6.734	7.654	8.476	9.109	9.518	9.942	10.338	10.748	11.174	11.614
Services	20.097	23.676	26.914	29.803	32.029	33.465	34.957	36.348	37.790	39.288	40.838
Equipment Rental and Leasing	0.212	0.250	0.284	0.314	0.338	0.353	0.369	0.384	0.399	0.415	0.431
Amusement and Recreation Services, N.E.C.	0.716	0.843	0.958	1.061	1.141	1.192	1.245	1.294	1.346	1.399	1.454
Engineering, Architectural Services	0.778	0.917	1.042	1.154	1.241	1.296	1.354	1.408	1.464	1.522	1.582
Accounting, Auditing and Bookkeeping	0.338	0.398	0.452	0.501	0.538	0.562	0.587	0.610	0.635	0.660	0.686
Research, Development & Testing Services	0.959	1.129	1.284	1.422	1.528	1.596	1.667	1.734	1.803	1.874	1.948
Government	14.630	16.697	17.548	18.377	18.962	19.203	19.441	19.938	20.445	20.964	21.492
Federal Government - Military	13.039	13.130	13.045	13.021	12.963	12.934	12.901	12.913	12.922	12.931	12.937
Total	93.848	106.305	116.162	124.410	130.667	134.305	138.048	142.400	146.886	151.524	156.295

Source: RPC

44

Table 17.2

Baseline Employment by Major Non-Farm Industry for the Florida Panhandle
(Panama City)
(in thousands of workers)

Sector	1995	2000	2005	2010	2015	2020	2025	2030	2035	2040	2045
Agriculture	0.50	0.48	0.52	0.56	0.60	0.61	0.63	0.64	0.66	0.68	0.70
Commercial Fishing	0.03	0.03	0.03	0.04	0.04	0.04	0.04	0.04	0.04	0.04	0.04
Mining	0.01	0.01	0.01	0.01	0.01	0.01	0.01	0.01	0.01	0.01	0.01
Construction	5.56	4.94	5.29	5.57	5.83	5.87	5.96	6.03	6.21	6.40	6.60
Maintenance and Repair Oil & Gas Wells	0.01	0.01	0.01	0.01	0.01	0.01	0.01	0.01	0.01	0.01	0.01
Non-Durable Manufacturing	1.28	1.35	1.42	1.42	1.42	1.40	1.40	1.40	1.42	1.44	1.46
Durable Manufacturing	1.52	1.19	1.11	1.03	1.02	0.97	0.94	0.92	0.92	0.92	0.92
TCPU	1.91	2.17	2.36	2.50	2.56	2.57	2.60	2.62	2.69	2.76	2.83
Water Transportation	0.31	0.36	0.39	0.41	0.42	0.42	0.43	0.43	0.44	0.45	0.46
Air Transportation	0.15	0.18	0.19	0.20	0.21	0.21	0.21	0.21	0.22	0.22	0.23
Wholesale Trade	2.49	2.78	3.03	3.29	3.45	3.55	3.67	3.71	3.82	3.93	4.05
Retail Trade	9.67	9.65	10.56	11.41	11.94	12.15	12.46	12.62	13.03	13.44	13.86
Eating & Drinking	6.20	6.19	6.77	7.31	7.65	7.79	7.99	8.09	8.35	8.61	8.88
FIRE Excluding Real Estate Rentals	1.85	1.98	2.24	2.46	2.64	2.72	2.83	2.89	3.00	3.12	3.24
Hotels, Lodging Places, and Rentals	5.14	5.52	6.24	6.85	7.33	7.57	7.87	8.03	8.34	8.66	9.00
Services	13.14	14.10	15.95	17.51	18.74	19.33	20.11	20.51	21.31	22.14	22.99
Equipment Rental and Leasing	0.16	0.18	0.20	0.22	0.23	0.24	0.25	0.26	0.27	0.28	0.29
Amusement and Recreation Services, N.E.C.	1.08	1.15	1.31	1.43	1.53	1.58	1.65	1.68	1.75	1.81	1.88
Engineering, Architectural Services	0.61	0.66	0.74	0.82	0.87	0.90	0.94	0.96	0.99	1.03	1.07
Accounting, Auditing and Bookkeeping	0.37	0.40	0.45	0.50	0.53	0.55	0.57	0.58	0.60	0.63	0.65
Research, Development & Testing Services	0.47	0.51	0.57	0.63	0.67	0.69	0.72	0.74	0.76	0.79	0.82
Government	11.60	12.16	12.94	13.58	13.99	13.99	14.11	14.21	14.58	14.96	15.34
Federal Government - Military	5.00	4.83	4.81	4.81	4.80	4.75	4.75	4.67	4.67	4.68	4.68
Total	69.06	70.81	77.15	82.58	86.51	87.93	90.15	91.25	94.09	97.01	100.03

Source: RPC

45

Table 17.3
Baseline Employment by Major Non-Farm Industry for the Florida Panhandle
(Pensacola)
(in thousands of workers)

Sector	1995	2000	2005	2010	2015	2020	2025	2030	2035	2040	2045
Agriculture	2.661	3.145	3.377	3.547	3.691	3.774	3.858	3.948	4.040	4.134	4.229
Commercial Fishing	0.135	0.159	0.171	0.179	0.187	0.191	0.195	0.200	0.204	0.209	0.214
Mining	0.322	0.310	0.307	0.306	0.311	0.310	0.309	0.310	0.310	0.310	0.310
Construction	17.462	19.211	20.539	21.886	23.069	23.522	23.979	24.709	25.458	26.228	27.019
Maintenance and Repair Oil and Gas Wells	0.039	0.038	0.038	0.037	0.038	0.038	0.038	0.038	0.038	0.038	0.038
Non-Durable Manufacturing	7.802	8.208	7.674	7.323	7.097	6.740	6.400	6.348	6.297	6.245	6.193
Durable Manufacturing	4.338	4.948	5.005	4.994	5.070	5.062	5.053	5.112	5.172	5.232	5.293
TCPU	5.869	5.821	5.982	6.192	6.362	6.353	6.341	6.439	6.538	6.637	6.738
Water Transportation	0.509	0.505	0.519	0.537	0.552	0.551	0.550	0.559	0.567	0.576	0.585
Air Transportation	1.166	1.156	1.188	1.230	1.264	1.262	1.260	1.279	1.299	1.318	1.338
Wholesale Trade	7.626	9.483	10.022	10.640	11.193	11.305	11.415	11.706	12.004	12.308	12.619
Retail Trade	23.426	26.650	27.897	29.149	30.409	30.656	30.899	31.587	32.289	33.003	33.730
Eating & Drinking	11.589	13.183	13.800	14.419	15.043	15.165	15.285	15.626	15.973	16.326	16.686
FIRE Excluding Real Estate Rentals	5.337	6.291	6.848	7.330	7.820	8.007	8.196	8.444	8.698	8.959	9.227
Hotels, Lodging Places, and Rentals	5.071	5.977	6.506	6.965	7.430	7.607	7.787	8.022	8.264	8.512	8.767
Services	53.877	63.501	69.128	73.995	78.937	80.822	82.737	85.234	87.800	90.435	93.141
Equipment Rental and Leasing	0.575	0.678	0.738	0.790	0.843	0.863	0.884	0.910	0.938	0.966	0.995
Amusement and Recreation Services, N.E.C.	0.789	0.930	1.013	1.084	1.156	1.184	1.212	1.248	1.286	1.325	1.364
Engineering, Architectural Services	2.151	2.535	2.759	2.954	3.151	3.226	3.303	3.402	3.505	3.610	3.718
Accounting, Auditing and Bookkeeping	1.068	1.259	1.371	1.467	1.565	1.603	1.641	1.690	1.741	1.793	1.847
Research, Development & Testing Services	0.545	0.643	0.700	0.749	0.799	0.818	0.838	0.863	0.889	0.916	0.943
Government	30.804	37.745	38.570	39.223	40.196	40.008	39.813	40.426	41.047	41.673	42.305
Federal Government - Military	10.010	10.966	10.846	10.822	10.987	10.969	10.950	10.959	10.967	10.975	10.981
Total	193.173	223.342	234.998	245.820	257.169	260.036	262.943	269.060	275.322	281.728	288.279

Source: RPC

Table 18.1

Baseline Output by Major Non-Farm Industry for the Florida Panhandle
(Fort Walton Beach)
(in millions of 1994 dollars)

Sector	1995	2000	2005	2010	2015	2020	2025	2030	2035	2040	2045
Agriculture	60.02	66.24	74.90	77.87	83.62	83.56	83.47	86.52	89.66	92.91	96.26
Commercial Fishing	3.68	4.06	4.60	4.78	5.13	5.13	5.12	5.31	5.50	5.70	5.91
Mining	4.57	3.48	3.46	3.46	3.45	3.45	3.44	3.45	3.46	3.47	3.48
Construction	510.00	565.41	629.80	679.97	719.85	744.01	768.75	796.51	825.15	854.76	885.25
Maintenance and Repair Oil and Gas Wells	0.17	0.13	0.13	0.13	0.13	0.13	0.13	0.13	0.13	0.13	0.13
Non-Durable Manufacturing	172.64	210.43	226.14	234.45	242.12	250.15	258.37	265.05	271.86	278.83	285.92
Durable Manufacturing	406.52	402.42	400.44	400.31	399.15	386.60	374.32	381.14	388.03	395.01	402.04
TCPU	308.76	355.72	388.22	410.93	432.50	443.42	454.48	469.20	484.33	499.91	515.88
Water Transportation	16.38	18.87	20.60	21.80	22.95	23.52	24.11	24.89	25.69	26.52	27.37
Air Transportation	27.81	32.04	34.97	37.01	38.95	39.94	40.94	42.26	43.62	45.03	46.46
Wholesale Trade	202.51	239.99	289.08	301.56	313.21	325.27	337.69	350.41	363.55	377.16	391.20
Retail Trade	417.57	483.91	534.80	580.01	611.77	629.74	648.03	671.15	694.99	719.63	744.99
Eating & Drinking	270.00	312.90	345.80	375.04	395.57	407.19	419.02	433.97	449.38	465.31	481.71
FIRE Excluding Real Estate Rentals	562.25	663.43	755.32	837.69	901.66	943.54	987.12	1,027.99	1,070.41	1,114.55	1,160.28
Hotels, Lodging Places, and Rentals	840.41	991.64	1,129.00	1,252.12	1,347.73	1,410.33	1,475.47	1,536.57	1,599.97	1,665.94	1,734.31
Services	1,022.29	1,206.24	1,373.32	1,523.09	1,639.39	1,715.54	1,794.77	1,869.09	1,946.22	2,026.46	2,109.62
Equipment Rental and Leasing	16.38	19.33	22.01	24.41	26.28	27.50	28.77	29.96	31.19	32.48	33.81
Amusement and Recreation Services, N.E.C.	33.02	38.96	44.36	49.20	52.95	55.41	57.97	60.37	62.87	65.46	68.14
Engineering, Architectural Services	55.50	65.48	74.56	82.69	89.00	93.13	97.44	101.47	105.66	110.01	114.53
Accounting, Auditing and Bookkeeping	19.03	22.45	25.56	28.35	30.51	31.93	33.40	34.78	36.22	37.71	39.26
Research, Development & Testing Services	73.03	86.17	98.11	108.81	117.12	122.56	128.22	133.53	139.04	144.77	150.71
Government	548.55	627.05	660.02	692.27	715.43	725.62	735.74	755.73	776.14	797.07	818.38
Federal Government - Military	458.07	462.00	459.72	459.58	458.25	457.92	457.46	458.58	459.62	460.64	461.57
Total	6,029.15	6,878.38	7,594.91	8,185.52	8,646.71	8,925.60	9,214.25	9,538.07	9,872.68	10,219.46	10,577.20

Source: RPC

47

Table 18.2
Baseline Output by Major Non-Farm Industry for the Florida Panhandle
(Panama City)
(in millions of 1994 dollars)

Sector	1995	2000	2005	2010	2015	2020	2025	2030	2035	2040	2045
Agriculture	13.29	12.95	13.99	15.10	16.15	16.55	17.10	17.34	17.91	18.49	19.10
Commercial Fishing	0.72	0.70	0.76	0.82	0.88	0.90	0.93	0.94	0.97	1.00	1.04
Mining	1.61	1.52	1.52	1.52	1.52	1.51	1.51	1.49	1.49	1.49	1.49
Construction	497.84	442.75	475.13	501.08	525.36	529.40	537.91	545.18	562.88	581.00	599.72
Maintenance and Repair Oil and Gas Wells	0.08	0.07	0.07	0.07	0.07	0.07	0.07	0.07	0.07	0.07	0.07
Non-Durable Manufacturing	261.63	276.90	292.55	293.10	292.67	290.35	290.44	289.84	294.65	299.45	304.35
Durable Manufacturing	254.12	198.96	185.29	172.38	172.12	164.06	157.67	155.24	155.69	156.11	156.53
TCPU	326.32	371.15	405.07	429.02	439.96	442.18	448.10	452.08	464.60	477.36	490.47
Water Transportation	67.29	76.54	83.53	88.47	90.73	91.18	92.40	93.22	95.81	98.44	101.14
Air Transportation	21.54	24.50	26.74	28.32	29.05	29.19	29.58	29.85	30.67	31.52	32.38
Wholesale Trade	245.03	274.12	299.17	325.42	342.04	351.83	364.90	369.27	380.68	392.34	404.37
Retail Trade	358.66	358.61	392.91	425.28	445.71	454.20	466.70	473.41	489.19	505.36	522.08
Eating & Drinking	246.41	246.37	269.94	292.18	306.21	312.05	320.63	325.24	336.08	347.19	358.68
FIRE Excluding Real Estate Rentals	469.05	504.15	571.28	628.07	673.17	695.64	724.85	740.40	770.41	801.44	833.75
Hotels, Lodging Places, and Rentals	611.16	656.88	744.35	818.34	877.12	906.38	944.45	964.71	1,003.81	1,044.24	1,086.34
Services	695.18	747.19	846.69	930.85	997.71	1,031.00	1,074.30	1,097.35	1,141.82	1,187.81	1,235.70
Equipment Rental and Leasing	15.56	16.72	18.95	20.83	22.33	23.07	24.04	24.56	25.55	26.58	27.65
Amusement and Recreation Services, N.E.C.	50.77	54.57	61.84	67.98	72.87	75.30	78.46	80.14	83.39	86.75	90.25
Engineering, Architectural Services	42.34	45.51	51.57	56.70	60.77	62.80	65.43	66.84	69.55	72.35	75.26
Accounting, Auditing and Bookkeeping	23.94	25.73	29.16	32.06	34.36	35.51	37.00	37.79	39.33	40.91	42.56
Research, Development & Testing Services	26.83	28.83	32.67	35.92	38.50	39.78	41.46	42.34	44.06	45.84	47.68
Government	460.39	483.61	515.21	541.62	558.97	559.91	565.52	570.45	586.17	602.17	618.62
Federal Government - Military	168.70	163.14	162.78	163.09	162.85	161.56	161.61	159.11	159.57	160.00	160.43
Total	4,858.46	5,011.47	5,481.19	5,868.23	6,161.12	6,274.41	6,445.07	6,536.87	6,754.34	6,977.92	7,209.65

Source: RPC

48

Table 18.3
Baseline Output by Major Non-Farm Industry for the Florida Panhandle
(Pensacola)
(in millions of 1994 dollars)

Sector	1995	2000	2005	2010	2015	2020	2025	2030	2035	2040	2045
Agriculture	155.60	134.16	198.07	208.34	217.14	222.37	227.68	233.35	239.15	245.06	251.11
Commercial Fishing	2.92	3.45	3.71	3.91	4.07	4.17	4.27	4.38	4.48	4.60	4.71
Mining	18.05	17.39	17.23	17.22	17.50	17.50	17.50	17.54	17.58	17.62	17.66
Construction	1,489.70	1,641.45	1,757.60	1,875.82	1,980.24	2,022.28	2,064.77	2,130.82	2,198.83	2,268.81	2,340.79
Maintenance&Repair Oil & Gas Wells	0.27	0.26	0.26	0.26	0.26	0.26	0.26	0.26	0.26	0.26	0.26
Non-Durable Manufacturing	1,779.63	1,875.19	1,755.84	1,678.29	1,628.93	1,549.39	1,473.43	1,463.80	1,454.12	1,444.39	1,434.58
Durable Manufacturing	581.09	663.75	672.48	671.99	683.29	683.28	683.12	692.23	701.40	710.64	719.93
TCPU	1,140.68	1,133.13	1,166.25	1,209.12	1,244.25	1,244.23	1,243.94	1,265.05	1,286.42	1,308.04	1,329.90
Water Transportation	107.02	106.31	109.42	113.44	116.74	116.73	116.71	118.69	120.69	122.72	124.77
Air Transportation	179.11	177.93	183.13	189.86	195.38	195.38	195.33	198.64	202.00	205.40	208.83
Wholesale Trade	748.19	931.83	986.33	1,048.80	1,104.98	1,117.73	1,130.39	1,161.00	1,192.35	1,224.43	1,257.26
Retail Trade	892.06	1,016.38	1,065.59	1,115.13	1,165.14	1,176.42	1,187.57	1,215.90	1,244.82	1,274.31	1,304.37
Eating & Drinking	450.71	513.52	538.39	563.42	588.68	594.39	600.02	614.33	628.94	643.84	659.03
FIRE Excluding Real Estate Rentals	1,324.12	1,563.09	1,704.24	1,827.06	1,952.09	2,001.81	2,052.40	2,117.58	2,184.68	2,253.72	2,324.72
Hotels, Lodging Places, & Rentals	800.07	944.46	1,029.74	1,103.95	1,179.50	1,209.54	1,240.11	1,279.50	1,320.04	1,361.75	1,404.65
Services	2,711.97	3,201.41	3,490.50	3,742.05	3,998.13	4,099.95	4,203.57	4,337.08	4,474.50	4,615.90	4,761.32
Equipment Rental and Leasing	55.46	65.47	71.38	76.52	81.76	83.84	85.96	88.69	91.50	94.39	97.37
Amusement&Recreation Srvcs, N.E.C.	31.26	36.90	40.24	43.14	46.09	47.26	48.46	49.99	51.58	53.21	54.89
Engineering, Architectural Services	148.22	174.97	190.77	204.52	218.51	224.08	229.74	237.04	244.55	252.28	260.22
Accounting, Auditing & Bookkeeping	62.62	73.92	80.59	86.40	92.32	94.67	97.06	100.14	103.31	106.58	109.94
Research,Development&Testing Srvcs	24.80	29.27	31.92	34.22	36.56	37.49	38.44	39.66	40.91	42.21	43.54
Government	1,362.61	1,672.24	1,711.43	1,743.09	1,789.12	1,783.50	1,777.52	1,807.70	1,838.26	1,869.17	1,900.41
Federal Government - Military	385.08	422.51	418.56	418.25	425.29	425.28	425.18	426.19	427.17	428.11	429.02
Total	14,451.24	16,449.00	17,223.67	17,974.80	18,765.98	18,951.55	19,143.43	19,599.57	20,067.56	20,547.44	21,039.27

Adjusted distribution of migrants within a metropolitan area to make the model's baseline population projections consistent with BEBR / BEA at the county level.

To calibrate the MMS Florida Panhandle model, RPC ran iterations of the model to recreate BEBR's and BEA's baseline population projections by area and by counties within an area. RPC found that the allocation percentages in Table 19 produced a close approximation of these baseline population projections.   The model uses these allocations in all of its scenarios.

Table 19

Allocation of Economic Migration Between Counties in a Metropolitan Area
(in percent of total)

Area and Counties	1995	2000	2005	2010	2015 - 2045
Fort Walton Beach Area	100%	100%	100%	100%	100%
Okaloosa County	83%	70%	70%	70%	70%
Walton County	18%	30%	30%	30%	30%
Pensacola Area	100%	100%	100%	100%	100%
Escambia County	60%	65%	55%	45%	40%
Santa Rosa County	40%	35%	45%	55%	60%
Panama City Area	100%	100%	100%	100%	100%
Bay County	100%	100%	100%	100%	100%

The MMS Florida Panhandle model confirms that all three areas experience economic migration in the baseline from 1995 to 2045 (Table 20).

Table 20

Annual Migration in the Florida Panhandle
Baseline Scenario

Area	1995	2000	2005	2010	2015	2020	2025	2030
Fort Walton Beach	0	1,677	1,741	1,842	1,914	1,710	1,881	1,938
Okaloosa County	NA	1,174	1,219	1,290	1,340	1,197	1,317	1,356
Walton County	NA	503	522	553	574	513	564	581
Panama City	0	638	1,075	1,233	1,250	944	1,142	825
Bay County	NA	638	1,075	1,233	1,250	944	1,142	825
Pensacola	0	0	2,760	2,461	3,311	2,033	1,761	2,077
Escambia County	NA	NA	1,518	1,108	1,324	813	704	831
Santa Rosa	NA	NA	1,242	1,354	1,987	1,220	1,056	1,246
Total	0	2,316	5,576	5,536	6,475	4,688	4,784	4,840

Source: RPC.

Created a Baseline for Tourism Sector

Using information derived from the literature review of the tourism industry in the Florida Panhandle, RPC used an approach based on a paper to estimate tourist expenditures in the Pensacola area to approximate a tourism baseline for the MMS Florida Panhandle model.[8] This approach identifies a range of local services and retail trade by visitors from outside the Florida Panhandle as the model's baseline tourism expenditures. Using survey information on the distribution of tourism expenditures for various counties in the Florida Panhandle gathered by the Florida Department of Commerce in 1995 along with published figures on taxable sales on rental facilities, RPC estimated tourism expenditures in a way that highlights the expenditures of those visitors from out of state who would stay at hotels or other transient rentals, because those would be the people most at risk for choosing alternative vacation spots outside the Florida Panhandle, as opposed to residents of nearby counties who would visit on day trips.

In dividing the MMS Florida Panhandle model into 23 sectors, RPC combined hotels and motels (SIC 65) with real estate (SIC 70) in order to capture the range of rental expenditures subject to tourist development taxes. According to Section 125.0104 of the Florida Statutes:

> It is the intent of the Legislature that every person who rents, leases, or lets for
> consideration any living quarters or accommodations in any hotel, apartment
> hotel, motel, resort motel, apartment motel, rooming house, mobile home park,
> recreational vehicle park, or condominium for a term of six months or less is
> exercising a taxable privilege.[9]

A comparison of taxable sales for rental facilities in the Florida Panhandle with preliminary estimates of IMPLAN's hotel and motel sector confirmed that taxable sales of rental facilities were larger than the expenditures on hotels and motels in some locations.

Using tax on transient rental facilities, Tables 21.1 - 21.3 convert the sales subject to the tax on transient rental facilities and the distribution in other sectors. Tables 22.1 - 22.3 show RPC's projections of tourist expenditures (final demand) from 1995 to 2045.

---

[8] Florida Department of Commerce, 1995; Huth and Stewart, 1995; Florida Legislative Committee on Intergovernmental Relations, *Local Government Financial Information Handbook*, September 1998.

[9] Florida Legislative Committee on Intergovernmental Relations, *Local Government Financial Information Handbook*, September 1998, page 384.

Table 21.1

**Distribution of Expenditures by Tourists in the Fort Walton Beach Area
(in millions of 1995 dollars)**

Item	IV	III	II	I	Average	Percent of Total	Expenditure ($ million)
Transportation	5.48	5.50	10.99	32.72	13.67	1.90%	9.16
Gasoline	38.14	31.95	46.21	55.36	42.92	5.98%	28.74
Food (Grocery)	59.94	84.52	61.09	70.38	68.98	9.60%	46.20
Food (Restaurant)	110.65	133.90	159.98	148.19	138.18	19.24%	92.55
Lodging	83.19	425.28	383.21	255.61	286.82	39.94%	192.10
Entertainment	22.02	66.35	87.05	53.43	57.21	7.97%	38.32
Gifts	57.17	49.56	50.32	69.50	56.64	7.89%	37.93
Other	58.95	69.79	54.95	31.48	53.79	7.49%	36.03
Total	430.06	861.35	842.81	683.95	718.22	100.00%	481.03

Sources: RPC.
Florida Department of Commerce, 1995.
Huth and Stewart, 1995.
Florida Legislative Committee on Intergovernmental Relations, *Local Government Financial Information Handbook*, September 1998.

Table 21.2

Distribution of Expenditures by Tourists in the Panama City Area
(in millions of 1995 dollars)

Item	IV	III	II	I	Average	Percent of Total	Expenditure ($ Million)
Transportation	8.74	4.37	2.98	5.47	5.39	0.79%	3.22
Gasoline	55.60	46.85	55.44	57.46	53.84	7.89%	32.19
Food (Grocery)	79.73	55.91	62.49	76.78	68.73	10.07%	41.09
Food (Restaurant)	128.35	145.11	135.94	129.12	134.63	19.73%	80.49
Lodging	191.98	246.70	346.80	296.51	270.50	39.64%	161.73
Entertainment	67.82	85.62	54.19	63.25	67.72	9.92%	40.49
Gifts	64.69	40.34	50.44	41.90	49.34	7.23%	29.50
Other	43.63	29.77	14.75	40.73	32.22	4.72%	19.26
Total	631.80	650.30	720.05	705.75	682.37	100.00%	407.97

Sources: RPC.
Florida Department of Commerce, 1995.
Huth and Stewart, 1995.
Florida Legislative Committee on Intergovernmental Relations, *Local Government Financial Information Handbook*, September 1998.

Table 21.3

Distribution of Expenditures by Tourists in the Pensacola Area
(in millions of 1995 dollars)

Item	IV	III	II	I	Average	Percent of Total	Expenditure ($ Million)
Transportation	15.38	8.74	3.59	51.77	19.87	3.39%	8.41
Gasoline	42.60	40.88	32.66	53.33	42.37	7.23%	17.93
Food (Grocery)	35.55	51.45	31.16	78.77	49.23	8.40%	20.84
Food (Restaurant)	99.64	102.26	151.69	148.70	125.57	21.43%	53.15
Lodging	113.82	154.52	274.88	279.87	205.77	35.11%	87.10
Entertainment	47.98	72.62	70.75	48.00	59.84	10.21%	25.33
Gifts	44.13	34.67	54.25	10.32	35.84	6.12%	15.17
Other	47.27	44.36	64.33	34.35	47.58	8.12%	20.14
Total	430.99	500.76	679.72	653.34	586.07	100.00%	248.07

Sources: RPC.
Florida Department of Commerce, 1995.
Huth and Stewart, 1995.
Florida Legislative Committee on Intergovernmental Relations, *Local Government Financial Information Handbook*, September 1998.

Table 22.1
Projected Expenditures by Tourists in the Fort Walton Beach Area
(in millions of 1995 dollars)

Sector	1995	2000	2005	2010	2015	2020	2025	2030	2035	2040	2045
Transportation , Communication, Utilities	9.2	10.8	12.3	13.6	14.6	15.2	15.9	16.6	17.2	17.9	18.6
Retail Trade Other than Eating & Drinking	148.9	175.4	199.4	220.8	237.3	248.0	259.0	269.3	280.0	291.1	302.6
Eating & Drinking	92.5	109.0	123.9	137.2	147.5	154.1	161.0	167.4	174.0	180.9	188.1
Hotels & Lodging Places	192.1	226.3	257.3	284.9	306.2	319.9	334.1	347.4	361.2	375.5	390.4
Amusement and Recreation Services, N.E.C.	38.3	45.1	51.3	56.8	61.1	63.8	66.7	69.3	72.1	74.9	77.9
Total	481.0	566.7	644.2	713.3	766.6	801.0	836.7	870.0	904.5	940.4	977.5

Source: RPC.

Table 22.2
Projected Expenditures by Tourists in the Panama City Area
(in millions of 1995 dollars)

Sector	1995	2000	2005	2010	2015	2020	2025	2030	2035	2040	2045
Transportation , Communication, Utilities	3.2	3.5	3.9	4.3	4.6	4.7	4.9	5.0	5.2	5.4	5.6
Retail Trade Other than Eating & Drinking	122.0	131.0	148.2	162.7	174.1	179.6	186.9	190.6	198.0	205.7	213.6
Eating & Drinking	80.5	86.4	97.7	107.3	114.8	118.5	123.2	125.7	130.6	135.6	140.9
Hotels & Lodging Places	161.7	173.6	196.4	215.5	230.7	238.0	247.6	252.5	262.4	272.5	283.1
Amusement and Recreation Services, N.E.C.	40.5	43.4	49.2	54.0	57.7	59.6	62.0	63.2	65.7	68.2	70.9
Total	408.0	437.8	495.3	543.7	581.9	600.4	624.6	637.1	661.9	687.5	714.1

Source: RPC.

Table 22.3

Projected Expenditures by Tourists in the Pensacola Area
(in millions of 1995 dollars)

Sector	1995	2000	2005	2010	2015	2020	2025	2030	2035	2040	2045
Transportation , Communication, Utilities	8.4	9.9	10.8	11.6	12.3	12.6	12.9	13.3	13.7	14.1	14.5
Retail Trade Other than Eating & Drinking	74.1	87.3	95.1	101.7	108.5	111.1	113.8	117.2	120.7	124.4	128.1
Eating & Drinking	53.2	62.6	68.2	73.0	77.9	79.7	81.6	84.1	86.6	89.2	91.9
Hotels & Lodging Places	87.1	102.7	111.8	119.6	127.6	130.7	133.8	137.8	141.9	146.2	150.6
Amusement and Recreation Services, N.E.C.	25.3	29.9	32.5	34.8	37.1	38.0	38.9	40.1	41.3	42.5	43.8
Total	248.1	292.4	318.3	340.7	363.5	372.1	381.0	392.5	404.3	416.4	428.9

Source: RPC.

57

Public Services and Fiscal Impact Module

Impact Triggers: Population (total, school age), Households (property valuations), Non-government Output (property valuation)

The module presents a set of representative impacts on local governments. This module converts a scenario's impacts on output and population generated in the economic-demographic interface into impacts on local public finance and services. The module uses the change in the number of households in some of the tax revenue impacts. The models estimates the change in households by taking the net impact of the population and dividing by 2.5, which is the average number of people per household in the Florida Panhandle (Bureau of Economic Business Research, Florida Statistical Abstract 1996).

Government Bodies

The module estimates impacts on county and municipal governments. RPC decided to measure the impacts on municipalities based on totals of all residents and property within municipalities in a given county rather than create a more elaborate model that would require a gravity model to specify where economic migrants would locate within a county. The impacts on special districts within the counties were deemed to be outside the scope of this project.

Fiscal Balance

RPC used data on fiscal year 1996-1997 from the Florida Department of Banking and Finance (1998). Tables 23.1 - 23.5 present a detailed breakdown of revenues and expenditures for each of the five counties of the Florida Panhandle. Table 23.6 shows the total expenditures per county. Tables 24.1 to 24.5 present the breakdown of all municipal expenditures and revenues in each of the five counties. Table 24.6 shows the combined municipal expenditures per county. Table 25 presents the percentage of each county's population that live in unincorporated areas. RPC assumed that this percentage stayed constant over time.

Table 23.1

County Government Revenues of Bay County
(FY 1996-1997)

Revenue Source	Dollars	Percentage
Ad Valorem taxes	24,774,514	19.80%
Other taxes, fees, and licenses	17,324,516	13.84%
Federal grants	514,368	0.41%
State and other govt sources	15,244,857	12.18%
Charges for services	29,003,403	23.18%
Fines and forfeits	1,477,214	1.18%
Special assessment and impact fees	149,506	0.12%
Other miscellaneous revenues	9,038,192	7.22%
Other sources / Interfund transfers	27,608,135	22.06%
Total	125,134,705	100.00%

Source: Florida Department of Banking and Finance, personal communication, November 1998.

Table 23.2

County Government Revenues of Escambia County
(FY 1996-1997)

Revenue Source	Dollars	Percentage
Ad Valorem taxes	50,841,280	23.19%
Other taxes, fees, and licenses	46,642,998	21.28%
Federal grants	8,430,148	3.85%
State and other govt sources	35,518,949	16.20%
Charges for services	40,156,659	18.32%
Fines and forfeits	2,402,829	1.10%
Special assessment and impact fees	5,462,213	2.49%
Other miscellaneous revenues	13,733,772	6.26%
Other sources / Interfund transfers	16,039,504	7.32%
Total	219,228,352	100.00%

Source: Florida Department of Banking and Finance, personal communication, November 1998.

Table 23.3

County Government Revenues of Okaloosa County
(FY 1996-1997)

Revenue Type	Dollars	Percentage
Ad Valorem taxes	21,471,797	14.78%
Other taxes, fees, and licenses	7,057,170	4.86%
Federal grants	4,048,773	2.79%
State and other govt sources	17,632,392	12.14%
Charges for services	40,900,772	28.16%
Fines and forfeits	116,272	0.08%
Special assessment and impact fees	82,200	0.06%
Other miscellaneous revenues	16,826,100	11.58%
Other sources / Interfund transfers	37,108,784	25.55%
Total	145,244,260	100.00%

Source: Florida Department of Banking and Finance, personal communication, November 1998.

Table 23.4

County Government Revenues of Santa Rosa County
(FY 1996-1997)

Revenue Type	Dollars	Percentage
Ad Valorem taxes	20,143,797	25.85%
Other taxes, fees, and licenses	12,332,627	15.83%
Federal grants	485,989	0.62%
State and other govt sources	10,720,043	13.76%
Charges for services	22,695,672	29.12%
Fines and forfeits	1,057,731	1.36%
Special assessment and impact fees	840,304	1.08%
Other miscellaneous revenues	4,122,335	5.29%
Other sources / Interfund transfers	5,527,789	7.09%
Total	77,926,287	100.00%

Source: Florida Department of Banking and Finance, personal communication, November 1998.

Table 23.5

County Government Revenues of Walton County
(FY 1996-1997)

Revenue Type	Dollars	Percentage
Ad Valorem taxes	14,959,773	33.57%
Other taxes, fees, and licenses	7,589,193	17.03%
Federal grants	3,237,898	7.27%
State and other govt sources	6,668,814	14.96%
Charges for services	5,272,988	11.83%
Fines and forfeits	708,020	1.59%
Special assessment and impact fees	365,313	0.82%
Other miscellaneous revenues	2,256,359	5.06%
Other sources / Interfund transfers	3,506,117	7.87%
Total	44,564,475	100.00%

Source: Florida Department of Banking and Finance, personal communication, November 1998.

Table 23.6

County Government Expenditures
(FY 1996-1997)

County	Dollars
Bay	115,386,094
Escambia	207,906,150
Okaloosa	142,661,764
Santa Rosa	76,521,782
Walton	38,144,204

Source: Florida Department of Banking and Finance, personal communication, November 1998.

Table 24.1

Combined Municipal Government Revenues of Bay County
(FY 1996-1997)

Revenue Name	Revenue Amount
Ad Valorem taxes	5,458,046
Other taxes, fees and licenses	20,694,195
Federal grants	4,500,556
State and other government sources	9,564,415
Charges for services	42,938,793
Fines and forfeits	1,108,136
Special Assessments and impact fees	400,922
Other Miscellaneous Revenues	13,166,022
Other Sources/Interfund transfers in	12,352,121
Total	110,183,206

Source: Florida Department of Banking and Finance, personal communication, November 1998.

Table 24.2

Combined Municipal Government Revenues of Escambia County
(FY 1996-1997)

Revenue Name	Revenue Amount
Ad Valorem taxes	8,158,937
Other taxes, fees and licenses	20,053,432
Federal grants	7,351,718
State and other government sources	8,176,547
Charges for services	55,711,991
Fines and forfeits	637,268
Special Assessments and impact fees	90,166
Other Miscellaneous Revenues	49,027,353
Other Sources/Interfund transfers in	51,265,337
Total	200,472,749

Source: Florida Department of Banking and Finance, personal communication, November 1998.

Table 24.3

**Combined Municipal Government Revenues of Okaloosa County
(FY 1996-1997)**

Revenue Name	Revenue Amount
Ad Valorem taxes	12,170,540
Other taxes, fees and licenses	18,931,351
Federal grants	2,774,656
State and other government sources	11,513,295
Charges for services	36,930,130
Fines and forfeits	940,874
Special Assessments and impact fees	147,720
Other Miscellaneous Revenues	19,606,591
Other Sources/Interfund transfers in	9,418,708
Total	112,433,865

Source: Florida Department of Banking and Finance, personal communication, November 1998.

Table 24.4

**Combined Municipal Government Revenues of Santa Rosa County
(FY 1996-1997)**

Revenue Name	Revenue Amount
Ad Valorem taxes	1,050,604
Other taxes, fees and licenses	1,411,136
Federal grants	130,002
State and other government sources	1,654,614
Charges for services	12,844,891
Fines and forfeits	320,584
Special Assessments and impact fees	20,300
Other Miscellaneous Revenues	4,274,459
Other Sources/Interfund transfers in	3,867,712
Total	25,574,302

Source: Florida Department of Banking and Finance, personal communication, November 1998.

Table 24.5

Combined Municipal Government Revenues of Walton County
(FY 1996-1997)

Revenue Name	Revenue Amount
Ad Valorem taxes	489,106
Other taxes, fees and licenses	1,823,892
Federal grants	1,014,119
State and other government sources	1,100,140
Charges for services	4,210,478
Fines and forfeits	159,043
Special Assessments and impact fees	0
Other Miscellaneous Revenues	333,830
Other Sources/Interfund transfers in	1,544,581
Total	10,675,189

Source: Florida Department of Banking and Finance, personal communication, November 1998.

Table 24.6

Combined Municipal Government Expenditures
(FY 1996-1997)

County	Amount
Bay	93,953,905
Escambia	169,567,112
Okaloosa	94,794,446
Santa Rosa	25,582,052
Walton	10,360,776

Source: Florida Department of Banking and Finance, personal communication, November 1998.

Table 25

Population of Florida Panhandle Living in Unincorporated Areas in 1996

County	Unincorporated	Total	Unincorporated as % of Total
Bay	57,439	142,159	40.40%
Escambia	223,603	286,301	78.10%
Okaloosa	96,665	165,319	58.47%
Santa Rosa	84,315	98,491	85.61%
Walton	27,112	34,328	78.98%
Total	489,134	726,598	67.32%

Expenditures: The module uses *per capita* expenditures to measure the impacts on local government expenditures. Table 26 contains *per capita* expenditures for county governments, as well as the average *per capita* expenditures for municipalities.

Table 26

Per Capita Expenditures for County Governments and for Municipal Governments in the Florida Panhandle

County	County Government	Average of All Municipal Governments
Bay	798.06	1,096.84
Escambia	714.12	2,710.52
Okaloosa	834.09	888.18
Santa Rosa	747.74	1,785.96
Walton	1,056.80	1,439.20

Revenues: Review of local government revenues by type show that Florida counties receive direct and indirect revenues. Direct revenues are taxes that individuals, households, and businesses pay in the form of *ad valorem* (property) taxes, sales taxes, tourist development taxes, fees, and licenses. Indirect revenues are grants, intergovernmental transfers, and other funds that local governments receive from sources outside the county itself, such as the State of Florida and the U.S. Government.

The MMS model estimates the direct revenue impacts as *ad valorem* taxes and *per capita* taxes and fees based on changes in population and economic activity in a given scenario. Given that county and municipal government budgets are in balance in the long-run, the model also estimates the amount of revenue these governments need from indirect sources to balance the budget each year in a given scenario (i.e., direct revenues plus indirect revenues equals expenditures).

Ad Valorem (Property) Taxes: The MMS model estimates the impact on *ad valorem* taxes from both residential and business sources.   The model estimates the change in commercial and industrial property valuation for county governments by multiplying the change in non-government output by the commercial and industrial valuation in each county per million dollars of expenditures in the area. The model estimates the change in residential property valuation by multiplying the change in households times the average value of residential property in the county. For the impact on municipal governments, the model multiplies the county valuation figures by the percent of the county's population that live in incorporated areas. The model then estimates ad valorem taxes by multiplying the change in property valuation by the millages (unit of taxation based on one tenth of a cent) of the county and municipal governments.

Table 27 contains the millage rates for county governments. Table 28 presents the taxation and average millage for municipalities in each of the five counties in the Florida Panhandle. Table 29 contains the average taxable value of residential property in 1997. Table 30 contains the value of taxable commercial and industrial property in 1997.

Table 27

Millage Rates for County Governments and Selected Special Districts
in the Florida Panhandle

County	County Government Operating	County Government Debt Service	Total
Bay	5.632	0.000	5.682
Escambia	8.260	0.000	8.792
Okaloosa	4.528	0.000	4.578
Santa Rosa	6.972	0.000	7.022
Walton	6.740	0.000	6.790

Source: Florida Department of Revenue, *Florida Property Valuations and Tax Data*, December 1997.

Table 28

Municipal Taxation in the Florida Panhandle in 1997
(in millions of dollars)

County	Taxable Value of All Property	Taxes Levied	Average Millage
Bay	2,509.6	6.1	2.4189
Escambia	1,663.5	8.3	5.0056
Okaloosa	3,079.8	9.1	2.9512
Santa Rosa	498.9	1.050	2.1058
Walton	124.8	0.5	4.2585

Source: Florida Department of Revenue, *Florida Property Valuations and Tax Data*, December 1997.

Table 29

Average Taxable Value of Residential Property in 1997

County	Taxable Value
Bay	47,513
Escambia	36,686
Okaloosa	62,065
Santa Rosa	37,869
Walton	48,689

Source: Florida Department of Revenue, *Florida Property Valuations and Tax Data*, December 1997.

Table 30

Value of Taxable Commercial and Industrial Property in 1997
(in millions of dollars)

County	Commercial	Industrial	Commercial and Industrial
Bay	732.4	90.6	823.0
Escambia	959.2	250.9	1,210.1
Okaloosa	755.6	84.6	840.2
Santa Rosa	225.2	35.5	260.7
Walton	173.3	15.2	188.5

Source: Florida Department of Revenue, *Florida Property Valuations and Tax Data*, December 1997.

Other Taxes, Fees: The model generates other direct taxes, fees, and licenses on a *per capita* basis. As with *ad valorem* taxes, municipal revenues for a county take into account the percentage of people living in incorporated areas in a given county. Table 31 presents data on taxes, fees, and licenses.

Table 31

Per Capita Revenues
(direct taxes, fees, and licenses)

County	County Government	Average of All Municipal Governments
Bay	330.64	755.80
Escambia	306.40	1,221.29
Okaloosa	281.07	808.34
Santa Rosa	352.62	1,017.64
Walton	375.97	860.32

Source: RPC model.

Schools

In the Florida Panhandle, each county has one school district.

Expenditures: The model estimates school district expenditures by multiplying the change in school-age population in the chosen scenario by a *per capita* expenditure per full-time equivalent (FTE) for each school district (Table 32).

Table 32

School District Expenditures per Full-Time Equivalent (FTE) Student
(in 1997 dollars)

County	Expenditures per FTE
Bay	4,952
Escambia	5,069
Okaloosa	4,643
Santa Rosa	4,657
Walton	5,130

Source: Florida Department of Education,
Profiles of Florida School Districts 1996-1997 Financial Data,
June 1998.

Revenues: The module estimates two types of revenue impacts for school districts: *ad valorem* and *per capita* revenue from state and federal sources. *Ad valorem* taxes multiply the increased valuation of residential and business property by school district millage. Table 33 contains millage rates of each school district in the Florida Panhandle. State and federal revenues are the product of the number of school-age children that the scenario generated times the amount of funding per FTE from state and federal sources. Table 34 presents Federal and State revenues that each school district received in the 1996-97 school year per full-time equivalent.

Table 33

Millage Rates for School Districts in the Florida Panhandle

County	Operating Budget	Debt Service	Total
Bay	7.3270	2.0000	9.3270
Escambia	9.5650	0.0000	9.5650
Okaloosa	8.5720	0.0000	8.5720
Santa Rosa	8.8460	0.0000	8.8460
Walton	9.3540	0.0000	9.3540

Source: Florida Department of Revenue, *Florida Property Valuations and Tax Data*,   December 1997.

Table 34

School District Revenues per Full-Time Equivalent (FTE) by Source (in 1997 dollars)

County	Federal	State	County	Total
Bay	415	3,375	1,747	5,599
Escambia	591	3,594	1,423	5,608
Okaloosa	431	3,224	2,247	5,902
Santa Rosa	399	3,430	1,549	5,378
Walton	516	1,960	3,642	6,118

Source: Florida Department of Education, *Profiles of Florida School Districts 1996-1997 Financial Data*, June 1998.

Public Services

Changes in local population change the demand on public services such as water usage, roads and highways to be maintained, and police and fire protection. The MMS model used community service multipliers for the five counties based on information from the Florida Bureau of Economic and Business Research and the *1992 Census of Governments* to project impacts (Table 35). The model projects these impacts on a *per capita* basis.

Table 35

Baseline Community Service Multipliers for Counties in the Florida Panhandle

Item	Units	Bay	Escambia	Okaloosa	Santa Rosa	Walton
Residential Water	Gallons per Person per Day	88.46	83.64	81.90	91.45	85.51
Residential Wastewater	Gallons per Person per Day	270.02	71.39	106.33	30.11	71.60
Solid Waste	Tons per Person per Year	1.78	1.60	1.41	0.74	0.70
Road & Highway	Miles per Thousand People	5.68	3.74	4.54	7.09	20.17
Police	Staff per Thousand People	2.70	2.43	1.95	2.04	2.22
Crimes	Number per Thousand People	66.76	61.97	30.60	36.56	29.60
Fire	Staff per Thousand People	1.08	0.47	1.04	0.27	0.70
Public Welfare	Staff per Thousand People	0.04	0.56	0.03	0.22	0.17
Physicians	Number per Thousand People	1.74	2.51	1.70	1.27	0.44

Sources: Bureau of Business and Economic Research, 1997 Florida Statistical Abstract; U.S. Bureau of the Census,Compendium of Public Employment, Volume 3, Number 2, 1992.

REFERENCES

Bureau of Economic and Business Research (BEBR). 1997. *1997 Florida Statistical Abstract.*

Chevron U.S.A. Production Company. 1997. Destin Dome 56 unit development and production plan volume I executive summary and project description. Filed with the Minerals Management Service, New Orleans, LA.

Chevron U.S.A. Production Company. 1997. Destin dome 56 unit development and production plan volume IV.B economic, fiscal and infrastructure impacts- 1994 data update and model re-estimation. Filed with the Minerals Management Service, New Orleans, LA.

Florida Bureau of Economic and Business Research, personal communication, June Nogle, 1996-1999.

Florida Department of Banking and Finance, Government expenditures and revenues for counties and municipalities, Jeanne Dowdrick, personal communication, November 1998.

Florida Department of Commerce, Visitor Profile Reports, 1995.

Florida Department of Education, *Profiles in Florida School Districts 1996-1997 Financial Data*, December 1998.

Florida Department of Labor and Employment Security, personal communication.

Florida Department of Revenue, *Florida Property Valuations and Tax Data*, December 1997.

Florida Legislative Committee on Intergovernmental Relations, *Local Government Financial Information Handbook*, September 1998, page 384.

Gramling R. and S. Brabant. 1986. Boom towns and offshore energy impact assessment: The development of a comprehensive model. *Sociological Perspectives* 29:177-201.

Hoover, E.M. and F. Giarrantani. 1984. An Introduction to Regional Economics, Third edition. Alfred A. Knopf, Inc. New York, NY.

Huth, W.L. and R. Stewart. 1995. Report on Escambia county tourism economic impact. University of West Florida. Pensacola, FL.

Leistritz, F.L. and S.H. Murdock. 1981. *The Socioeconomic Impact of Resource Development*: Methods for Assessment. Westview Press, Inc. Boulder, CO. 286 pp.

Leistritz, F.L., S.H. Murdock, and R.C. Coon. 1990. Developing economic-demographic assessment models for substate areas. Impact Assessment Bulletin 8(4): 49-65.

Leontief, W. 1953. Studies in the Structure of the American Economy. Oxford University Press. New York, NY.

Miller, RE. and P.D. Blair. 1985. Input-Output Analysis: Foundations and extensions. Prentice-Hall, Inc. Englewood Cliffs, NJ.

Minnesota IMPLAN Group, Inc. (MIG). 1997. IMPLAN professional version 1.1 Software, User's Guide, Analysis Guide, and Data Guide. Stillwater, MN.

Murdock, S. and F.L. Leistritz. 1979. *Energy Development in the Western United States: Impact on Rural Areas*. New York: Praeger Publishers

U.S. Bureau of the Census. 1992. *Compendium of Public Employment*, Volume 3, Number 2.

U.S. Bureau of the Census, *Population of the United States by Age, Sex and Hispanic Origin*, P25-1104 (November 1993) and P25-1130 (February 1996)

U.S. Bureau of Economic Analysis (BEA). 1998. Regional economic information system 1969-1996. U.S. Department of Commerce. Washington, DC.

U.S. Bureau of Labor Statistics website, http://www.bls.gov/emplab1.htm

The Department of the Interior Mission

As the Nation's principal conservation agency, the Department of the Interior has responsibility for most of our nationally owned public lands and natural resources. This includes fostering sound use of our land and water resources; protecting our fish, wildlife, and biological diversity; preserving the environmental and cultural values of our national parks and historical places; and providing for the enjoyment of life through outdoor recreation. The Department assesses our energy and mineral resources and works to ensure that their development is in the best interests of all our people by encouraging stewardship and citizen participation in their care. The Department also has a major responsibility for American Indian reservation communities and for people who live in island territories under U.S. administration.

The Minerals Management Service Mission

As a bureau of the Department of the Interior, the Minerals Management Service's (MMS) primary responsibilities are to manage the mineral resources located on the Nation's Outer Continental Shelf (OCS), collect revenue from the Federal OCS and onshore Federal and Indian lands, and distribute those revenues.

Moreover, in working to meet its responsibilities, the **Offshore Minerals Management Program** administers the OCS competitive leasing program and oversees the safe and environmentally sound exploration and production of our Nation's offshore natural gas, oil and other mineral resources. The MMS **Minerals Revenue Management** meets its responsibilities by ensuring the efficient, timely and accurate collection and disbursement of revenue from mineral leasing and production due to Indian tribes and allottees, States and the U.S. Treasury.

The MMS strives to fulfill its responsibilities through the general guiding principles of: (1) being responsive to the public's concerns and interests by maintaining a dialogue with all potentially affected parties and (2) carrying out its programs with an emphasis on working to enhance the quality of life for all Americans by lending MMS assistance and expertise to economic development and environmental protection.